OKAVANGO MEMOIRS

BY

E. CRONJE WILMOT

ILLUSTRATED AND EDITED
BY
C.T. ASTLEY MABERLY.

ORIGINALLY
PUBLISHED 1956
HOWARD TIMMINS
CAPE TOWN

What they said about
"Always Lightly Tread"

Rhodesia Herald - December 1956

For those Keen on wildlife

To those tourists and luxury hunters and also to the genuine hunters and government officials who spend months and even years far from civilisation, E.CRONJE WILMOT'S "ALWAYS LIGHTLY TREAD" (Howard Timmins), will appeal equally.

In fact the numerous graphic descriptions of wildlife in the book will entertain all outdoor lovers.

Whether shooting game in tsetse fly areas; fishing in the Hunyani, observing nature in the mysterious surrounding of the Okavango swamps or the equally unpredictable Makarikari Salt Pan, Mr. Wilmot casts a spell. Despite being badly mauled by a lion, contracting bubonic plague, experiencing many frightening encounters with crocodiles, buffaloes and deadly reptiles, his love and respect for nature is clear.

* * *

Northern News, Northern Rhodesia

Mauled by a lion, bitten by snakes – Quite a Story!

This is one of the best books on Africa to be published for a long time, and it is written by a man who has spent his while life observing the habits of wild game and studying the flora and fauna of Bechuanaland and Southern Rhodesia.

* * *

THE CAPE ARGUS, Thursday, November 22, 1956

Memories of Ngamiland Make Great Reading

Mr. Wilmot is one of those fortunate hunters who, after being mauled by a lion, have lived to tell the tale. He does so with remarkable vividness. But the lion episode as recounted here is merely a minor incident in a life that has been packed with adventure.

The author is a born observer of wildlife; a faculty which his expeditions in outland territory and his field work on tsetse fly eradication has sharpened.

Sunday Mail, Salisbury 26/1/1957
Leopards and Lions After His Life

Formerly a stock farmer and latterly an official of Tsetse Fly Control, the author has spent most of his life in the lesser-known parts of Bechuanaland and always on his tours he took his life in his hands.

Buffalo, lions, leopards, crocodiles and other wild animals were after that life, and once a lion actually mauled him.

"It is inexplicable..." he says, "why the lion left me (after inflicting 23 wounds) when I was approaching exhaustion, but I believe that my life was saved by the animal's inexperience".

Many excellent illustrations have been draw by C.T. Astley Maberly.

* * *

PRETORIA NEWS 10/12/56
Insight into the Wilds of Africa

This is a genuine narrative of unpredictable Africa. There is nothing superficial about it and it gives the reader much food for reflection.

Although the parts dealing with the trapping and destruction of wild animals will be saddening to those who are game preservationists, the book taken as a whole will give pleasure to all who are interested in wildlife and remote places.

Mr. Wilmot is a naturalist and he knows what he is talking about. He has a pleasantly informal style which is equally effective in his descriptions of the country and of his many experiences as a field officer in Ngamiland.

The book contains interesting accounts of the plant life and the habits of things that run and fly and creep.

One of the most interesting is of the deadly little poison beetle, whose grub is used in the making of arrow-poison.

There is a horrifying chapter which describes an outbreak of bubonic plague in an outpost which was without any means of communicating with the nearest help 120 miles away.

The book is one of the very few, scientific or popular, to give any information about the interior of the Okavango swamps – the largest in Africa and yet known to only a handful of Europeans.

* * *

Author's dedication

To the memory of my late wife,

Enid Maude Wilmot

whose inspiring great love of
all wild creatures and of nature
generally, immeasurably enriched
our companionship, this work
is affectionately dedicated

About the Author

Author Eric Cronje Wilmot came to the Bechuanaland Protectorate (now Botswana) in the early 1900s, and after a stint as a stock farmer, worked for the Protectorate Government in various capacities in the field, including as a Stock Inspector, Tsetse Fly Control Officer and Ranger.

The events documented in this book took place while he was employed on the Tsetse Fly Control programme in the Okavango between 1944 and 1948. He had two sons and a daughter, with his son Bobby becoming a well-known Okavango crocodile hunter, and then founder of Crocodile Camp outside Maun. Bobby was a pioneer in the development of photographic safaris in the Okavango.

Cronje's grandson Lloyd, hunter turned conservationist and professional safari guide, carried on the family's close involvement with the Okavango, establishing Xaxaba Camp and later Lloyd's Camp in Savuti.

The picture below shows E Cronje Wilmot after his mauling by a lion, and the inset at right: E C Wilmot in later years. He died in the Eastern Cape in 1967.

CONTENTS

NEW MATERIAL

EDITORS' NOTES

C. T. ASTLEY MABERLY - 1955

WHEN Mr. Cronje Wilmot honoured me by requesting that I should glance through and arrange his original manuscripts recording his observations and experiences in Ngamiland and neighbouring areas of the Bechuanaland Protectorate, I felt that this would be indeed a worthwhile task. There is at present little literature concerning this fascinating, in many ways mysterious, portion of Southern Africa.

Mr. Cronje Wilmot's book is essentially a genuine narrative of that wild, unpredictable Africa which we — who have been fortunate enough to know it — have come to love so well.

This is no superficial record of a few, hastily conducted trips. It is the account of a man who has spent a lifetime in the area concerned: first as a stock farmer, and later as an official in the Tsetse Fly Control Department — to whose service he is still attached. In it, he gives us some insight into the various activities of the Tsetse Fly Control, takes us on tiger fishing and crocodile shooting expeditions into the mysterious Okavango swamps, relates numerous adventures with buffalo, lions, leopards, and other less well-known game of the swamplands — such as lechwe and sitatunga.

One of the most interesting chapters is that devoted to some of the local snakes, including the justly respected Mamba! His account of his mauling by a lion is one of the most vivid I have read.

In addition to his obvious experience as a hunter, the author is clearly a most keen and reliable observer, and as great a lover of trees and plants as he is of animal life.

Apart from mere entertainment value, however, the author has given us much food for reflection. For instance, his suggestion that the prevalence of Bubonic Plague throughout the territory may largely result from the intensive persecution of the smaller carnivorous mammals by the natives who find a profitable trade in their skins (thereby permitting an unnatural increase of the rodents which act as carriers), demands serious attention. His remarks and observations concerning the strange water systems and annual inundations of the Okavango and its tributaries are equally interesting.

I hope that naturalists, botanists, hunters and anglers, as well as all those who have experienced and enjoy the acrid smell of the camp fire, and love our beloved African veld for its own sake; will enjoy this book as much as I have done!

FRANK NUNAN - 2017

I GREW UP in Francistown during the 1960s at the time of the Bechuanaland Protectorate's transition to an independent Botswana. In the early 70s I spent just more than a year as a young geology intern for a large South African mining company, prospecting for diamonds and copper in the area around Lake Ngami. I know many of the places mentioned this book well: Maun, Sehitwa (where we bought our beer!), Toteng, the Kwebe Hills (modern spelling Kgwebe) - our main base camp was at Nwako Pan, not too far from the Hills.

I had been to school with two of the Wilmot sisters (Joyce and Daphne - Cronje's granddaughters) in Francistown and had recently "re-connected" with Daphne - and many other "Francistonians" from those days - through a Facebook Group called "Historical Francistown". At the instigation of members of this Group, I had become involved with the reproduction of an iconic little recipe book - *"Recipes from Bechuanaland"*, published by the Francistown Women's Institute in about 1959.

I found this gem: *"Always Lightly Tread"*, amongst a number of other examples of Africana collected by my late father, and neglected by me for years. I felt there may be some merit in bringing it back to life in the same way as the recipe book - it had been out of print for many, many years. I contacted Daphne via the Facebook Group, and put my suggestion to her. Her response was immediate and enthusiastic! She conferred with her brother Lloyd (legendary Okavango and Savuti professional safari guide), and his response was also immediate and very enthusiastic!. The project quickly became a "Wilmot Clan" project, and this wonderful book is the result.

I have, in the main, respected Mr Maberly's editing and have kept the book largely as it appeared in 1956, including Mr Maberly's excellent illustrations. However, two new chapters, previously unpublished, have been added: "The Baring Expedition" - an account of the visit to the Okavango by Sir Evelyn Baring, then British High Commissioner for Southern Africa, and his wife Lady Mary. The second is an article written by Cronje in later years on the Bushmen or "Masarwa".

I thank the Wilmots - in particular Lloyd and Daphne - for the opportunity to work on this wonderful project.

I hope you enjoy reading the book as much as I enjoyed working on it!

* * *

Chapter 1

INTO NGAMILAND

Kalahari Sand-Veld

'OCTOBER 4th, 1944. Radio message from Crawshaw reading as follows: '32 C. Oct. 3rd. Your appointment approved of stop You should proceed Maun by Govt. Lorry leaving Maun for Francistown tomorrow. Fly con'."

This message from Mr. Crawshaw, the Tsetse Fly Control Officer, was the result of an application I had made to the Director of Veterinary Services, Bechuanaland Protectorate Government, for employment in one of its establishments as a field officer. The appointment referred to was that of Assistant Overseer in the Tsetse Fly Control: with headquarters at Maun, Ngamiland. The duties consisted of office work at headquarters, erection of game fences, expulsion and destruction of game where necessary, and other field work in connection with the eradication of Tsetse fly, a real scourge in that country.

As I had for years nourished a great desire to get to Ngamiland: a desire which was strengthened by everything which I had heard and read about the country; I was greatly elated by the successful outcome of my application, and I lost no time in making my preparations to get away on the date given.

My son and daughter-in-law came into Francistown to see me off; and at 4.45 p.m. on October 6th, 1944, I joined the truck to rattle away on the three hundred and twenty mile trip   much the greater portion of which was across the northern extension of the Kalahari desert. Here (at that time at any rate) considerable miles of travelling had to be covered in auxiliary low gear. On account of the heavy going and the great extent of waterless stretches which have to be crossed, it was rarely that the journey was undertaken except with vehicles in convoy; and on this occasion our convoy consisted of three heavy trucks belonging to the Tsetse Control Department. Each was heavily laden with fencing wire, petrol and other equipment. The truck in which I travelled was driven by a European, and it took the lead. After three hours we arrived at Mosetse, one of the "Wenela's" (Witwatersrand Native Labour Association's) rest camps, where, after a couple of hours wait for the other trucks, we decided to sleep. One of the trucks arrived at midnight: its African driver reporting that it had been necessary for the other one to be taken back to Francistown on account of mechanical trouble.

After an early breakfast, my driver decided to carry on to Nata Drift and there to await the other trucks. Half way between the two places I met old friends in the persons of Mr. and Mrs. Bruce Rutherford. Mr. Rutherford had been the District Commissioner at Maun and was coming out on transfer. They both looked terribly worn out after a fatiguing trip in their light truck, having battled incessantly for two days through the heavy sand and fierce heat by day. A little over an hour after bidding them farewell, I reached the Nata, where I was destined to be held up for two days.

"Wenela" has a fine camp on the west bank of the river, and here I met a couple whom, sometime later on at Maun, I came to know quite well. They were Mr. and Mrs. E. Kendall, and during my brief stay at their camp they were most hospitable. Mr. Kendall was a road engineer in the employment of the recruiting corporation, and he had to do much travelling; having to supervise work over hundreds of miles of country.

At Nata I was back in familiar surroundings. Ten years previously, when acting as temporary Government Stock Inspector, I had done months of work up and down the river from its spillway into the Great Makarikari Salt pan right up to the Rhodesian border, as well as over a great deal of surrounding country. Therefore although I was impatient at the enforced delay, I considered myself fortunate that it should have occurred here among pleasing surroundings. I was able to point out to my friends where I formerly had an interesting encounter with and had killed my first lion — to be related later in this book.

At five o'clock on the afternoon of the 8th October, the Convoy being at long last re-assembled, we left Nata. Darkness soon set in, rendering any observation of our surroundings difficult, but a northerly extension of the great salt pan — a few miles wide — was traversed; its smooth, whitish alkaline surface showing up clearly in the starlight. I had never previously travelled in a heavy truck, and now found that my body ached from fatigue caused by the cramped position in the not very comfortable cab.

We had long since entered the heavy sand, and one has to become accustomed to the slow heaving motion and the shrill screaming of the extra low gear as the engine battles with a heavy load through the loose, resisting surface.

On the following day we left early, and drove straight through to Maun. The trip was most wearisome and monotonous. In all that vast stretch of wild, unoccupied country we saw only one gemstone, a wildebeest, and a few small buck. After all the heat and dust it was indeed enjoyable to reach the beautiful tree-lined Thamalukane River, and to hear the frogs rattling away in their throbbing chorus. The trees there were magnificent, some of the finest I have ever seen. Here we stopped for half an hour, and I stood to watch the fish leaping continuously in their efforts to negotiate the rapid beneath the wooden causeway by which we crossed the otherwise smoothly flowing stream. Finding a little backwater where there was no danger from crocodiles we bathed and rid ourselves of much of the filth collected during that trying, dusty journey. Nowhere else in the Protectorate had I seen so glorious a waterway, and I was as much enthralled by the grandeur of the trees as by the masses of lotus lilies dappling the unruffled surface of the water. Faintly quivering reflections lent depth and warmth to the tranquil and lovely scene. Maun being another six miles downstream, I reluctantly dragged myself away; but I then and there determined that whatever hours of leisure I might have, it would be on this river that they would be spent.

The road wound and twisted beneath the trees of the fringing forest, whence glimpses of the reed-lined channel were frequently obtained. Both known and unfamiliar bird calls echoed through the open woods, and much interesting vegetation and strange trees fascinated me. I felt I had entered a new and glamorous land.

Next to come into view was the "Wenela" Depot, nestling among trees at the water's edge; and shortly afterwards the tall masts of the Broadcasting Station. Finally appeared the main camp: scene of my future labours; where all the Government offices are situated. I had to consult my chief here before I finally settled into a comfortable room at Riley's Hotel.

Maun, the administrative centre of Ngamiland, had at the time of my arrival a European population of something over forty. These included Government officials of various departments, a resident staff of the "Wenela" Depot, a hospital run by the S.D.A. (Seventh Day Adventists - this was later taken over by the Bechuanaland Protectorate Government) and a London Missionary Society mission station. Four trading stores provided practically everything in the form of foodstuffs for both the white and African communities, but other requirements were generally imported. There were also a small school and a butchery, while the Meteorological Station (which provided the only means of rapid communication with the outside world) was run by a couple of young Air Force officers.

The little settlement straggles along the beautiful Thamalukani River for a distance of about three miles. Although it is so scattered (perhaps even on account of that) the community is a happy one, and the social life leaves little to be desired. Parties and dances are of frequent occurrence, and generally a fair percentage of the residents gathered at Riley's Hotel for an evening's entertainment: singsongs, impromptu dances, billiards, cards, dice, and the inevitable "Sundowners". Good pictures are shown at the weekly cinema, and the entertainment is made the occasion of pleasant sociability. Tennis on Saturdays was another of the social events which brought the people together, and there were some rattling good players, particularly among the ladies.

The settlement was connected with the main line at Francistown by a weekly mail and passenger service run by the enterprising Hotel Proprietor, whose fleet of trucks catered for most of the transport requirements. Large convoys of trucks belonging to "Wenela", carrying native recruits for the Rand mines, travelled the long, heavy track regularly. This organisation was largely responsible for the existence of the road, which extends for hundreds of miles beyond Maun to Mohembo and into South West Africa. It maintains continuous gangs of labourers engaged in maintenance and extensions.

There were several boats on the river: good, bad, and indifferent, which, during the fishing season, were invariably in demand. Fish could generally be caught along the fine reaches of the river, but for the best possible bream fishing one had to go out to the Botletle River - some eighteen miles distant - where amazing catches were secured.

I spent my first evening at Maun with Mr. Crawshaw, who had invited me for sundowners and a chat. I had met him a year or two previously, so we were not entirely unknown to each other. Also enjoying his hospitality was Lieutenant Ross Owens, who was in command of the local Police force. I had first made the latter's acquaintance during the 1933-34 Foot and Mouth campaign, when he was stationed at Tseaghaki on the Great Makarikari salt pan. Today he commands the Bechuanaland Police. The evening was pleasantly passed, and some of the comments I heard (as recorded in my diary) were: "'Choba' Weskob killed twenty two duck with a single shot as they rose off the water", and: "Harry Riley caught forty good bream yesterday afternoon, but he reckons that the fishing is not yet worthwhile but will improve as the season advances!" Fantastic and incredible as this sounded to me at the time, a short sojourn in the country soon convinced me otherwise, for I myself had killed nine duck in the same way (and that

" MOKOROS ".

with a charge of buckshot), and had by then seen Harry bring in bags of bream from Chanogha, on the Botletle, numbering more than double the number given. Anyhow, the information which I received that first evening augured well for enjoyable future free weekends, and it raised my enthusiasm to redhot pitch!

After a day in the office, I accompanied Mr. Crawshaw and Dr. Royle to the Xnaragha River where about one hundred employees of the Tsetse Fly Control had to receive anti-sleeping sickness injections. A rendezvous had been arranged where the ranger in charge of the gang — a Mr. Casalis — had been instructed to have a small boat and a couple of mokoros (dugouts) awaiting our arrival. Later on causeways were constructed over the various streams, and the picturesque, but unreliable, river craft ceased to be used. In this case, through a misunderstanding on the part of the Africans, the craft were taken (unknown to us of course) to a place other than that arranged, so we had a lengthy wait.

Walking along the margin of the river, I watched immense shoals of young bream which seemed fairly to stiffen the water, and I longed for a casting net. As I approached, they dashed away into deeper water, just as I had seen mullet do in the shallows of tidal rivers, only in vastly greater numbers. I speculated as to what happened to these finny multitudes when the waters of the annual inundations had seeped away, as they do year after year. From immemorial times, waterfowl of numerous description had, no doubt, fed to repletion from the "silvery hordes": and when no water remained, hyenas, jackals, the various cats and other carnivores probably did the cleaning up. I think though, that there

is some truth in the theory that these fishes dig themselves into the sand, remaining in a comatose condition deep down until they can emerge once more with the advent of new water. How, otherwise can one account for their presence in isolated pools shortly after the coming of rain?

There were a lot of buffalo tracks in the moist sand, and apparently a small herd had been there during the early hours of the morning. After their drink they had grazed a while on the lush river grass. I little imagined then that this very area was to be the scene of many affairs with these creatures in die future!

Returning to my companions, I joined them in an enjoyable cup of tea. No one in that country undertakes a lorry journey without the old "scoff box" containing tea, sugar, powdered milk, and odds and ends of canned foods, because to be held up for many hours through being bogged, or stuck in heavy sand, is a most common occurrence.

It was a good deal later before the boats finally arrived, and we lost no time in getting away. This was my first trip by water in the swamp lands, but unfortunately a bad headache and an aching body spoiled my enjoyment of it. Having had a good deal of malaria in the past, I was shrewdly suspicious of what was brewing!

En route, on a little sandy knoll at the waterside, I saw the heads of two newly killed buffalo bulls. Further along, festoons of their flesh draped over rods resting on forked poles reminded us that

we were nearing our destination: though owing to perpendicular banks at the camp, we had to disembark about a quarter of a mile before reaching it. The Mopani trees were by then casting lengthy, lazy shadows; and by the time the syringes were sterilized, the sun, like an immense globe of crimson fire, was dipping to the horizon. The doctor was soon busy, but it was nevertheless quite dark before, straightening himself, he at last remarked: "Well, I'm through!" The following morning it was my own turn for an injection, as I had sustained a sharp attack of malaria — contracted probably on the banks of the Gwebe River in Rhodesia, whence I had arrived prior to my departure from Francistown. However I was soon over it, and back at work.

After a couple of weeks at the office, I was sent a few miles up-river to supervise a gang engaged in clearing undergrowth. A few fly persisted in the area, and occasional ones were caught in the cabs of passing trucks. Some scattered kraals of native-owned cattle grazed the locality, and it was necessary to take all measures to eliminate the pest: particularly as horses belonging to the police and local headmen frequently wandered into the danger zone, with resulting isolated cases of Nagana.

I pitched my cottage tent within a couple of hundred yards of the river, thoroughly enjoying the outdoor life and work. However, on the very first night I discovered that conditions were not to be as pleasant as I had anticipated.

The whole area was overrun by mice and gerbilles. They rendered a night's rest impossible by running over my face and hands and into everything during the hours of darkness. Within a few days I was worn out for want of rest, and I sent a runner to headquarters with a minute explaining the position and requesting traps and poison. At the same time I mentioned that I had noticed some mortality among the rodents — though I did not, at that time, attach as much significance to this phenomenon as I should have done.

No traps were available, but the messenger brought a large, lidded pail containing some disinfectant or preservative, and a letter instructing me to kill, with the aid of my staff, as many mice as possible. These had to be dropped into the pail, which was to be returned with its contents the following morning. Accordingly, after supper I collected the boys and, with flashlights and sticks, we began a great mouse hunt. In half an hour over sixty were accounted for: more than the preservative could cover, and the remainder were incinerated. That night I had little peace, and at dawn I sent off the specimens before starting on the day's work.

During the afternoon a carload of officials arrived, and a heavy, empty truck followed shortly afterwards. My chief came up and issued instructions that my camp was to be broken forthwith. He gave me no specific reason, though I already had my suspicions on that point. There were several doctors, one of whom — together with a Health Officer — hailed from Southern Rhodesia, having been lent by the Rhodesian Government to advise on the best measures for stemming a widespread outbreak of bubonic plague which was then raging in Ngamiland.

I immediately set about packing all my effects, while the officials supervised the burning of all grass shelters erected by my gang, and also the pumping of cyanide gas into the innumerable burrows scattered widely over the sandy terrain. I observed that all officials wore bandages wound puttee-wise and tightly round their trousers: presumably to hinder the entrance of fleas. At length, when a pretty thorough clean-up had been made, and all was ready for our return to headquarters, Rodent boys were summoned and the officers, one at a time, had themselves thoroughly dusted with odoriferous insecticide.

It duly transpired that the specimens which I had sent in were carrying plague-infected fleas, hence these elaborate precautions. Thus, remembering the fact that I had been in the thick of the infestation, that fleas had gambolled over and fed on my person (only on the previous night I had written in my diary: "have been flea-bitten and shall be lucky to escape the disease"), it now struck me as decidedly amusing that everyone else had been far too engrossed about ridding themselves of possible fleas to notice that I was escaping the attentions of the pump gang!

At this period, Maun was the centre of a good deal of trouble. This is well illustrated by the following brief extracts from my diary:

26/10/44: "Plague is rife, and there has been a number of deaths. Today we hear that Small Pox has also broken out. Ye Gods! What with Plague, Small Pox, Malaria, Sleeping Sickness and

Mumps, the doctors are having a hectic time. It has been recommended that all women and children be sent out of the country, and this is being done. Chicken Pox has also appeared, and Dr. Fox tells me there have been numerous deaths from dysentery at Mohembo".

30th October: "This afternoon all Europeans assembled at Riley's Hotel, at 4.30, to receive anti-plague injections."

November 4th: "Another four doctors arrived — two from Rhodesia."

November 5th: "There are altogether now seven medical officers with about the same number of European assistants. Sir Walter Johnson and the Resident Commissioner left for Francistown this afternoon."

GERBILLE.

Chapter 2

GAME FENCE CONSTRUCTION AND SOME UNCOMMON NGAMILAND FISHES

I WAS disappointed that my work had been cut short by the outbreak of plague at my camp on the Thamalukane. The place was just a mile or so below the causeway at Motlapeneng where Burger and I had bathed on our way from Francistown, and I had looked forward to a month or two in this area. I soon discovered, however, that I would be in equally pleasant country at Khantsaang where I was to supervise the same sort of work.

The river at Khantsaang is an extension of the Thamalukane, but it is necessary to study a map of the river system in order to appreciate the complicated network of waterways which intersects the country. This branch of the Thamalukane at Khantsaang is called Nghabe, but as it meanders towards Lake Ngami its name changes several times: indeed, it ceases to be a river further along; no water having reached the lake along its sandy channel for many years.

Early on the morning of November 17th, 1944, Mr. Crawshaw, Burger and I set out for Drotsky's camp, which was situated in an ancient waterway near the Kwebe hills. Mr. Drotsky was the Department's official well sinker, and here he was down twenty two feet and had, on our arrival, just encountered rolled rubble and fragments of limestone. The overburden consisted of silt and blown sand. The possibilities of finding water at this place seemed quite good, but — typical of the contrariness of Africa — after months of work, and at a depth of over one hundred feet the site had to be abandoned.

The distance from Maun to Kwebe is about fifty two miles, and on our way we passed two wells which had been put down by Drotsky. The first was at a place called Patikwa, the only really satisfactory site as here a fair supply of sweet water was struck. I was subsequently sent to erect a fly-proof building for experimental work at this spot, so shall refer to it again later.

The Kwebe hills appeared interesting, but I had no opportunity to explore them. A few local bushmen mentioned that leopards frequent the hills: and from a different source I learned that certain types of vegetation exist there that are found nowhere else in Ngamiland.

Gold was at one time located near the nearer end of the range, but I could collect little information about this lonely working. It appears that the B.S.A. (British South Africa) Company opened the prospect in 1896, but obviously they had closed down not long afterwards as there are no indications of prolonged work. Old concrete plinths, with embedded holding-down bolts, showed that heavy machinery had been installed, and I have often wondered how supplies were taken to the working.

The ancient river bed joins the Botletle near Makalamabedi, and it appears to have been the probable route from the old Palachwe-Toteng road. The distance was great, though, and there were several long "thirsts" (one of at least three days between Makalamabedi and Palapye) so that the prospects must have been fairly auspicious for any work to have been begun at all in so remote a locality. Perhaps, with easier and faster modern transport facilities, some enterprising small worker will find a living in the workings.

On our return, I remained at Khantsaang while the others proceeded to Maun. I erected my tent about a quarter of a mile from where the boys had settled in, soon making myself comfortable. There was no indication that I would be disturbed by rodents here; and, with the river just below me, I anticipated an enjoyable and interesting time. For the present period I was to have about ten days work here. Thereafter — early in January — I was to proceed to the Xnaragha River, which was to be spanned by a wooden causeway. The site indicated was a few miles up from the large Tsoda pan.

On the completion of a day's work at Khantsaang there always remained about an hour during which I could enjoy some fishing or shooting. Though the river was low, it still had some current, and I spent all my leisure time along its margin. After a day's absence, Burger returned to my camp. The causeway spanning the river there needed antheap "topping", and he had been given this work, which occupied nearly a week. He was a crack shot with a catapult, and, when I needed bait, was usually able to get a bird — the intestines of which served reasonably well when nothing else was available. Sometimes we went out at night and with the aid of a flashlight found numerous francolin roosting in the big thorny Acacias. Burger always managed to knock off several which, with the bream which I caught, formed a tasty addition to the "pot".

I was walking along the riverside one morning, when a number of Whistling duck, startled at my sudden appearance, rose noisily off the water and I immediately fired into the midst of them with my last cartridge, an AAA. The distance was probably forty yards, and I was surprised to see a number of the birds fluttering to the water. Here was food, and bait, to last me several days. However, the floating birds were some distance out in the river, and, with crocodiles present, there was undoubtedly some risk in collecting them. I was determined not to leave them, so, having stripped, I waded slowly towards the birds. The latter were scattered in a broad line, and I reached the nearest before the water had risen to my waist. My companion shouted to me, emphasising the danger of venturing further into the river. Only a few yards separated me from the last of the birds, so I took the risk: moving on up to shoulder depth and gathering the last of the lot — nine in all!

The Khantsaang pool is probably half a mile in length, and deep over long stretches, and I had seen several crocodiles there, both out of and in the water. It was therefore undoubtedly foolish to have entered the pool at all, of course, and I was quite aware of the fact: having previously been rebuked for similar acts of stupidity! That was in Southern Rhodesia when on one occasion I entered the crocodile-infested Hunyani River to free a snagged fishing line at the one end of which a fine Yellow fish was jerking. In this case I also waded breast deep, and then had to go down head first to loosen the line. Again I was lucky, for there were crocs about, and I eventually landed my fish. Such acts, nonetheless, are worthy only of a madman as crocodiles are real killers; and in its own element even a half-grown one would be a match for any man. Later in this narrative some account will be given of a terrifying experience which I had with a croc in Southern Rhodesia, as well as some more recent adventures.

Owing to Burger's wife being suddenly taken ill, he had to return to Maun for a few days. These included the weekend, I was in desperate straights for bait. There had been a brisk lower of rain,

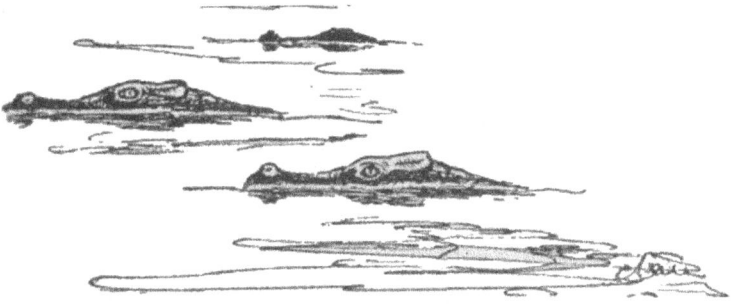

and the veld swarmed with small "thousand-legs" (Millipedes) of a grey-brown colour. Horrid little brutes icy appeared to me, but I wondered vaguely whether that opinion would be shared by the local bream, pike, etc., so I decided to experiment with them as bait. I am squeamish about handling "goggas" at any time, and my first attempts to thread these on the hooks sent little shudders up and down my spine: but the results they brought were so astonishing that I quickly lost my aversion to handling the revolting things. The fish literally went mad over them, and I had grand sport in consequence, but unfortunately they vanished almost as suddenly as they had appeared. One evening, while still at Khantsaang, and while engaged in preparing a fish fillet for a pike hook, I glanced casually down the long reach of the river. I immediately spotted an object which I expect few anglers have beheld under similar circumstances. About forty yards away the head, and perhaps a yard of body of a huge serpent emerged from the water and remained poised, as if about to strike some object. Hardly able to believe my eyes, I stared at the nasty looking creature which remained in this alert posture for perhaps a minute, when it submerged with hardly a ripple left on the surface, grabbed my rifle, and ran at full speed down the river opposite where I judged the snake had disappeared. But though I waited a long time I never saw it again.

The snake was as large as the biggest python I have ever beheld, and I cannot think otherwise than that it was a python, though it looked almost black. That, however, could have been caused by the fact that the sun was setting, and the high banks were casting deep shadows across the water. I have often since

wondered why snakes appear to be immune from attacks by crocodiles. They certainly never hesitate to enter water infested with these brutes, and pythons particularly often occur in such places.

I was working at Khantsaang during the hottest time of the year, and at times the heat was most trying, particularly when we got into the thick, low *Moselesele* and *Grewia* scrub. Also the hours were long for we were nearing the longest day of the year, and I always worked according to the sun. In spite of this I thoroughly enjoyed my brief stay; though, apart from guineafowl, waterfowl, and francolin, the area was practically devoid of wild life, and I got little shooting. One of the official hunters was attached to my gang, and twice during my stay this man procured big buck (one of which was a fine gemsbuck bull), but he had to go immense distances for them, and work was delayed through having to send men to bring home the meat.

In due course I returned to Maun, and here I was given additional equipment and sent out to Xnaragha River, where the causeway had to be built, and where about sixty boys awaited my arrival.

Large quantities of heavy Mopani poles had been cut in the surrounding forests, and many of these had already been trundled in on small hand-operated wagons, fitted with pneumatic tyres. I immediately began to expedite this work, as it was necessary to have all materials on the spot before the construction could be begun. Under continuous supervision, the work progressed rapidly, and by the tenth of January I was able to start on the actual building. From an engineering point of view, the methods we had to employ were of the crudest: the one purpose being to have some cheap means of crossing the streams which carry a lot of water during a few months in each year. All such work had to be done at speed: appearance and "finish" not entering the picture at all.

A fine tree grew near the bridge site, and I had my tent erected beneath it. It was a pleasantly wild and lonely spot, and it suited me very well for I was at least half a mile from the noise and racket of the large compound which the natives had established before my arrival. During my first two nights at this camp, lions roared grandly, but thereafter I never heard them again: the activities of a large gang of boys in the surrounding bush probably causing them to retire to more secluded parts. A wretched hyena, however, used to serenade me nightly, as it passed on towards the compound, where, doubtless, odd bones and scraps of hide formed an attraction.

By the nineteenth, the causeway was complete except for the antheap topping, and that I left for the attention of the lorry driver with half a dozen assistants. Of the temporarily large gang, I sent all but sixteen back to Casalis's camp where they belonged, and then began work on the game fence which would, in due course, pass within a mile of where I was then camped.

Enormous numbers of posts had still to be brought in and laid along the line cut through the bush. Many of these posts had to be conveyed from four to six miles. They had all been barked, but still required to be cut to an even length. The majority of these could be put down with ground augers, but there were long stretches where digging bars had to be employed.

The fence (very many miles of which had already been erected from the Toteng (Lake Ngami) end by Rangers Casalis and Odendaal) consisted of an eight-strand job, seven feet high.

The posts were chiefly of Mopani and they were supposed to average eight inches at the base. They were spaced thirty six feet apart, and four or five wooden droppers were used in between. Altogether, about one hundred and twenty miles of fencing had to be erected (this was later doubled), about half of which had been completed when I arrived. The purpose of the fence was to prevent game entering the country on its eastern side. All animals trapped in that portion (and there were many thousands of them) had to be shot out. This was being done, systematically, by some hundreds of native hunters under the supervision of the European rangers.

These hunters were camped down at regular intervals on, or near, the marked out line of the fence, and they covered a huge extent of the fly-infested country. It is not necessary to state how they were controlled, but methods were employed which enabled the rangers to handle them pretty efficiently. A strict tally of all animals destroyed was always available at the month's end, when many returns had to be submitted. The hides and skins were trucked to Headquarters, and regularly disposed of from there.

All pay was taken out to the men in the field. Month after month I shared in this duty, and was thus able to see a great deal of the country: slowly gaining a little insight into the amazingly complicated network of waterways which comprises the delta of the Great Okavango.

Those trips usually entailed sleeping out at least one night, but not infrequently two or even three when we met unforeseen delays such as being stuck in bad tracks or sand or mud, or through mechanical break downs. I found such outings a wholly enjoyable break from the uncongenial indoor work at Headquarters.

For a couple of weeks I was able to carry on with the fence without having to shift my camp at the bridge. The work was of a kind which I was accustomed to perform periodically over many years during my previous farming career; and my principle worry was to get a fair day's labour out of Africans, completely unused to heavy work as they were unable to comprehend why a certain length of fencing had to be completed on each succeeding day. It would be so much easier and more reasonable too — to leave a portion over for completion on the following day! It was a long while before they became accustomed to steady production work, from the boredom of which they frequently sought release by pleading for "muti" for an aching head, or belly, or for time off to "bury brother". On the whole, however, they were a cheerful, light-hearted crowd which, in time, hardened up excellently to the heavy manual labour. A couple of hunters was attached to each labour gang, and there was seldom a shortage of meat in the camp, and this of course worked wonders!

Although I had encountered Tsetse during pay trips, or when other duties brought me into the fly belt, I had never previously seen so many of the pests as appeared in this area. I was bitten literally scores of times each day, and often during moonlight nights as well. To me, the bite was just like a jab from a needle — painful for a few moments, then over until another fly came for a feed. I suffered no irritating aftereffects, nor even the slightest swelling, and I was probably fortunate in this respect. I have seen many people, allergic to the bite, suffer great inconvenience resulting from the attentions of Tsetse flies.

On the other hand, minute sand flies rendered my life a misery. There are many kinds of these: some so minute as to be almost invisible; but all loaded with a type of venom sufficiently irritating almost to drive one mad. Moreover, in my case the dreadful itch lasted about a week and was always accompanied by some swelling. The natives call the larger species Letoba, and the others Moetsana. For my part, I most feelingly called them a lot of things! Unlike Tsetse, these sand flies, fortunately, were only in evidence during about four months in a year. During that period they certainly made the most of their opportunities. Eventually I found that I could ward off their attacks by frequently rubbing all exposed parts with a swab impregnated with citronella oil, and I thereafter always carried a shoe polish tin containing my swab. It was never left in camp, which is more than I can say about the Snakebite outfit which was seldom seen for months on end.

While citronella is so effective against sand flies and midges, it causes Tsetse no discomfort whatever, and I never discovered an effective repellent for these flies. Tsetse are resolute, quick and silent in attack; and it is only by sheer good luck that you are aware of their presence before you receive their painful "sword thrusts". If the latter are delivered in a nerve, they will make you jump!

Tsetse are equipped by nature with the ability to alight, even on sensitive portions of the human skin, without being felt. Should you happen to see one and attempt to slap it to pulp you will immediately realise its lightning speed. With a little practice it becomes possible to kill them by striking with both hands open and in such manner that the palms slap together just above where the fly is resting, but even then there will be as many misses as hits!

During the time I was engaged on fencing work I seldom had a midday meal. It was usually too hot even to think about eating and I also became accustomed to going without a drink for many hours at a time. On occasions, though, I suffered from intolerable thirst, when I simply had to search for water, or else go miles back to camp. One such incident comes clearly to mind, as in this case my search for water led me to the discovery of some very interesting natural history specimens.

The head of the fence was then at a place called Maropi, where at one time some hunters were posted. I had passed there once, and now recalled having seen ground periodically swamped, and rather imagined that I had noticed a string of small, shallow pans. I was by no means certain, though, that this was indeed the place I had in mind. However, by a lucky chance I walked right on to the little pans.

They contained nothing more than rapidly drying mud, but as they lay in a slight depression with clumps of reeds here and there, I pressed on a little further and presently noticed egrets, divers, and a few other waterfowl on some low bushes and tussocks of stiff swamp grass. There I found a fairly large pan containing a lot of water — rather muddied by the birds, but still a welcome sight to a partly dehydrated human. The water was lukewarm: but — well it was wet! I drank my fill, and sat down for a smoke. Tracks on the sandy margin of the pool indicated that buffalo and wildebeest had also visited the pan. Their spoor, plainly visible, obliterated that of many other creatures.

I wandered a little further, and presently came on another puddle which had obviously been receiving a lot of attention from the larger aquatic birds. It contained just a ribbon of shallow water — probably two yards across and some six or eight feet in length — all that remained of quite a considerable pool. I was immediately intrigued by movements in the water, so, slipping off my boots, I waded in and found that a number of fish of different kinds thronged the sandy bottom. Using both hands with quick, sweeping motions I soon managed to fling several fish on to the dry, muddied sand. Just the merest glance revealed that two of these were quite unknown to me, so, hurriedly, I renewed my efforts, and in a very little while I had a dozen out of the water.

It was necessary to return to work now, so I collected some water grass in which I firmly bound the specimens, hoping that they would remain reasonably cool in the wet covering: though having no preservatives in my camp I had no hopes of finally saving them. My object was merely to get them to camp in the best condition as I had an excellent book on the freshwater fishes of South Africa with which I could identify the various species. It duly turned out that the specimens consisted of the following fishes:

FAMILY	GENUS & SPECIES	COMMON NAME
1. *Paratilapia*	*P. Longimans*	*Large-mouthed Bream*
2. " "	*P. Angusticeps*	" " "
3. *Mormyrididae*	*Mormyrus anchietae*	*Bottle nose*
4. *Anabasidae*	*Anabas multispinnis*	?

I was particularly pleased to see the "bottle noses", for, oddly enough, I had made several enquiries about these fish; but no one, not even the Makuba (the River folk) seemed to know them. Possibly my description was insufficiently clear for these latter to recognise the fish in question, for the Makuba are great fishermen, and should be acquainted with all local species. I found that the three specimens I had collected from the pool were different to the Rhodesian Bottle nose, which is named: *M. longirostris*. Of these latter I have caught a dozen in various Rhodesian rivers; the largest weighing 5 lbs.; but I know of specimens over 10 lbs. being taken. *Longirostris* is a golden-brown when taken from the water: but those in Ngamiland are blue-black with milky white bellies, and their snouts are shorter. In East Africa, *Mormyrus* generally are called "Elephant snout", and this species is also known as the Egyptian Sacred fish and it is figured in Ancient Egyptian, hieroglyphics. The homely Rhodesian name "Bottle nose" is not a particularly dignified appellation for this finny aristocrat.

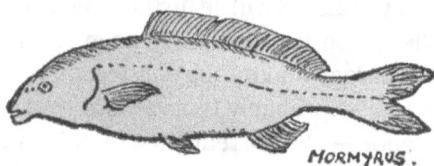

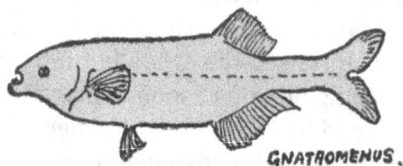

MORMYRUS.

GNATHOMENUS.

If angled for in deepish water, with earthworms as bait, these fish are sooner or later bound to be caught in Ngamiland. I never, afterwards, saw either *Mormyrus* or *Anabas*, though I caught numbers of *Paratilapia*, which greedily go for a tiny spoon or large artificial flies and spinners, as well as the usual baits used for *Tilapia*. Some time later on I was fortunate in securing a rather rare fish which was included in a bunch of fresh Tilapia which a native had just removed from his non-return trap. This was also a *Mormyr*, and it is scientifically known as *Gnathonemus macrolepedotus*. This specimen was sent to the Grahamstown Museum, and it is probably still there.

Chapter 3

MY FIRST BUFFALO HUNT

I CANNOT remember spending a weekend in my camp while I was engaged in fence construction.

Invariably by the first streak of dawn I was fortifying myself with cups of hot coffee: bread and butter, or just a chunk of cold cooked game. Then, as soon as it was possible to see, I would set off for a day's shooting, or perhaps merely a ramble to see more of the country. I walked immense distances during that time, toughening myself to such an extent that I rarely became aware of fatigue.

Game, though still plentiful in the Xnaragha Valley, was excessively wild — owing to the persecution to which it had been subjected. One had to work hard for a shot, and there were many blank days from a shooting point of view, though not in other respects. It was then that the wild, unspoilt veld: the endless varieties of birds: the vegetation: the myriads of tracks dotting game-paths or the margins of pans, and much else besides, held my interest in thrall and proved ceaselessly fascinating.

My boys (who invariably evinced a greater liking for their homes than for the "Bundu") wasted little time in getting away on Saturday afternoons, and I never attempted to persuade them to stay. In any case I preferred being on my own when making long tramps. Occasionally permission was sought to accompany me from men whose homes were a long way off, and these I never refused, and on occasions they proved to be very useful.

I spent much time trying to circumvent the local buffalo which, from constant persecution, had become amazingly cunning. But it was a long time before I was successful. It had been an indifferent rainy season. The many small pans which should have been full of water contained nothing but mud or a mere covering of slimy, odoriferous fluid which — owing to the wallowing habits of both warthog and buffalo — became filthier and smellier day by day.

The tracks of most of the game were converging on Tsoda Pan which still contained perfectly clear and, in parts, deep water. All other adjacent waters had soaked away so — though it was some distance out of my way — I found it advantageous to proceed to the first, and then follow whatever tracks suited my purpose.

It befell, therefore, that one morning I reached Tsoda at sunrise. Even at that early hour, however, all the game had already departed. A pair of belated reedbuck spotted me, whistled shrilly; galloped, with "rocking-horse action" and fanned tails, for a short distance along the water's edge; paused to glance back. They made a charming picture, as their reflections with that of their background embellished the ripple-free water.

Among an abundance of spoor, that of a large herd of buffalo was evident. The buffalo had wandered between the trees and bush surrounding the pan, grazing on patches of lush grass; and I frequently caught fleeting whiffs of the strong bovine smell so often noticeable after the recent presence of these beasts. Apparently they had not lingered long, for the tracks of a considerable number made off in a south-westerly direction, straight towards the heavy sand belts.

I followed the spoor, noticing that the herd was composed of a number of small parties which had evidently united at the water; because ever and anon groups of tracks led off at a tangent — either to one side or the other — and these did not again join up. My camp (quite a few miles away) lay well to the right of the direction pursued by the animals, so I followed the spoor bearing most nearly in that direction.

Though there was no evidence of alarm, it was clear that the buffalo had neither loitered nor paused to nibble. I was clearly involved in a long walk, and I decided to make a day of it, if necessary. One hour, two hours, passed; but the spoor still doggedly held the same direction — though by now it had been reduced to that of two animals, both big bulls. The country was dreadfully sandy and heavy to walk over but no art was required to hold to the tracks which were plainly visible.

After a while I found that the buffalo were constantly veering a point or two in the direction they were following. That this was intentional was confirmed by the spoor leading first to one, then to another, and so on, of several small pans of mud, where the beasts had stopped for a brief wallow before moving on again. Buffaloes always have a plastering of mud over their bodies in dry weather: doubtless finding it a protection from the attentions of Tsetse and the many other biting flies which abound in Ngamiland.

After several more hours of fairly fast walking on my part, I began to wonder if the old brutes had no intention of lying up at all! One small patch of good grass revealed signs of a feed, and as there was a fair amount of heavy timber on three sides ahead, I felt a surge of hope that I might soon come on terms with my quarry, as the heat, by now, was becoming terrific. There was no danger of the game scenting me, as it had steadily travelled up wind.

Reaching the outskirts of the thicker bush, I stood on an old fallen trunk in deep shadow and carefully peered all round, for often buffalo will, on reaching forest land, remain motionless for a long period: waiting beneath a tree or bush and staring in various directions, but particularly in that whence they have come.

No! Not a sign! So moving on cautiously I entered some juke thick bush with a good canopy: the very place they would be likely to choose. I now advanced with considerable care, but, oddly enough, the buffalo had not halted in what seemed an ideal resting place, but had at length moved out of it into very broad expanse of scrub Mopani with a few tall trees a long way ahead. I must confess that at this point my enthusiasm began to weaken, and I was sorely tempted to leave the old brutes and try for something else in the long belt of tall timber through which I had just passed. However, since the buffalo were now moving almost directly towards my already distant camp, and the first craving for something cool to drink was becoming urgent, I doggedly stuck to the spoor for another half hour and then decided to return to camp: intending, after a long rest and some food to try up river for pig, pallah, or any other of the smaller game.

Meanwhile my present need for water was becoming sufficiently urgent to put most other thoughts out of my mind, when, on walking through a perfectly dry, small pan, I again noticed very fresh buffalo spoor. I was no longer sufficiently interested to slacken my speed.

Thus it was that, rounding a huge termite heap with a thick, thorny acacia at its edge, I practically walked right on to the two old bulls! The first indication I received was a startlingly sudden and loud snort — as arresting as a rifle shot — and a simultaneous vision of two massive black forms advancing in my direction. As I instinctively recoiled from so unexpected an apparition, my heel encountered an obstacle which all but set me heels over head! However, as I recovered myself, the two bulls stood facing me, with characteristic uplifted muzzles, at a distance of not more than ten yards. I lost not a moment in placing a bullet in the chest of the foremost, whereupon they both swung round and crashed off into the bush in the twinkling of an eye. It all happened so quickly that, as I rushed forward, they were momentarily lost to view and I was unable to tell which was the wounded one.

Suddenly the two buffaloes doubled round and galloped past me at about seventy yards. The great beast I had fired at was now running very heavily, and a considerable distance behind its fellow. I expected its imminent collapse, and stupidly refrained from giving it another bullet. The opportunity passed in a couple of seconds and was never again presented.

I walked after them, but they were soon out of my sight and I had to take up the spoor which was easy enough to follow. Very soon it led me into really nasty, thick Moselesele scrub, and thereafter the utmost caution was necessary. The beasts had turned downwind: a thing which harassed or wounded buffalo often do, and which renders the following of them very dangerous as they are able to scent you from a considerable distance.

Considering its bulk, no other living beast is more difficult to see in cover — however slight — than a buffalo. The ease with which their mud-daubed hides blend with the shadows of even thinnish forest is matched only by the cunning which they display in selecting positions which the hunter (who usually has all his senses concentrated on the thicker, darker patches of cover) hardly stops to notice. A wounded one, having taken up such a position, will charge without fail the moment a suitable opportunity is presented: and the hoarse grunts accompanying such a charge — usually from a quite unexpected quarter — have an unpleasant effect on the nerves, and only the most accurate shooting will stop the beast.

It is very unusual, though, for a buffalo (unless it is very severely wounded) to turn away and remain behind when its companions are in full flight; and I have followed hard-hit ones for hours without coming on terms with them.

The beast I was after now was severely wounded, and as I advanced into the scrub — one step at a time — I braced myself for instantaneous action.

A few gnarled and twisted Mopani trees reared high above the Moselesele, and I hoped that the spoor (which I dared not for one moment abandon) would skirt closely one of the trees so that I could climb the latter and locate my quarry from a greater height. However, this was not so, and I continued with even greater caution than before: feeling very certain that at any moment the now almost unbearable tension would be broken by the grunting onslaught of the wounded bull.

I am of opinion that just as a situation develops in intensity, so also does a hunter's every sense sharpen when he is in pursuit of dangerous game; so that precautions which, under less tense moments he would probably consider unnecessary, are taken quite unconsciously yet with utmost accuracy. It is man's ability to reason rapidly that has preserved his comparatively frail body down the ages!

These two buffalo provided (during a brief period of perhaps fifteen minutes) the sort of experience that makes the following of these beasts surely one of the most exciting types of sport in existence. However, the affair was to end tamely after all because in a short while the forest thinned out into the usual low Mopani scrub once more, and this was bounded, a long distance ahead, by another belt of dense bush. I could see no sign of the game ahead, so they must have already entered the timber. The inevitable reaction set in; all my leg weariness and torturing desire for water returned in a rush. The spoor now led directly away from my camp, so I decided to give up the hunt and return to camp.

* * *

It was at this time that I received instructions from Headquarters to move in the matter of stopping all shooting outside the area bounded by the fence, now under construction. It was most desirable that this area should be recognised by the wild creatures as "sanctuary". We knew that our own hunters were violating this rule, in spite of repeated warnings. It therefore became necessary to catch them at it. It was while on a patrol of this sort that I had a rather amusing experience with buffalo.

I set out one morning while the stars were still shining, accompanied by a young Bushman whom I had promoted to the status of a hunter. He was a cheery, intelligent lad; and I had liked him from the time he had first come to me with other labourers from Maun. I followed a north-westerly direction which would take me past the left of Maropi — near which place we crossed the fence line.

The going was heavy: the sandy surface being riddled by myriads of rodent burrows. One broke through the crust with nearly every step and this made even a few miles of such progress exhausting. I wondered, as I struggled along, how the tens of thousands of mice and gerbilles found sufficient sustenance in the scanty, tussocky herbage.

At length I came to a waterway of considerable size and obviously quite deep. Teal and cormorants and other water fowl were passing up and down the stream, and they contributed in no small measure to a scene which, typical of the swamp lands, was the embodiment of peace and quiet. Resting here a while, I envied the birds and longed, with them, to plunge into the cool depths; but the terrible, watchful crocodiles discourage all such liberties and pleasure!

Suddenly the peace of the scene was dispersed by the vicious bark of two rifle reports, in quick succession, sounding from some distance across the water. After a brief interval, several more shots rang out, followed after a slight pause by a final bang whose echo hurtled through the woods. We were now thoroughly alert. The Bushman declared that the hunters had killed something, and I had heard the unmistakable thud of a bullet.

The shots had been fired perhaps half a mile away. I immediately realised that, lacking a craft in which to cross the river, it would be impossible to reach the poachers who obviously must have had a dug-out hidden somewhere up or down the stream. There were too many crocs about to make swimming attractive!

While I was still debating this point, eight buffalo came diagonally galloping towards the stream on the opposite side. When close to the water, they pulled up and stood gazing in the direction from which they had come. They bunched up, then separated, then again drew together - they were obviously both excited and scared. Wondering what they were about to do, I watched interestedly, but they seemed in no hurry to move away. They were quite unsuspicious of danger from any side but the one from which they had come: and though we were on open ground they had failed to make us out, which was extraordinary for buffalo because generally they are very keen sighted.

At length two began to walk down stream, and presently the remainder trotted after them, and joining up they all galloped slowly along the edge of the river. For just a brief while they again halted; looking back on their tracks. They were troubled; and I wondered if an old, trusted leader had been laid low in the bush beyond the stream. However, after a few seconds, they swung round with a snort and almost immediately entered the water and were soon swimming to our side of the stream.

About three hundred yards ahead of us, a narrow strip of bush extended almost to the water's edge. As it was apparent that the buffalo would emerge thereabouts, I ran at full speed towards the place while the "Buffs" were yet swimming. However, they landed first, and had already entered the jutting strip of cover before I could reach the spot. I had no intention of shooting at them, but merely wanted to obtain a close view.

As I entered and passed through the tongue of cover I was just in time to see the tail end of the small herd reach the fringing forest. To amuse the Bushman at my heels, I called out: *"Dumela Banna!"* ("Good day! Friends!"). To my astonishment, the buffalo immediately turned and came trotting out of the wood and they lined up in a closely packed bunch within ten yards of where I was standing, right in the open, grassy glade.

They were all young but adult bulls, and they acted like a lot of young bloods out for a bit of fun. Had they been especially trained for the part, it could not have been more neatly executed. As they gazed at the curious, pale-coloured biped, I could see every detail of their faces — even their eyelashes! They stood with raised muzzles; their gleaming, massive horns well back against their shoulders, evidently as interested as I was: and they formed a fine picture. As I watched them closely, I held my rifle in readiness, though I hardly expected to use it. Those buffalo were just about as friendly as such beasts can ever be!

I again shouted: *"Dumela Banna!"*, but not a move did they make. It was an opportunity for a priceless photograph, for such chances come but rarely in a lifetime. Alas, I had no camera!

As I shouted the second time, I heard a snigger some little distance back from where I stood; but I did not take my eyes from the buffalo. When, after a moment or two, they swung round and galloped away, I glanced round, and there was my Bushman — perched on an antheap in the strip of bush, grinning broadly. I think we both enjoyed that little bit of fun.

We hung about for some time, hoping to discover something about the men whose shooting we had heard across the river. Nothing further was seen or heard of them, so finally we departed on the long, homeward tramp. On the way I again heard a snigger behind me, and turning round I asked the lad what ailed him —

"Kheen yano?" Whereupon he remarked, with a delighted chuckle, *"Dumela Banna!"* And as, later while I regaled myself in camp, I heard these words once more accompanying a vivid conversation with my cook, I realised that my simple companion would also likely remember this experience for the rest of his life.

* * *

As buffalo figure quite often in these reminiscences of mine, perhaps a few personal observations on the habits of these fine animals may be of interest. Contrary to popular belief, I have not found them to be naturally morose and aggressive.

Indeed, so far as human beings (whom they have greater cause to fear than all their other enemies put together) are concerned, buffalo are timid and are always ready to get out of the way. It is only when they have been wounded that, as a rule, they become dangerous to man.

When suffering from any injury of a serious nature — inflicted, perhaps, by a beaten-off attack by a lion, from bullet wounds, or severe injuries wrought by a rival, a buffalo will absent itself from the herd for a period depending on the length or extent of its injuries, and the recovery therefrom; and will lie up in a secluded place. Woe to the unwary, unarmed man who should happen to intrude upon one in such circumstances! Lucky indeed will he be if he escapes to tell the tale.

A wounded buffalo is a perfect devil, and among the most dangerous of all game. Buffalo are most difficult to stop in a headlong charge: the courageous beasts generally fight until they drop dead, and there is surely no other beast more tenacious of life. A shot through the heart will not always immediately kill them, and they can do fearful damage before expiring from such a wound: sometimes, in fact, actually themselves becoming the hunter in their furious, whirlwind search for their persecutors during the brief spell of life remaining.

Hoarse, pig-like grunts are usually uttered by charging buffalo; and as they plunge through the heaviest undergrowth they present a picture of vindictive strength and ferocity.

Unwounded buffalo, in my experience, always retreat from the sight or scent of a man; though quite frequently — if you should happen to walk on to one or more when they are upwind of you — they may snort and trot a few yards in your direction; presently halting to stare with characteristic uplifted snouts. This need never be taken as the prelude to a charge, and indeed offers the best opportunity for a chest shot at very close range. After satisfying their curiosity for a moment or two, they will invariably swing round, and with another snort gallop heavily away. I have heard it suggested that this habit of swiftly advancing for a few yards is an attempt to intimidate the intruder, failing which the animals make themselves scarce as quickly as possible. Be that as it may, the habit, until one becomes accustomed to it, can be alarming. No man who hunts buffalo will fail to experience it sooner or later, nor will he be long in learning to recognise the vast difference between the demonstration and a genuine charge, which not even a mortal wound will always arrest.

The beef from these animals is always tender, even that of the oldest bulls, provided they are not in very low condition. It is dark in colour but well flavoured — though too much of it palls after a time and one is pleased to turn to something else for a change! The tails make wonderful soup: in fact I often found a bowl of buffalo-tail soup equal to a warm blanket on a cold winter's night! The tongues were always good, either hot or cold. But as for the marrow bones! Well, the mere thought of them makes my mouth water right now! It is perhaps not generally known that animals in low condition have hardly any marrow in their bones. At any rate, after some experience in the veld, I never troubled about marrow bones unless the animal brought in was in good condition.

Chapter 4

"BEHOLD, A GREAT LAKE!"

SHORTLY after my arrival in Ngamiland, I became friendly with Mr. George Scholtz, a Government Agricultural and Livestock officer, who had assumed duties at Maun a few days before my arrival. At Riley's Hotel we sat at the same table; and having many interests as well as friends in common, our acquaintance soon developed into a close friendship. As our respective offices adjoined we saw a lot of each other. Later he suggested that I should share his quarters when I was at Headquarters; and as he was then unmarried, and had a fine large house to himself, I gladly accepted this offer.

I had no conveyance of mine own, but George had a light-delivery Chevrolet truck. In this he often invited me to accompany him on various outings: shooting, fishing, or just visiting the various homes along the river. Our weekend jaunts, when we would travel a number of miles up or down the river for fishing or duck shooting, were always most enjoyable. On one occasion we travelled out to Chanogha, on the Botletle River, where we camped for a couple of days and had some splendid bream fishing.

Harry Riley had a couple of boats on the Chanogha pool, and we had permission to use one of these. This was a most enjoyable outing though on the way there I had the misfortune to lose an excellent and almost new metal fishing reel, full of new line. It was an irreparable loss, for at that time (just prior to the ending of the war) fishing tackle was virtually unprocurable. I immediately sent a runner back along the road, with a promise of a substantial reward if he found the reel, but, alas, he failed to do so and I never saw that reel again. George, and a mutual friend, Sergeant Plenderleith, who was accompanying us, searched their bags and collected bits and pieces of tackle, which at least enabled me to have a line in the water. Apart from the usual Tilapia, of which a large variety exists in these waters, we procured a number of Pike, Squeakers, and Barbel. The latter — which run to quite large sizes in Ngamiland — are, owing to their very wide distribution, well known to anglers generally: but the two former I had not previously seen. In water the local Pike strongly resembled freshwater Tiger fish — to which they are closely allied. They both belong to a family of fishes called *Characinidae;* but the "pike" still more closely resembles the true pike, and it has a mouth full of fierce-looking teeth, of which the larger ones occur in pairs on either side of the strong, narrow jaws. They have the same lines, speckled fins, and minute adipose dorsal fin as occur in the tiger fish. However they do not compare favourably with the latter as a sporting fish, neither do they attain the same size.

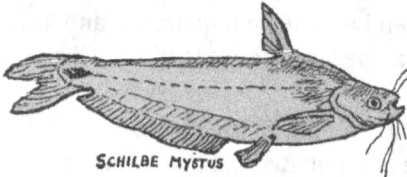

The term "Squeaker" is applied commonly to the various species of cat fish occurring in northern waters, of which several are found in Ngamiland. The one particularly referred to here (known scientifically as *Schilbe mystus*) at times becomes a great nuisance to anglers: by whom it is detested on account of the sharp, poisonous main spines on both the pectoral and the dorsal fins. Nevertheless, it is an edible fish. In East African rivers and lakes, where this fish attains a fair size, it is known as the "Butter Fish", and is prized for culinary purposes. In appearance it is quite the most attractive of any of the cat fishes I have seen. The feelers, or "barbels" — characteristic of all members of the family — are present, but they are rudimentary (almost hair-like) in fact, and they are not branched, as is the case in several other species.

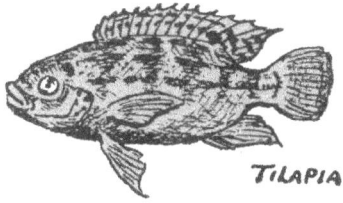

I have caught bream (Tilapia) in variety in the majority of the rivers of Southern Rhodesia, and in other parts; but for abundance, variety and size, I have never experienced anything to equal bream fishing as it can be enjoyed at Chanogha, and in many another of the deltaic rivers of Ngamiland.

TiLAPIA

Tiger fish, unfortunately, do not occur in the Botletle, and I do not think that this species occurs more than a day's journey downstream from Seronga, where the various channels spill into the great swamps. Very occasional ones might reach the Botletle during years of exceptionally heavy inundation, but they have never become established there, and so can definitely be said not to occur in that river.

We saw no more than a small portion of the pool at Chanogha, which is said to be seven miles in length and, in parts, up to three hundred yards in width.

Though bearing only about two thirds of the water conveyed by the Thamalukane, the upper reaches of the Botletle (or Zouga, as it was formerly known) are much finer and greater than the Thamalukane itself. A century ago Livingstone, so enthralled by the aspect of the noble stream, enthusiastically described it in the following glowing terms:

"It is a glorious river; you never saw anything so grand. The banks are extremely beautiful, lined with gigantic trees, many quite new. One bore a fruit a foot in length and three inches in diameter. Another measured seventy feet in circumference. Apart from the branches it looked like a mass of granite! And then the Bakoba in their canoes — did I enjoy sailing in them? Remember how long I had been in a parched land, and answer!"

Of the Thamalukane, he had the following to say:

"I enquired whence the Tamak'le came. 'Oh, from a country full of rivers!' (referring, obviously, to the innumerable waterways of the Delta). 'So many no one can tell their number, and full of large trees'."

The Botletle is certainly very beautiful here, and many magnificent trees line its banks. Reed-fringed islets abound over the fine reaches of the river, and the best bream fishing is usually to be had right up against the edges of these reed banks. We saw great numbers of Egyptian geese, of which a big percentage were goslings, disporting themselves in the quiet, reed-bound bays. The presence of goslings of various ages proved that they were locally hatched. Waterfowl, generally, are drawn to the perennial waters of the upper reaches, and there bird lovers may spend many enjoyable days studying a great variety of birds, including many species not always met with in the vicinity of open waters.

While on the subject of fishing experiences, I might record that during a lengthy sojourn of several seasons in Southern Rhodesia, I found — in common with many other anglers — that one of the best baits for bream consisted of the repulsive larvae of the Dung, or Rhinoceros, Beetle.

These huge, fat, cream-coloured maggots can be obtained by digging in the manure of cattle kraals at all times of the year excepting the winter months. I introduced the bait at Maun, where hitherto the insides of birds had constituted the favourite bait. A fair amount of good-natured leg-pulling followed my recommendation, but it was not long before the "Kraal Worms" were being fairly widely used. Indeed, long before I left the country I was pleased to note that the grubs, and tiny spoons and spinners, were saving the lives of quite a lot of birds!

***

About this time — March 1945 — I had a turn of doing the Nokaneng (150 miles) Pay trip. Owing to the distance, hunters stationed on the Taokwe River, south east of Nokaneng, were visited at irregular intervals only. There was a fair amount of official work needing attention, apart from the collection of "Game Destroyed" tokens, reports on the incidence of Tsetse fly, temporary migration of buffalo and other game, etc. The men of course also had to receive their pay and rations.

I was pleased to have an opportunity to visit these parts, and I was fortunate to have Martinus Drotsky, who had to collect some Government equipment in his charge at Nokaneng and Xlaxla, as a travelling companion. A few years previously he had done a great deal of work in that region and, knowing the country and the local swamps exceedingly well, he provided a mine of information on the area and its inhabitants, including a few small scattered clans of Bushmen, whose dialect he was able to speak.

The road to Nokaneng is a continuation of the one on which I travelled to Khantsaang: from which place it runs more or less parallel to the Nghabe River until it reaches Toteng, where the basin of Lake Ngami is entered.

When, on August 1st, 1849, Oswell's party, which included Dr. Livingstone, Murray of Lintrose and J. H. Wilson, reached the lake, the Batawana chief — Lechulatebe — was living very near Toteng, and his town later became the rendezvous of the majority of the trader-hunters. One reads of Joseph McCabe, Charles John Andersson, Wilson, Samuel Edwards, Fred Green, Petrus Jacobs, Jan Viljoen, Baldwin, and a host of others being there at various periods. All fine men, and as intrepid a set of pioneers as ever faced the hazards of travel in inhospitable, waterless Kalahari tracts. It was the lure of ivory in abundance which brought them to this remote locality, and for a few brief years the trade resulted in huge profits. For instance, the usual price for a pair of bull elephant tusks was an obsolete musket valued at about 15/-!

Lechulatebe had a vast accumulation of the commodity, and it is said that stockades of bull elephant ivory around the kraals were no uncommon sight. The wily chief, however, soon began to recognise the value of ivory, and in less than a decade the trade could no longer be profitably carried on. Baldwin bemoans the fact that the chief "wants your things on his terms and asks outrageous prices for his", but he naively adds:

"Lake Ngami, 15th. We arrived here on Friday, 11th, not until I had received several messages from the Captain to make haste and be the first wagon at his "state"; since which time we have been haggling and wrangling about the price of two horses, till my interpreter and I were utterly exhausted, the former drinking half my cask of sherry to keep his throat moist, till today I gave in and let the Captain have them for thirteen teeth of ivory and a saddle and a bridle into the bargain. I only gave £9 for one nag and the ivory I got for him is worth at least £60, so that it was worth a little patience".

The tracks of the discoverers of the lake were trodden continuously by increasing numbers of traders and hunters. At all seasons, the journey was a formidable one which could only be undertaken with the heavy old Cape wagons drawn by teams of native oxen, which were found to be the best able to endure the appalling hardships of traversing a region, whose scanty, unreliable waterholes were separated from one another by two, three and even four days of unceasing toil through deep and heavy sand. Whole teams of oxen perished thus, and few journeys were accomplished without losses due to the cruel suffering entailed. The sands and waterless tracts of the Kalahari have taken a heavy toll in human and animal life.

Among the most remarkable journeys to the lake was that made by Joseph McCabe, who reached it from Kanye (near Kolobeng), shortly after Livingstone's discovery.

This dauntless man struck out through entirely unknown country; travelling in a north-westerly direction for two hundred and fifty miles, and then directly north for another three weeks. No water was found for several weeks of this journey, and both man and cattle subsisted on Tsama melons which, providentially, grew in great abundance during that season. McCabe visited the lake on several subsequent occasions, but then travelled the eastern route—that first broken by Wilson, and later by Oswell's party. McCabe died and was buried at Molepolole.

There can be no doubt that Lake Ngami was great and impressive when first beheld by white men. Livingstone records:

"It is of such magnitude that we could not see the farther
shore and could only guess its size from the reports of the
natives that it took three days to go round it."

Baldwin, writing nine years later, seems to have gleaned similar information as to the size of the lake:

"I gather from the natives that it is three days ride round the
lake but that Tsetse render it impossible for horses. The natives are afraid to cross it in their frail canoes, as when a wind
rises the water is very rough. Three canoes were swamped
not long since and their crews drowned."

C. J. Andersson laboured under the curious misapprehension that the lake was tidal! He was deceived by the known phenomenon of banked up water, which occurs in situations where large expanses of the element lying in flat, exposed land are driven by strong prevailing winds to opposite shores, and, with the ensuing nightly calm, resume their natural level. In Andersson's case, he was coasting the lake in "dug-outs". Stopping for the night, he was obliged to wade through the shallows to dry land. As he awakened in the morning, he was completely mystified to see the craft lying on wet sand with no water anywhere near! His astonishment was still greater when he was informed that the water would return later — which it did.

The enthusiasm and joy expressed in the writings of the early travellers when they arrived suddenly in a land of clear streams and lakes can be appreciated: and if some of their accounts of the new land are, perhaps, too glowing, it is easy to understand that their reaction was born of a sudden, glorious change of environment.

As I entered the present travesty of Livingstone's great lake, these fragments of history were recalled in my mind. The lake's former glory contrasted sadly with the reality I had just entered: notwithstanding that my tireless enquiries had prepared me what to expect. Nothing had been exaggerated. Ngami was truly dead, and seemingly gone for all time.

Extensive groves of big, but not ancient Camelthorn, Mosho and Makwelekwele flourish where — in Livingstone's time — their uttermost tops would not have pierced the water's level. Wherever my eye roved, there were roads and game paths, hillocks of blown sand, lowing herds, springbok, wildebeest. Who, but the specially informed, could exclaim: "Behold, a great lake!"? The producers of the latest Government maps have not troubled to outline the former lake. There are Government establishments, trading stations, native villages and schools; cattle, sheep, and goats; horses — real beauties, and native owned; the ubiquitous donkeys, and a generous sprinkling of wells 50 feet and more in depth, in Ngami's ancient floor. It is a fine pastoral area, and many wealthy Africans have their permanent homes in and along the margin. At the native village of Sehitwa are two European-run stores, and in the neighbourhood the Government has established a Bull camp for the benefit of the natives.

The road traverses the lake for a number of miles, then passes out on to slightly higher ground with alternating belts of thorn bush and great open spaces until it reaches Setaten, where are a number of fine pans of water. Here I procured a brace each of Yellow-billed duck and Teal, and might easily have made a big bag including other species as well. There were a lot of impala about also, but these were exceedingly wild, as a result of being shot at by passing motorists. The bush seemed ideal for kudu, in fact for most types of game.

There was evidence in plenty of sticking cars and trucks in the slippery Setaten clay, and I, too, later on had my share of troubles along that road. Shortly afterwards we arrived at Tsau, and stopped at one of the several stores for the ever desirable cups of tea. Apart from the usual school, there is a Government clinic for the benefit of the large native community. It is said to be most efficiently run by a highly trained African attendant, under our own Medical Officer at Maun.

From Tsau there are two roads to Nokaneng, one of which traverses the country well to the west of Taokwe and passes through rather charming savanna woodland with occasional small pans which — during the rainy season — hold water sufficiently well to cause game to congregate in the area. Being for the most part uninhabited, it is in fact still excellent game country — notwithstanding the heavy slaughter that has taken place.

On the forward journey we travelled this road, and the fifty miles of its length passed all too quickly. I saw two small lots of kudu, which antelope (judging by the amount of spoor) must here be very plentiful. We passed within easy range of several Roan antelope — the first I had seen in Ngamiland, though I had enjoyed a good deal of sport with these magnificent creatures along the Southern Rhodesian border, east of Francistown.

Small buck: duiker and steenbok, were spotted at frequent intervals, and three reedbuck, and two troops of impala, were also encountered.

We were soon at Nokaneng, where we received a hearty welcome from the residents of the trading station. Both having a little business there, we stopped for the night.

Mr. Andrew Wright, the proprietor of the establishment, was an old Ngamilander with a pretty wide experience of the country, and I found him immensely interesting. Living with him in the establishment were Mr. and Mrs. Hardus Pretorius and their two small

children. Mr. Pretorius — "Uncle Hardy", as he was affectionately known — was a government stock inspector, and he was reputed to know the swamplands better than any other living European. His cheery, jovial nature, which made light of any hardships or discomforts, was very attractive, and won him the multitudes of friends which were his. Those swampy regions which he understood and loved so well eventually caused his untimely end, for he was attacked by a kidney complaint which brooked of no delay. In these places there are no means of speedy transport, and by the time he reached hospital, there was no longer any hope for him.

The following morning we proceeded to Xlaxla on the Taokwe, as Drotsky had to collect his equipment there. En route we passed the mile wide clearing he had supervised some time previously, as already indicated.

This clearing — one to one and a half miles wide and some sixty miles in length — was one of the major measures adopted by the Government for controlling and confining the fly scourge to the eastern side of the Taokwe which was, and still is to the best of my knowledge, heavily infested with the pest. As Tsetse will not remain in terrain denuded of vegetation, the clearing extended all along the western bank of the river. The results of the scheme were markedly good: so much so, in fact, that that long strip of splendid pastoral and agricultural country is now carrying a lot of stock where, formerly, domestic animals could not exist. It also had the effect of reducing to a minimum the spread of the fly into the clean area westwards. A small percentage of Tsetse did come across on the bodies of game, notably buffalo — hence the presence of T. F. C. Hunters in certain strategic localities.

Drotsky's vast undertaking, in which local chiefs and their followers co-operated, was a great achievement accomplished at an incredibly low cost of time and money. On the completion of that work he was given the task of making a canal through the Karangana channel and also the clearing of papyrus in the insignificant waterway which is the Taokwe at Xlaxla. This, I understood, was a preparatory effort in the larger scheme of restoring a perennial flow of water along the now totally choked up Taokwe (Teoghe), which has long since ceased to flow. The westernmost of all the branches of the delta, it was at an earlier period the most important of them all and, in 1853, the traveller Charles John Andersson wrote:

"The lake is fed by the Teoghe at its north west extremity. The river never, perhaps, exceeds forty yards but it is deep, and when at its greatest height contains a large volume of water. Its annual overflow takes place in June, July and August, and sometimes even later. The source of the Teoghe is unknown, but it is supposed to be very distant. It may have its rise in the high tableland of the Quanza and other streams of importance .... as far as I proceeded, however, it was navigable for smaller craft, for only in three places that I can remember, did I find less than five feet of water, and, generally speaking, the depth was considerable."

I was interested in the old shack which had been Drotsky's headquarters, and the manner in which he had tackled the clearing of the papyrus from the stagnant, festering water. The conditions were about as bad as could be imagined, and the fact that the man survived at all was eloquent proof of his amazing natural resistance to malaria, sleeping sickness, and other ills. For a while his wife shared the discomforts of the life he was then leading, and from his own account they appeared to have had few grumbles.

I had to spend a considerable while at the camps of the hunters, and it was late before I had finished with them. At one camp I found the skin of what must have been a princely lion. It was included with other tokens and was shot by one of the men. I requested the skin from my chief, and it is today a fine wall exhibit in the Albany Museum, Grahamstown.

On our return trip, we used the river road; and I found it both shorter and more interesting than the one by which we travelled

from Tsau. Unfortunately it becomes unusable shortly after the advent of the rainy season.

Drotsky pointed out the *Sediba ya de kubu* — pools of the hippopotami. They were entirely dry, and I am not certain whether present day inundations ever reach them. They are in black river silt and when full would be of considerable depth.

On the way down we passed Kakanaga: a place I am never likely to forget, for it was there that I subsequently endured an experience as trying as any that I can remember. We saw a great number of waterfowl of various species, particularly geese and duck. I had a shot at some spur-winged geese at a range of 200 yards, and was surprised to see two fluttering on the ground as the remainder took wing. Later I shot another of these excellent table birds: in which respect they are far superior to the more showy, smaller Egyptian goose.

Chapter 5

SHOOTING FOR THE POT

BACK at my camp, I now lost no time in making arrangements for an immediate departure to a spot a mile or two beyond the head of the fence. I had previously made a mental note of a fine camping site where two splendid trees would provide shade throughout the day, and we set off for this place within a couple of hours.

Ploughing through deep sand, the truck, heavily laden with fencing material, my own equipment, and a great deal of junk which the men habitually accumulate and insist upon taking with them, laboriously but successfully negotiated the journey: but only after branches and quantities of long grass had been laid crosswise over the tracks through a particularly bad patch of loose, powdery sand.

After unloading, half a dozen boys — each with a spade — were soon engaged in clearing away the tussocky grass, dead branches, and undergrowth from beneath the selected trees; and when the trash had been raked away and the clearing neatly swept with branches and generally tidied up, but a few minutes were required to pitch the tent and get my things under cover.

The new site — a very desirable one in other respects — had the drawback of being nowhere near water. As the area had to be covered, there was no remedy other than transporting all we required from a distance of several miles. As there was plenty of other work for the truck, which also had to make periodic trips to

Maun, the necessity of having to remain in such a place was — to say the least — awkward. When one returned to camp hot, weary, and covered with sweat after a hard day in the fierce sun, the evening tub was always eagerly anticipated: and when the cook greeted one with the information that the lorry with the water had not yet arrived, the news was not conducive to an amiable frame of mind - particularly when thirst was added to the discomfort of grime! Such occasions were generally brought about by either a blowout or through the truck being stuck in a heavy stretch of sand which could not be bypassed save by a wide detour.

In other ways, however, I liked this camp, and I occasionally went for short evening rambles after returning from the day's work. There were a lot of impala and warthog about, but all were extremely wild owing to the amount of shooting that had taken place all along the marked outline of the fence. On the east side there were some fairly extensive open flats, and the pig favoured these places where they excavated industriously in search of uintjies and other bulbs. By taking advantage of what cover I could find behind the aromatic little Mokodi shrubs, I tried frequently to circumvent them in these places. Always, however, they evaded me: not that this vexed me unduly, especially when there was a meat supply in camp, as I found ample compensation in the fun of the stalking.

Ever on the alert, and with exceptional eyesight and other senses developed to a corresponding degree, warthog are difficult to bag when in open ground, and the manner in which these hideously ugly but interesting creatures have contrived to hold their own amid innumerable dangers is no doubt due to the extreme wariness they display where there is a lack of cover. Apart from man, their chief enemies are lions and leopards, and cheetahs also prey on them though I doubt if these half-cats would attempt conclusions with any but immature animals. I have heard of orphaned youngsters being killed by jackals, and hyenas and wild dogs may also account for some — though no such instances have come under my own notice.

I have always been attracted by the sport of pig-hunting, and I never had cause to complain of the scarcity of these animals in Ngamiland. They were exceedingly plentiful throughout the swamp regions of that country.

The fact of being stationed in an area teeming with game is not necessarily a guarantee of an adequate fresh meat supply for a large camp. When game discovers freshly sprouting grass in regions previously swept by veld fires, or there is too much human activity in its favourite haunts (or, again, perhaps through the drying up of veld waters) temporary local migrations will occur, and so suddenly can this happen that, literally, the game can "be here today, and gone tomorrow".

At other times sheer bad luck seems to trail the hunters, when one wounded beast after another successfully gets away — after many hours and often a full day laboriously expended in the pursuit. Such runs of ill luck are by no means uncommon, and as they frequently resulted in a succession of meatless days, the hunters attached to my gang would for the time being become more than slightly unpopular with the labourers! These gentry, thoroughly spoilt by lavish supplies of fresh game in variety, complained loudly whenever there was an occurrence of even the shortest of meat famines. This they invariably contended as being due entirely to the incompetence of the so-called hunters — "they should be forced to take a turn at the heavy labour, or sent unarmed into the bush: there to subsist like the Masarwas (Bushmen) on tortoises and snakes, frogs, grasshoppers and roots, and be regarded as not fit associates for proper men", etc. "Just hand them a rifle, and none of the manual workers would fail to provide all the meat they could eat" — and a lot more besides! Was not the whole land swarming with buffalo, wildebeest, *kabole* (sassaby), kudu, pallah, *kolobe* (pig), and so on?

"Why should they, who had to slave harder even than donkeys, be forced to exist on stamped mealies? Was that food or men? No! No! that was womens' food! How were they going to handle great Mopani posts or heavy coils of wire on such stuff? They required MEAT — lots of meat, for their exhausting work" — and so on.

Immediately, however, that word came round that a buffalo or big buck had been accounted for, the shares of the successful hunter would instantly soar, and grouses would magically resolve themselves into voluble anticipation of the coming feast.

Irrespective, of time (whether early afternoon or after sunset) six to a dozen of the erstwhile grousers — depending on the size of the animal shot — would be detailed to fetch the spoils, and I do not recall ever observing the slightest unwillingness to perform this particular duty. Occasionally the distance was too great to permit of a return to camp that same night, but sleeping out was never regarded as hardship when a plentiful supply of meat was at hand. The choicest morsels — including the intestines — were taken as perquisites of the carriers. A thoroughly good gorge, extending over several hours and a roaring fire — nothing could be more idyllic to the African heart!

It so happened that on the eve of my first weekend at this camp some discontent due to a shortage of meat was observable. I noted the fact without remarking thereon, but told one of the hunters — N'Dashiwa by name, a thoroughly experienced and plucky fellow — that he would be required to accompany me at early dawn, and to tell one of the fence boys to come as well.

I awakened at 4.30 a.m., and was soon settled down to a cup of coffee with something to eat as well, as I am no believer in starting the day on an empty stomach. The two men who were each to accompany me were both given a big pannikin of strong, heavily sweetened coffee, and to judge by the amount of lip-smacking plainly audible outside my tent this went down very well! It was a treat seldom enjoyed by any of the Africans, who lived chiefly on meat with a small grain ration — washed down only by water — while on field work.

At grey dawn we were already a mile or two from camp, trudging heavily across a very broad area of scrubby bush — mostly Mopani — where the going was rendered arduous by the manner in which the surface soil had been riddled by rodents. Breaking through into their burrows at every step becomes fatiguing to a degree that can only be appreciated when experienced. Areas affected by these warrens (if the term can be applied to the abodes of mice and gerbilles) are unbelievably vast, and the burrows are so labyrinthine in nature that the upper soil is often positively sponge-like. These colossal communities of rodents are responsible for the continuance of the dreaded bubonic plague, which is transmitted by the fleas which they harbour, and outbreaks are of almost yearly occurrence.

I have earlier referred to the incidence of plague in the country, and my subsequent trying experiences of this dreadful malady created in me a loathing of these rodents which I find difficult to describe. I believe that only those who have experienced situations where plague is rife can appreciate how truly revolting and full of horror such contacts with the foul disease can be.

Through a deficiency of natural enemies, these rodents multiply at a rate quite beyond human control: except in small settled areas where concentrated and costly campaigns are periodically instituted against them. This system can never effect anything much beyond a local safety measure as the areas affected are too vast in extent to be efficiently controlled by ordinary methods. One feels that here is an instance where aid should be sought from nature herself.

Snakes, raptorial birds, and nearly all the numerous species of the smaller carnivorous mammals prey on rodents. Let us consider these as they occur locally!

Snakes have always seemed less in evidence to me in Ngamiland as compared with other more closely settled areas. This is one reason, perhaps, why rodents have gained so strong a hold in the country, though it is not suggested that the ophidian (snake) population should be augmented by importations!

Birds of prey are useful up to a point but these burrowing rodents are largely nocturnal, and have evolved a mode of life which affords them maximum protection from feathered enemies.

With regard to the part played by the carnivorous mammals, I, am not aware of what the position is today; but while I was still in the country, pelts of the most efficient killers could always be seen hanging in bunches in every trading establishment! Natives bring them in for barter; and goods to the value of a few pence are given for a little skin whose original possessor was an invaluable ally in man's endless, costly battle against noxious rodents.

If granted absolute protection, the lesser carnivores, such as genets, ichneumons, mongooses, polecats, weasels, and possibly even servals and jackals, might conceivably in time restore a balance that would eventually lead to an end of epizootics and fell diseases affecting humans. If all trade in these skins was entirely prohibited there would be less incentive for the merciless destruction of the animals concerned: though seeing that the flesh of all the smaller catlike creatures is high in the scale of veld deli-

ALLIES AGAINST PLAGUE!

cacies, some killing would certainly continue. At least it would be in lesser degree.

Native youths, armed with sticks and a pack of half starved dogs at their heels, wantonly kill every living thing not sufficiently cunning or agile to elude them, and it is certain they will continue to do so until the custom is "educated" out of them. This, admittedly, is a tall order: but one hopes that something can be done to save animals of such vast economic importance. But let me now return to our hunt!

The fact that a single buffalo represented a week's meat supply for my large squad of boys, caused these unfortunate creatures to be more frequently the objective of my hunts than any other of the numerous species of game. The excitement inseparable from the following of these unquestionably dangerous beasts, and the ease with which their tracks could be held, were contributing factors to my preference for buffalo as quarry. They were, moreover, more plentiful than the other game animals, and they were undoubtedly the most guilty of all as carriers of Tsetse.

I had left camp that day determined to shoot a buffalo, and had set out with the intention, if necessary, of going a long distance. From the very outset, however, and quite contrary to expectation, we found game in abundance. Even as we plodded over the rodent-infested areas warthog, impala, wildebeest and sassaby were sighted at regular intervals, and then, on suddenly reaching

and skirting a drying marsh, we startled a couple of reedbuck and a small troop of lechwe — the latter all females.

As the sun rose above the trees, I spotted a belated hyena; and anxious to secure a specimen for the museum in my native Grahamstown, I would have bagged it, but was deterred therefrom by simultaneously noticing perfectly fresh buffalo spoor. This was revealed clearly over the dew-laden couch grass near the margin of the partly dried up swamp, and we immediately followed it at a brisk pace. There was only a breath of wind, and that constantly changed, with the inevitable result that the buffalo presently scented us and broke from heavy cover just as we were about to enter it. I refrained from following them, feeling certain that more would be found under more favourable conditions. Changing direction, I crossed the swamp and entered a narrow strip of fringing forest.

As we emerged from the timber, we were suddenly brought to a halt by a loud crashing through the undergrowth, but for a short while could see no glimpse of any animals responsible for the noise. Obviously they were now standing and listening, or else they had gone off noiselessly over the open ground beyond. I moved on again, and had just reached a well-trodden game path when a slight sound from N'Dashiwa caused me to glance round. He was already squatting, and I instantly emulated him: endeavouring simultaneously to glimpse some object he was pointing at. I soon realised that it could not be visible to me from my position,

and as soon as I had crept back to where the boys sat crouched, I saw the cause of their excitement.

A small troop of sassaby (tsessebe) which had been startled by something came bounding towards us. A fine bull held the lead, and he was less than forty yards away when he apparently saw us, for he pulled up so sharply that those behind him actually shot past him before being able to stop. Fleeing obviously from one danger to another, the animals — dependent solely on their incredible speed and vigilant senses — stood in a bunched group, taking nervous stock of the unfamiliar objects squatting on the ground. Their intensely alert bearing, with every sinew braced for instant evasive action, formed an unforgettable picture. The hunter in search of "something for the pot" is not generally given to considerations of this nature, but this close-up view of the fine creatures before me removed all difficulty in shaking my head to N'Dashiwa's urgent whispered suggestion to "shoot the bull"! In a flash they were off, their purplish coats flashing in the rays of the early sun. I watched their curious bouncing action until they had passed through the sedges and coarse, tussocky grass of the marsh.

Turning, I caught N'Dashiwa's eye. A curious expression on his face, and a half smile, seemed to suggest that though he could not comprehend the reason I held my fire, he was at least certain that it was highly foolish to allow such good meat (practically "in the bag" so to speak) to escape.

The wind, what little there was, had veered again, and not wishing to have it behind, I turned away towards the south-west, where I would be entering familiar ground. This new direction soon led us into more extensive swamp lands — though very little water remained. Presently we entered a small patch of softish grass, different to that usually found in the marshes. It was dry and bleached and about eighteen inches in height. I noticed immediately that something had either been lying down there for a while, or had indulged in a roll. The soil beneath was baked as hard as brick, so there was no hope of seeing any spoor. Not particularly interested, I pressed forward, but N'Dashiwa asked me to wait a little. He was closely examining the trampled area. I waited a minute, but quickly losing patience at what seemed to be an unnecessary delay, I called to him to hurry. He straightened and immediately came up to me, remarking that a lion had been there not long before us, and that it was probably still close by.

I failed to notice any sign of freshness about the crushed grass. So far as I could tell it might have been flattened the day before, and I was unable to understand how he could possibly tell that something had been rolling there so shortly before, let alone that that something was a lion! Later, however, he admitted that he had seen a hair or two from the animal's mane. I was unable to ascertain from him why he was so certain about the freshness of the indications left by the animal. Here, in the open, the dew had long since evaporated, though just a little ahead on the turfy margin of the island and in the shade cast by the tall trees the lawn-like surface was still bespangled with moisture. About twenty or thirty yards of this wet grass separated the swamp proper from the forest line, and clearly visible across this were the tracks of some animal. Simultaneously, the man following N'Dashiwa shouted that he had seen a lion enter some thick cover on an island to our right front.

Feeling that there was no immediate hurry to attend to "His Majesty" who, I felt sure, would not leave the island with such excellent cover, we continued to follow the spoor ahead, and it presently led us to a partly-eaten carcass of a buffalo bull of immense size. We realised at once that the lion seen was responsible for the spoor we had been following, and that indeed it was the same one that had been breakfasting off the buffalo which it must have abandoned just before our arrival.

The buffalo had obviously died from a bullet wound and was already slightly "high". What astounded me was that the carcass had been dragged for a distance of some forty feet towards the bush, and that by the effort of a single lion. Great fang marks and saliva showed on the dead bull's muzzle, by which it had evidently been grasped and dragged backwards. The carcass had only been partially disembowelled, and some of the entrails had been devoured — rather unusual for a lion — but a lot of flesh had been eaten out between the hind legs, and the skin over the brisket was torn. Had we been five minutes earlier, that lion would probably have been bagged at the carcass. However, it seemed worth while to follow it to the adjacent island, which indeed was no longer an island as the water had evaporated around it and only a few ribbons of thick fluid remained here and there.

Turning back, we quickly reached the spot where the lion had been last seen, and immediately entered the bush. This consisted almost entirely of *Letaga (Royena pallens)* — small evergreen bushes, much given to coppicing. Here it was so thick that we had to crawl on hands and knees, but found no difficulty in following the tracks, plainly visible in the soft, spongy ground. With every sense on the alert, and rifle at full cock, I advanced cautiously, expecting at any moment to see or hear something of the lion. The boys kept at my heels, and after some minutes of this tense procedure N'Dashiwa touched my foot, and pointed straight ahead. I could see nothing, but raised myself on one knee with the rifle ready for an instant shot. Beyond the thumping of my own heart, not a sound reached me as, maintaining my attitude of extreme readiness I waited in silence. Suddenly there sounded a low murmur of a growl, followed immediately by a violent crashing worthy of a buffalo itself, as the old brute - breaking cover within fifteen feet of us - was gone.

Forcing our way out of the *Letaga* thicket in amazingly good time, we ran at full speed over heavy sand, of which the remainder

of the island more or less consisted, and along which the great pug marks were clearly visible. To sprint over two hundred yards of such going is not the best practice for rifle shooting, but at least we saw the lion again, and a shot would have been possible for anyone less winded. I did not attempt it, but watched the lion enter a small growth of stunted Hyphaene palms beneath some tall trees on another island. After a momentary rest, we again followed him. A few minutes later we again heard the lion running, and we followed at our best pace and quickly came to the end of this small island and found that he had crossed the drying marsh and continued on to the island where he had breakfasted less than an hour before. Here the growth was dense and heavy, and judging that the lion's temper was becoming rather frayed, I decided to leave him. My decision was much to the relief of the two natives who had stuck to me in commendable fashion!

After a short rest, and a smoke, we walked off westwards with the sun behind and a nice breeze in our faces. We continued to see buck — chiefly impala and sassaby — but as I was bent on getting a buffalo I did not fire a shot. Fresh tracks of the latter were soon found, and clearly the herd was not far ahead.

As we rounded some small bushes, we came on a tiny pan containing just a patch of water and a great deal of mud in which an immense old warthog was indulging in a glorious wallow. We were within a few yards of him before he became aware of our presence, and then in a split second he was off at lightning speed, the mud flying from his flanks. I laughed aloud at his absurd appearance, but unfortunately he ran right in the tracks of the buffalo, through the midst of which he tore with unabated speed; and I was just in time to see them take fright and go galloping away in a cloud of dust.

It seemed useless to follow that herd now, so I turned south: making for a line of pools known to me, as the rising heat had now developed a thirst. Before reaching the water more buffalo spoor was crossed, but as the beasts were moving almost directly downwind, they were ignored, and a few minutes later, as I reached the first pool, I spotted two more warthogs trotting rapidly away. A little to one side of the retreating pigs, a mixed herd of impala — rams, ewes, and youngsters — made a charming picture as they grazed and frolicked about on a patch of lush young grass, freshly sprung up on a patch of recently burnt ground. A couple of ostriches and a small troop of wildebeest were in sight further ahead some of the latter enjoying a sandbath. Having slaked my thirst at the pool, I was about to proceed when a honeyguide began to chirp insistently on a nearby tree. The boys instantly followed it, and within a minute or two heard them shouting. On coming up, I found N'Dashiwa already about ten feet up a sloping *Lonchocarpus* tree, busily enlarging a small hole with his little native axe. The bees were low swarming out, and the boy up the tree literally fell out his haste to escape their onslaught. We all got some stings, but having retreated some distance we started a fire and got e rotten wood smouldering, with which we returned to the live. Those bees were really vicious, but the stupefying fumes soon subdued them somewhat, and a number of magnificent sealed white combs were successfully removed. After a luscious repast of the sweet honey, I instructed one of the boys to remove a trough-like section of bark from a handy tree, which, when the ends were knocked back, formed an excellent container wherein the remaining combs could be carried back to camp.

It was now becoming unpleasantly hot, and as camp was several hours distant, I decided to hunt in that direction.

After a few moments of walking, I suddenly became conscious that the boys were no longer at my heels, and looking round saw them some distance back, peering into thick cover.

N'Dashiwa, evidently sensing that I had stopped, glanced my way and beckoning, pointed into the thicket on his right. On my arrival, I noticed a fleeting grin on his intensely black, cheerful countenance, as he held his fingers to his lips to enjoin silence. After the dazzling sunlight I was at first unable to make out anything in the dark shadows, but as my eyes focussed to the dim light, the form of a medium-sized ratel (honey badger) slowly merged into the field of my vision, and presently was clearly defined.

The stocky little animal was facing me directly, and even as I watched it advanced just a step or two and then again halted. There was a droll, questioning air about the creature as it raised its muzzle high, blinking enquiringly in our direction with its small, beady eyes, that caused me to grin. "He wants our honey!", exclaimed the downright N'Dashiwa, but the sound of his voice caused Mr. Ratel to turn about and unhurriedly disappear in the thicker stuff.

N'Dashiwa's suggestion that the ratel had been attracted by the smell of our honey would have been more satisfactory had we been stationary at the spot — if only for a few minutes.

About an hour later, after crossing an open valley and having climbed the rise on the opposite side, I was surprised to note a solitary buffalo walking down the valley but still a long way off. Why it was abroad at all in that heat was a puzzle which I did not try to solve, and the possibility of procuring a meat supply after all caused me to crawl into the sombre shade of a nearby tree where I sat in readiness for the buffalo to come along. It approached steadily, without a single halt, and was evidently making for some cool retreat where perhaps its mates - if it was not solitary - could be found. A few moments later it came abreast of where we sat at a distance of perhaps one hundred yards.

The old fellow dropped to the shot like a pole-axed ox and gave no more than a few kicks. The boys gave expression to their joy in a few congratulatory yells, quickly cutting down a number of branches with which to cover the carcass. This accomplished, we set out directly for camp — which was reached in the late afternoon.

A dozen boys were immediately sent out to bring home the meat, guided by one of the two who had accompanied me. In return for a chunk of meat and a bag of tobacco, he was quite content to undertake the long walk once more!

I remained up late that night, dealing with a pile of neglected correspondence and weekly returns. As I turned in about midnight I had only just extinguished the light when I heard shouts a great distance away. Realising that the carriers had probably strayed from the correct direction in the darkness, I fired a couple of guiding shots, and started a fire where I prepared a great pot of coffee for them. Occasional shouts, to which I replied, guided them back. In the flickering glare of the campfire they came staggering in under great loads of their beloved *nyama* (meat), and, happy though exhausted, they jabbered away over their coffee while a few grilled choice cuts on a pile of coals outside. Soon they were gorging contentedly, and it was another hour before they drew off to their own bush shelters.

As I was dropping off to sleep I was suddenly brought to a sitting position. The tent was flapping wildly in a strong wind which had arisen, but it was not that which had awakened me. I had only just regained consciousness in time to hear the final moaning sighs of a lion's roar. I sat listening for its renewal, and had not long to wait before the grand, full-chested grating roars again resounded above the racket of the wind in the surrounding trees.

Never before, or since, have I heard the King of Beasts roar more grandly: the very air seemed to tremble with the huge volume of sound. He could not have been far away, and the repeated roarings, ending in their sequence of ruggedly harsh grunts, came as a fitting finale to a delightfully interesting day.

Shortly after this, I moved my camp forward to a place called Xabaracha, and there selected a site beneath a magnificent Mochaba tree (*Ficus sycamorus*) with a massive, heavily buttressed trunk and colossal lateral roots showing above the ground for a yard or two. It was an attractive and interesting spot, and the few weeks spent there were happy ones. My most vivid recollection there is of a pan of rapidly diminishing water about a mile from the camp where a wonderful display of bird life was always to be seen. I soon formed a habit of wandering thither as soon as the day's work had ended, armed only with fieldglasses; and it was the waning light alone which drove me back to camp. What was the main attraction for the smaller birds I never discovered, but the larger fowl had undoubtedly gathered to feed on the unfortunate fish which had been trapped in the ever-narrowing confines of the pan.

Marabou storks and Sacred Ibis predominated: but evening after evening I saw various waders — stilts, curlews, spur-wing and blacksmith plovers, sandpipers, and several grebes. Though not regularly present, two grand wattled cranes also favoured this pan; while a majestic saddle-billed stork, and several African spoonbills, periodically visited the place.

As they became accustomed to my presence, the birds became more confiding each evening: finally permitting me to watch them at very close quarters. I was always fascinated to observe the beautiful pied avocets waggling their curious long, slender and upcurved bills over the surface, skimming off minute forms of aquatic life. They are surely among the most handsome of all the wading fraternity! Their snowy plumage, black "bracer" markings, and black crown and nape render them real ornaments of the waterside. They wade more deeply than other birds of similar habits, and as they wander out of their depth, they swim unhesitatingly.

The stilts I have never seen outside Ngamiland — though doubtless they occur in most places where conditions are suitable. They are almost as noisy as the spur-wing plovers; and it always seemed to me that, when flying, their long, vividly pink legs were somewhat of an embarrassment.

I spent many hours watching the grebes (the Cape dabchick). As they dibbled happily they frequently puzzled me by the quick and apparently aimless turns they executed at intervals, as they floated on the water. Nowhere else had I noticed them doing this, and I could think of nothing to suggest a reason for the action.

A few teal evidently spent their nights at the pan — like the grebes becoming more confiding with approaching darkness.

Generally, however, the teal were wilder than any of the other numerous birds congregated at this spot. A few pelicans used to cram their pouches at sunset every evening, and then, after a short pause, and with the air of being immersed in solemn thought, they would take off simultaneously: their magnificent flight action always claiming my undivided attention.

On two Sundays I visited the pan in the early afternoon, when the heat was at its height. On each occasion a large number of both Egyptian and spur-winged geese were present, and also several kinds of duck. The geese passed the time grazing off the new shoots penetrating the recently exposed "drowned" land, and I found — curiously enough — that both herons and egrets were also more in evidence during the hours of extreme heat.

This pan, only a little over one hundred yards in length, was the deepest portion (and all that remained) of a very considerable lagoon that regularly fills with the arrival of the annual inundations: and it is but one of many thousands of similar ones that occur throughout the swamps region. In some cases they are of considerable depth and contain some water right up to the time of the next flooding. Those at Mochaba were a real delight.

At dawn, on the morning of my departure, I paid the lagoon a final visit. Not many birds were present, so I walked all round the margin, endeavouring to interpret the complicated lacework of myriads of footprints. In so doing, I walked right on to the tracks of a pair of lions which had slaked their thirst just before my arrival. This I assume from the belief that they must have heard or winded me, as the departing tracks were made by running animals. Lions like to loiter after their drink, and do not normally hurry away.

Chapter 6

CHIRPING GECKOS AND THE
ARROW-POISON BEETLE

MY fencing work came to an end at Mochaba camp, and though I later frequently passed there, I never again camped at the same place. It was, I think, the pleasantest of all the numerous camps I occupied while I was employed by the Tsetse Fly Control.

I now returned to Maun for another brief spell in the office. In fact, I had been back several times, but always just for a day or two. I was never sorry to get away again, and when my chief informed me that again I had to take charge of my Khantsaang gang who had worked their way a long distance down Nghabe, I was elated, and prepared to leave the following morning.

My instructions were to move on to a place called Gwexwa — about five miles downriver from Khantsaang. Here, formerly, a previous Tsetse Fly Control Officer had a camp and a small shack, the ruins of which could still be seen. There was an attractive but not very tall *Moetsintsila* tree at the place, and I placed my tent next to it. These *Berchemias* give splendid shade, and I always admired this specimen.

It was while at this camp that I first witnessed the curious phenomenon of a large river suddenly begin to rise and flow with a strong current after months of cloudless skies; though the 1945 inundations were not very spectacular. A strange native passing the place where we were working mentioned that a strong stream of water was filling the pools between Khantsaang and my camp: so in the afternoon I walked upstream until I met it, and for a while remained to watch the swirling volume. At the head of the stream, closely bunched on a sandbank, was a flock of about one hundred pelicans which had apparently fed to repletion. For pelicans, they were astonishingly tame, and I crept up to within thirty yards of where they remained tightly packed on the bank, occasional swirls of water washing round their feet. There was a strong wind blowing, and I was intrigued to watch the loose yellow skin of their throat pouches fluttering in the blast like garments on a line. In a short space their sandbank was awash. The water was still rising, and the birds began to float down to where I sat crouched in a clump of reeds. They seemed to be quite indifferent to my presence, drifting past very close to me.

By the following morning the pool at Gwexwa had increased tremendously in size, and a large flock of Whistling duck were disporting very near the bank. It was pleasant to get a supply of fresh, sweet water again. What had previously remained in the pool had become very stagnant and slightly smelly.

It was also while I was at Gwexwa camp that the Conroy Expedition passed through, en route for South West Africa, after its short stay at Maun. One of the trucks drew up near where I was working, and its occupants seemed interested in the Anti-Tsetse measures being carried out.

The finding of a site suitable for further research work into the mechanical transmission of Nagana had occupied my chief for some considerable while. After a protracted search he eventually decided on Patikwa, where, apart from a good water supply having been struck not long previously, the place had the additional advantage of being in an area free of Tsetse and yet not too distant for operation from Maun: thus fulfilling all natural requirements. A fly-proof building, together with kraals and a "Cattle-crush", were also required. The difficulty of finding suitable material for such was overcome by the utilisation of two "Smudge" huts, which, during a former anti-Tsetse campaign, had been erected respectively at the N. E. and S. W. Limits of the then existing Fly belt. As these had now become redundant, I was instructed to dismantle them and transport the materials to Maun.

A brief digression here will explain the purpose for which smudge huts are employed. Where a main road passes through a fly area it is essential to reduce to a minimum the danger of conveying Tsetses, by means of passing cars or trucks, from infected into clean areas. These flies are always prone to enter cabs of vehicles, or even to travel on the loads or passengers sitting

61

at the back. Consequently huts, wherein all passing vehicles are enclosed and thoroughly sprayed, are erected — barrier-fashion — across the road. The strict recording of all fly found in or about the vehicles assisted also as a useful indication of the incidence of the pest in the area served by the huts at all seasons of the year.

I began work on the one to the north-east, which was at a place called Sherobe, thirty odd miles distant from Maun. The work took me into an area where I had not previously been, and I found the journey full of interest. From the bridge at Letapanen the road — a sandy, seldom used track which is, in fact, the main road from Maun to Kasane on the Chobe River via the Mahabe depression, and on to the Victoria Falls — follows the Thamalukane River all the way to Sherobe, passing in many parts actually along the water's edge. So the drive was a delightful one, and I obtained some very good duck shooting on the forward journey.

Within a few miles of Sherobe, the road passes into a belt of country thickly studded with stately Hyphaene palms which, towering above the surrounding bush, are a notable feature of the area. The stems of this variety of palm (which is also known as the "Ivory" Palm) are often thicker near the middle than they are at the base. Thinly interspersed, the trunks of dead ones, minus their feathery tops, stab upwards like masts among the lower vegetation. The wood, which has an attractive speckled grain, is intensely hard, and I believe the species attains a great age. Fruits, about the size of tennis balls, cluster thickly beneath the crowns from which they are most difficult to dislodge. A percentage is occasionally gathered by natives, who, in famine years, take much trouble to remove the toughish skins to get at an edible substance which occurs in a thin layer beneath. I have sampled this prickly, powdery product — very like sweetened sawdust — and conclude that none but the highly specialised digestive organs of the African could cope with it.

The kernels, about two inches in diameter, constitute the well known Vegetable Ivory: so familiar to visitors to the Victoria Falls; where it is largely and ingeniously employed by native craftsmen in the manufacture of ornaments and toys for which the multitude of tourists have created a never failing market. Common, also, is a dwarf variety of this palm.

Incidentally, I found that the long, half-round stems to which the huge fan-like leaves are attached, can be most successfully

used for the manufacture of light, and very serviceable fishing rods. If cut green, and allowed to season thoroughly in a shady place, these canes are tough and easily straightened and worked; but as only about a third of the blanks are free of defects, a little experience is necessary in selecting them. I still possess a rod with an extremely thin 31/2 foot long tip with which I have landed a great number of fish, including a ten pound Barbel which, after putting up a game fight for several minutes, sulked after the manner of its kind! It took a long while to dislodge him from the bottom by the old method of vigorously twanging the taut line.

Having arrived at Sherobe, I succeeded not only in dismantling, without damage to the material, a well-constructed building some fourteen feet by twenty five feet, but also getting it loaded and back to Maun on the same day — quite an achievement!

A few weeks elapsed before I was able to attend to the dismantling and removal of the second smudge hut, which was situated at Toteng, right at the bottom end of the fly belt. This, also taken down in sections, I dumped at Khantsaang: to be later picked up when the work of converting two smaller buildings into a larger one at Patikwa would begin.

At length I was handed a rough plan of the Patikwa building and told to proceed to that place as soon as sufficient labour had been collected.

Patikwa, which is on a limestone formation carrying, in parts, a heavy overburden of Kalahari sand, was practically devoid of any attractions, and very little game existed in the locality, and yet I enjoyed the few weeks spent there.

In accordance with my usual practice, I spent my weekends roaming round the huge sandbelts. Though I found nothing of greater interest than the occasional spoor of big buck — Roan, Gemsbuck, Kudu, wildebeest — the long tramps in the exceeding stillness of those huge, waterless tracts were always fascinating.

The vegetation was poor. It consisted of the usual sandbelt trees: *Terminalias*, *Boxias*, Camel thorns, *Commiphoras, Bauhineas, Grewias* in variety: some of the smaller Acacias, and here and there belts of fair Mopani intersecting the low bush. On the exposed limestone sizeable specimens of *Zisiphus* mucronata grew; and I also saw occasional *Mosilabele (Rhus lancea)* trees, believed by many to be an indication of underground water. The Bauhineas were in profuse bloom, when I was at Patikwa, and they formed a fine sight. The blooms of this species — *B. Macrantha* — are a snowy white, practically identical with some cultivated varieties.

There is another Bauhinea: a stiff, woody climber, which may trail untidily over the ground or into other vegetation. This has beautiful crinkly white blooms. Yet another is the Momma of the natives, quite a small shrub. This plant bears pods which contain large brown beans which, when roasted on live coals, pop open and are well flavoured to the palate. They are among the countless plants which have enabled the Bushmen to eke out an existence in the inhospitable regions to which these people have retreated. Where the Bauhineas and the *Mogonono (Terminalia sericea)* abound, knowledgeable travellers expect to encounter heavy sand; so as far as is possible they steer clear of this vegetation.

During these exceedingly long tramps, I saw almost unbelievably little animal or bird life, but to some extent this was no doubt due to the complete absence of surface water. The veld was beautiful, and it appeared to be ideal for such animals as gemsbuck, hartebeest, eland, etc., all of which are independent of water. As

the area was quite unoccupied by natives, there seemed to be no other reason why it should not be teeming with game. Occasional tracks indicated that some big buck passed through periodically, but I was puzzled by the apparent general avoidance of this excellent country by game animals as a whole.

On the first evening of my sojourn at this camp, just at sunset, my attention was attracted by an unknown chirping call. I spent some time walking around trying to locate it. It was a cheery, bird-like sound, but quite unfamiliar to me. I threaded my way through the surrounding bush, ever expecting to encounter the bird that was uttering the sound, and when within a few yards of its apparent source would approach with the greatest stealth. Always the same thing happened! When the note next sounded, it would always be a little further away: either to the right, or the left, or straight ahead. With the advancing darkness there sounded a perfect chorus of chirpings. With the failing light I had to abandon my quest, determined, however, to solve the mystery in due course. The following evening, as I had been out late on an unsuccessful venture after duiker, I had no time no renew my researches, though plenty of the calls were audible.

On the next evening it was the same again, but by this time I had become convinced that the sounds were in no way connected with the surrounding bushes, and that birds, at any rate, had nothing to do with them. What remained then? Insects? No, I was sure no insect ever uttered those clear notes which I could hear one hundred yards or more away. I became more than ever determined to find out. Obviously I was being deceived by some ventriloquial quality of the sounds.

The following evening the mystery was at last solved, though not through any special effort on my part. It so happened that one of Drotsky's Bushmen, who was spending the night at the camp, was asked about the sounds. He grinned, and, beckoning to me to follow, walked into the scrub. He soon stopped and, kneeling, pointed at a tiny sloping hole in the sandy soil, saying: *"Kgatwane!"* (Lizard!) I procured a spade, and with the Bushman's help unearthed, before it was dark, three sound and one mutilated specimen of what obviously were a very small species of Gecko — entirely unlike any I had ever previously seen. It would appear that these little creatures only raise their tunefull voices in the breeding season — early spring — when they have the habit of sitting in their front doors of an evening and sounding their not unmusical serenade. As to their size, I might say that the living ones fitted comfortably in a match box! Hoping that they would survive the journey, I posted them in that way to the Albany Museum, Grahamstown: and, though the journey in those confined quarters lasted a week, they arrived safely. In the following extract from a letter written by the Director, it will be seen that they might have fared worse:

> "Soon after I had posted my letter, the Geckos arrived and, as I suspected, they prove to be *Ptenopus garrulas*, the Chirping Gecko. Two of them are alive and very fit. Indeed one of them gave me quite a vicious bite, chirping excitedly as I handled him. I am keeping them alive for the study of their behaviour, these Geckos being quite different to any found in the Eastern Province, or, indeed, in any part of the Union.

> There are other Geckos in the Kalahari, any of which would be of interest to us. I think some of them may make a much bigger noise; at any rate the creatures themselves are much larger than *Ptenopus*."

CHIRPING GECKO

Just two years ago I came across quite a colony of *Ptenopus* in the Moselebe valley, Southern Protectorate - about eighty miles W. S. W. of Mafeking. Their cheery voices recalled me to Patikwa and those great sand belts over which I had so enjoyed to roam.

I was anxious to procure some of the pupae of the Arrow Poison Beetle *(Cladocera nigro-ornata)* for the Albany Museum. I asked Drotsky, who was still engaged at the well near Kwebe, and who passed my camp periodically, to persuade the Bushmen in the hills to collect some for me. These people are no longer secretive about their arrow poisons, but nevertheless they demand payment of a new blanket and other trifles of a total value of about twenty five shillings for the service. This I considered reasonable enough, so I arranged for the articles to be sent out to me by the next runner from Maun. A few weeks later, I was in possession of several dozen of the deadly things, and was able to examine them with interest. So far as I know, the beetles themselves are not used in the manufacture of arrow poison, though no doubt the contents of their bodies would also be highly toxic. Both the larvae and the pupae are used.

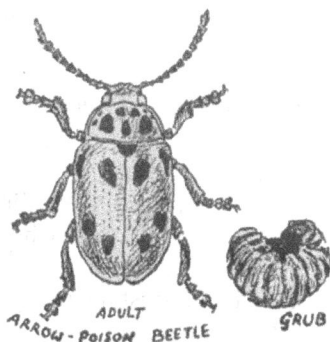

ADULT
ARROW - POISON BEETLE
GRUB

The beetle *C. Nigro-ornata* is about half an inch in length, a quarter of an inch in breadth and about the same in dept. It is smooth and glossy and of a rich chestnut brown. On the thorax there are five very dark — almost black — spots (these are said to vary in number though this does not hold good of those I have examined), and in appearance the little creature conveys the impression of being a defenceless and not unattractive object. It lays its eggs on a dwarf *Commiphora* bush which grows very plentifully in the sandy stretches of Ngamiland, and a great number occur around Patikwa. I was unable to identify the plant for certain, but believe it to be *C. Kwebensis* (several species of *Commiphora* are markedly similar, and my knowledge of botany does not rise to fine distinctions).

The grubs feed on the fresh young foliage of this bush, and when the pupal stage approaches they descend to the ground and dig themselves well in under the mass of roots. Here they form cocoons about three-eigths of an inch in diameter, which closely resemble the pellets of sheep dung, though of a light brown colour. The tiny cases seem to be formed of a mixture of chewed bark and sand: and so fragile are they that they fracture if dropped on a hard surface from a height of twelve inches.

It is among the roots of the *Commiphora* that the Bushmen excavate for the cocoons. The little curled grubs which they contain are soft and of a creamy colour. Six minute caterpillar type feet are present on the inner curve, just below the head. When using the poison, the Bushmen grasp the tail end of the tiny maggot between forefinger and thumb of the left hand. Using the same members of the right hand, one of the rudimentary feet is deftly caught between the nails and pulled off the body. A pale, amber-coloured fluid then immediately exudes, and the bone arrow point is steeped all over with the toxic substance. When dry, the point appears to be speckled with a thin film of gelatine. The fragment of skin — all that now remains of the grub — is carefully dried and saved. According to Mr. Drotsky, these little skins are collected, and when required are powdered and used as a specific for stomach ills.

I was unable to ascertain exactly how long this poison retains its potency. Two Bushmen whom I questioned, unsatisfactorily, through an interpreter, replied vaguely enough: "a very long time". I procured my cocoons in the middle of August, 1945. They had then probably been in the pupal stage since the Autumn. As they were unlikely to emerge as beetles until the rains in November or December, the poison must be available to the Bushmen for the greater portion of each year. I was informed, however, that the venom was usually preserved at full strength by being incorporated with the latex of a certain *Euphorbia* and gum, but was unable to obtain full details in this connection. The Bushman name for this poison is "*Ngwa*".

Livingstone refers to the poison as follows:

> "The Bushmen of the northern part of the Kalahari were seen applying the entrails of a small caterpillar which they termed "*Nga*", to their arrows. The venom was declared to be so powerful in producing delirium that a man in dying, returned, in imagination, to a state of infancy and would call for his mother's breast. Lions, when shot with it, are said to perish in agonies".

Thomas Baines who, in 1861-62 accompanied Chapman on his journeys between Walvis Bay and the Zambezi River, stated of the arrow poison caterpillar, that it fed on a tree called by the natives

Maruru papeerie. In Ngamiland there is a small tree or bush known as "*Marupapiri*"; but this is a *Rhus* and not a Commiphora, and it bears slightly acid but edible berries which "hang in bunches, like currants" (Miller). The native name of this bush is similar to that recorded by Baines, and perhaps *Cladocera nigro-ornata* lays its eggs also on this plant.

At the first possible opportunity, Mr. Crawshaw and I experimented with the poison obtained from the grubs. We used a couple of guinea pigs belonging to our Department, and the results left us in no doubt of the deadly nature of the poison.

No. 1. guinea pig was prepared for the experiment by having a small patch of hair (about the size of a shilling) closely sheared from its side. One of the minute grubs was then crushed, and the small amount of liquid obtained from it was simply rubbed on the bare skin, though there was hardly sufficient of the substance even to dampen the latter.

The effect of the application of this fluid must immediately have caused intense pain — probably severe burning — as, when liberated, the little animal immediately licked the spot, rolling and rubbing itself against the side of the large cage. In a few moments it began to career round, uttering shrill whistling cries. This it continued to do throughout the period — perhaps a quarter of an hour — in which we remained near its cage.

Meanwhile we tried the effect of a subcutaneous injection on a second guinea pig. We used the smallest syringe available, and a very fine needle was employed. With a little difficulty, the small amount of one minim of the venom was administered. The poison took effect in a matter of three seconds, and it resulted in apparent paralysis of the hindquarters as the little creature sank into a sitting attitude — its whole frame jerking convulsively. Within a minute it fell over on its side, and was apparently dead, though violent spasmodic muscular contractions of the body continued at increasing intervals. Actually fifty eight minutes elapsed before life became finally extinct.

During this time the first guinea pig continued to race around like a thing demented, and I was strongly wishful to end its misery, but it quietened soon afterwards. For days it remained very sick; and a week later a lump of flesh sloughed away from the place where the venom had been applied, leaving a cavity in which I could have put the end of my thumb.

The horribly deadly effect of the poison was now apparent to me, and I carefully put away the remaining cocoons. A good supply of these was later sent to Dr. John Hewitt of the Albany Museum, Grahamstown.

I was very busy at this time preparing for my departure to Boayankwe — whither I was being temporarily transferred — and completely forgot about the rest of the cocoons, which I had put away in an old Polish tin with perforated top. During my absence, some of these completed their cycle, and I found, on my return, three defunct and somewhat broken beetles. Just what had happened to the container I never discovered, but the specimens were not so badly smashed as to prevent my recognising a beetle which I had seen before, and one that must be familiar to many residents of the country: though few indeed are aware of the deadly nature it assumes during some of its life stages.

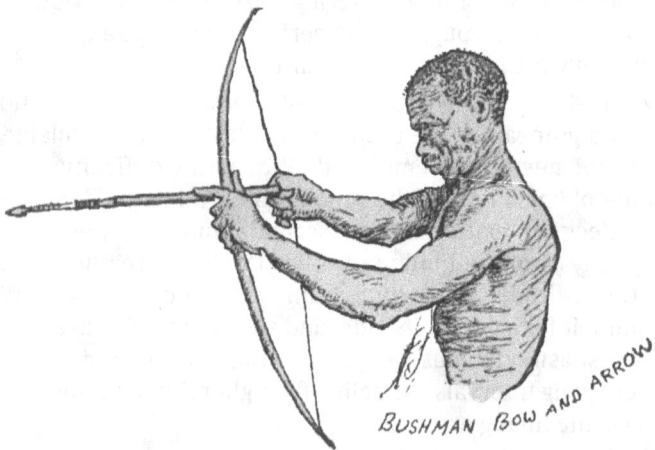

BUSHMAN BOW AND ARROW

Chapter 7

AFTER LECHWE AND SITATUNGA

DURING the many weeks I was at Patikwa, I did little shooting. A wildebeest, one of a small passing troop, was all that fell to my rifle. In fact it was the only animal fired at, and I was obliged to get my meat supply from Maun by the weekly mail carrier. I was extremely busy during the day, and at knock-off time I was pleased enough to relax after the evening sponge down.

Towards the end of September 1945 I received instructions to prepare for a temporary transfer to Boayankwe (135 miles from Maun) where I was to engage and again take charge of a squad of bush-clearing boys. There was a good deal to attend to. My preparations occupied a few days, and as it was expected that I would be absent for several months, I packed and loaded the greater part of my kit, including several dozen books — all cherished volumes. Ready at length, and for the second time having the company of Mr. Drotsky, we got away just before sunset on the evening of October the seventh, which was a Sunday.

When we reached Toteng, the African driver refused to proceed any further: complaining in a thick, maudlin voice that he was tired and wished to slumber. He repeated several times: "I want to slumber! I want to slumber!" So, as we had only done about forty miles I told him to "slumber" on the load at the back, and Drotsky, who knew the road like the palm of his hand, took the wheel.

We had on the truck a quantity of cement which, at the request of the Veterinary Department, had to be dumped at the Government Bull Camp, near Sehitwa; and as it was midnight when we reached there, we decided to remain over for the night. We were again on our way before sunrise, stopping for a welcome cup of coffee with Mr. Farber, who was running the Sehitwa Store.

Pushing on from there, we reached Gwedau at noon, and as I had instructions for Keemetsikgosi, the senior hunter, we remained there awhile. The next stage brought us to Boayankwe.

The work at this place did not consist of the ordinary bush clearing such as I had to carry out at Khantsaang and Gwexwa, but of the cutting back of a considerable amount of regrowth which was developing in the clearing which Drotsky had made. It was found that all this new growth was affording Tsetses, from the heavily infested eastern side of the river, the means of crossing the mile wide clearing which had, hitherto, acted as an almost perfect barrier to the pest. A small focus of fly, which had been causing some concern, already existed in the savanna forest west of the clearing; and it was desirable to prevent all reinforcements from reaching it.

It was due chiefly to the presence of these few fly that the hunters at Boayankwe and Gwedan (respectively fifteen and twenty five miles south of Nokaneng) had been maintained. The job of these hunters was to discourage as far as possible the movement of all game into and across the clearing. The work they did was useful and needful, but it became necessary to determine just what the incidence of the few fly in the savanna forests to the west of the clearing amounted to. This could only be established by the regular patrolling of fly rounds in the area affected, and it became my task to determine where best these rounds should be marked through the bush.

I must have tramped approximately one hundred miles to reconnoitre the area concerned, and, by a process of elimination, to satisfy myself as to the exact location of the greatest density of the fly: though nowhere could I find any part in which they occurred except in sparing numbers. Having acquired this very necessary information, I immediately established — by the "blazing" of trees and the numbering of sections at convenient intervals — a round that would occupy about four hours to patrol, and this was put into operation at once.

This patrolling is carried out always by the men, two of whom carry on their shoulders a long staff, to which is fixed a sheet of dark green canvas. Each is armed with a small, short-handled net, with which experienced "fly" boys most deftly catch Tsetse alighting on the canvas, or on their persons. The third man, who is the head "fly" boy, and who is selected for the post on account

of superior intelligence and reliability, walks behind. Besides a net to cope with flies alighting on his own person and those to be seen on the back of the man immediately ahead of him, he carries a small cage made of perforated metal which, in addition to a slip-off lid, has a small tube soldered to one end through which the flies are imprisoned. This is closed with a cork for easy handling. He also carries a board to which is pinned a printed record sheet. On these record sheets (which have headings covering sex; age (old-young); hungry or fed; pregnant females; etc.) he records each fly and the section number where it was taken. On completion of the round, he hands in the record and cage for the further attention of the ranger, who checks up on captured flies and any information furnished by the head fly boy.

The daily patrol revealed surprisingly quickly how very few Tsetses really existed in this area, and danger of their ultimate permanent establishment did not now appear to be so imminent as had been feared. The heat had been terrific, and I felt completely dehydrated after the few days of almost continuous "foot-slogging" which the patrols necessitated. The brassy glare of the sun on the parched grass and fallen leaves; the former long since bleached to a surprising whiteness; resulted in the sensation that my eyes were too large for their sockets. They ached to such an extent as to keep me awake at night. To add to the trial, I was at this time suffering with some deep-seated pain in my left ankle, from which, no matter how I tried, I could obtain no relief.

Boayankwe is right on the Teoghe Channel, and though it is now rather unattractive in aspect owing to the elimination of its splendid riverside forest, I found the work and the remoteness of the locality interesting. All my leisure time was spent in exploring the surroundings, hunting, and fishing.

Enormous numbers of Egyptian and Spur-winged geese, and duck in variety, congregated along the few stagnant pools which still remained in the loops of the greatly winding river. Often when they were not actually visible I could hear these and other waterfowl, but the Egyptian geese always held the palm for sheer noisiness. Their lives seemed largely to consist of domestic arguments, when, with outstretched wings and perfect volleys of gaggling invective, they would chase each other around.

The huge spur-wings, on the other hand, are silent fellows which only occasionally utter their absurdly thin: "Koo-weet, Koo-weet!" Both species of goose are wonderfully handsome, but there is as much difference in their respective colourings as there is in their vocal attainments. I took toll of these fowl for my own requirements, with just an occasional one for the boys; and, using my very excellent small rifle exclusively, the sport was good.

There were a lot of reedbuck and kudu about also, and one day I procured a splendid specimen of the former at a range of 212 yards (measured). It was a curious shot. The ram was lying under a thorn tree, but the slanting rays of the late afternoon sun striking full on its glossy hide made it a conspicuous mark against the dark background of shade. I sat down for the shot, and clearly heard the thud of the bullet.

The buck rose on its hind feet but remained kneeling for a few seconds: finally standing with low-hanging head. I was about to give it a second shot, when it began to take a few backward steps, staggered, and suddenly collapsed. I paced the distance, and was delighted to find an exceptionally fine male with beautifully symmetrical horns and a perfect coat. But I was puzzled to find two bullet holes in its left shoulder. Later, while skinning and opening the buck, I found that the little slug had pierced the heart and, breaking a rib on the far side, had somehow deflected backwards, emerging within a few inches of where it had entered! The trophy was carefully prepared for the Grahamstown Museum; and as the leg bones and skull had to be cleaned of all fat and flesh, and suitably preserved against the attacks of insects, I was well occupied until after midnight.

Just previous to my departure on transfer from Headquarters, I had successfully applied for two weeks occasional leave. This was due to commence within a fortnight after my arrival at the new camp.

I looked forward eagerly to this break, especially as I had also received permission to collect certain of the more rare, protected birds and mammals — all intended for the museum. So a stock of preservatives was ordered, as well as an extra supply of food stuffs and ammunition: and by the time the leave was due, I was reasonably well equipped.

My original intention had been to hire two good "dugouts", complete with paddlers, and to go a good distance into the swamps. Unfortunately the water was now so low in the available channels that the idea had to be abandoned in favour of a walking expedition. This was a great disappointment, as apart from the nuisance of having carriers, their food supply would be difficult in such an isolated area. Also I would be cut off from the very parts — the heart of the swamp lands — which I was most eager to penetrate. Carriers proved to be difficult to secure, but I managed to collect four men who agreed to follow wherever I cared to proceed.

Among the specimens which I most ardently desired, and for which I had permission to search, was that rare and elusive antelope, the sitatunga (*Nakong*, or more correctly *Naakoe*, of the local natives). I felt that my course should be largely determined by localities wherein there was a reasonable hope of securing this animal. Numerous enquiries, however, invariably produced the information that there was little probability of my obtaining a specimen of a sitatunga, and that if one was brought to bag at all, it would be by sheer good luck. I learnt that a few existed in most

parts of the marsh lands where large tracts of reeds occurred; and that the direction followed would not necessarily be important.

Mr. Andrew Wright, my friend at Nokaneng, had suggested that I make a central camp at a place called Karanamoxgee, which is about sixteen miles north of Nokaneng and on a westerly inclined extension of the marshes. He insisted that as the place was easily reached from Nokaneng, little time would be lost in travelling. He further assured me that a good deal of game existed in the vicinity, and that fair fishing would be obtainable. For want of a better plan, I acceded to this suggestion, and in view of subsequent events it was fortunate that I did so. I was becoming rather worried about the pain my ankle was causing. In spite of hot fomentations and all other available treatment it was steadily becoming worse, and it would have been wiser to postpone my vacation. It was nearing the end of the year, however, and as the allowable occasional leave had either to be taken during the current year, or forfeited, I was loath to alter my plans. The rainy season was also due. This meant that any postponement would lead to further difficulties arising from the necessity to carry tentage for myself and boys.

At Boayankwe, my tent was pitched beneath a couple of fine Motsaudi trees (*Garcinia livingstonei*), and the place became known as Motsaudi Camp. Thence, a good deal of the fifteen miles to Nokaneng was over alluvial flats, which in the distant past must have been covered with water from the annual inundations. Ancient, ditch-like hippo paths criss-crossing the area are still visible. No doubt traces of them will remain for hundreds of years to come. I spent a couple of hours, one Sunday afternoon, pottering around and following one of these paths. In places I found it to be shoulder-deep. It exactly resembled those to be found in the centre of the waterways still frequented by the great beasts, and which are a familiar feature to those who have travelled through the marsh lands of the Okavango.

During my brief ramble I unearthed two hippopotamus tusks from the sloping side of the old pathway. I first caught sight of what I took to be a piece of bone sticking out of the ground. A little scraping and digging revealed the two teeth, but these must obviously have been trampled into the mud at a remote period for they were in an advanced state of disintegration and, of course, utterly useless as specimens. They must have belonged to a half grown hippo, but the find was not without interest. A further search yielded nothing more than some pieces of decomposed bone: probably fragments of the skull to which the teeth had belonged. The great depth of this ancient track testified to the ages which must have elapsed during its formation.

On Friday the nineteenth of October, 1945, Mr. Crawshaw and his second-in-command Captain McGiles arrived at Motsaudi Camp. After some refreshment, and a discussion on the future anti-fly campaign, Mr. Crawshaw offered to convey me with all my carriers and equipment to Karanamoxgee, expressing his intention of remaining over the weekend for some shooting and fishing. This of course meant a great saving of precious time, so I gladly accepted the offer, and soon had my belongings stowed in the "Bug truck". We reached Nokaneng in time for lunch. Here we received the usual hearty welcome and, chatting gaily through the meal, we persuaded our friends to join us on the morrow. Later, after a few belated purchases, we set off for the camp: reaching this in time to settle in comfortably for the night, after a short unsuccessful round for duck.

At dawn we set out in different directions in search of game, and it certainly proved to be my lucky morning. I had not proceeded for more than a couple of miles when one of my accompanying boys noticed some lechwe grazing over a small alluvial flat some distance away. Dropping to my knees, I began to stalk the game; and after taking advantage of odd tussocks of grass and rushes and with much painful crawling, managed to approach within reasonable range without awakening suspicion. Rising suddenly, I fired and knocked down what seemed to be the best ram. It struggled frantically to regain its feet, and had just succeeded in doing so when, to my amazement, it was savagely set upon by another ram, which butted it violently to the ground once more. The unfortunate animal contrived to regain its feet, only to be once again knocked flat on its side by a savage renewal of the assault by its companion. Was it perhaps a cowardly attack by a vanquished rival? The incident, which occurred exactly as related, is unique in my experience.

In order to terminate the sufferings of the wounded ram and to prevent further assaults, I ran forward. The unwounded lechwe went bounding away in the wake of a mixed mob of ewes and youngsters, while the stricken buck struggled to its feet and made off towards a papyrus-filled watercourse away to the right. I missed it disgracefully, though to some extent I was hampered by the tall grass through which the buck was running. I was relieved to note that it ran up the side of the rank stuff and not into it, as I expected it to do, and I followed at my best pace. Losing sight of it at a bend in the waterway, I now advanced quietly, noting how profusely the animal was bleeding, and I felt certain that it would not go far. Nevertheless, I covered at least a quarter of a mile before I again saw the buck, which suddenly broke from a small clump of reeds almost at my feet, and tore away as if nothing was amiss with it. I immediately bowled it over for the second time.

My boys rushed forward, but by the time they had reached the lechwe it had once again staggered to its feet. Turning, with a threatening hiss, and with lowered horns, it attempted to poke the men. I soon reached them, and, successfully avoiding its vicious lunges, we managed to pull down the gallant beast, which I immediately piked, and so spared all further suffering.

Lechwe are amazingly tenacious of life, and the manner in which they elude their pursuers when bearing appalling wounds is perfectly astounding.

This specimen was as fine an example as one could wish to see, and I determined that it should grace the Antelope Section of the museum for which I was collecting. It carried a splendid pair of long, wide-spreading horns which had tips so sharply inclined forwards that it was almost impossible to suspend the head by

them from a crossbar. I once saw a head from the Chobe River possessing this characteristic, and remember thinking at the time that it was the most beautiful specimen which I had ever beheld. Excluding, perhaps, Grant's Gazelle, I do not believe that there is another species of antelope in the whole of Africa which carries longer horns for its size than the lechwe. The females are hornless and, shaggy as the males, lack the gazelle-like daintiness of impala ewes. Nonetheless, they are lovely creatures. There are lengthy periods when they are not accompanied by the rams, and it is no uncommon sight to see large herds of them, with kids at foot, grazing over the alluvial flats with no male in sight. These cousins of the waterbuck are not much larger than impala or reedbuck: but, being stockily built, they are a good deal heavier. Their large, broad hooves splay widely when the animals run: enabling them to negotiate easily the marshy regions they invariably frequent.

Normally tame and confiding in their habits, lechwe, where much hunted, become excessively wild: more so, in fact, than is the case with most other buck, and they them become exceedingly difficult to circumvent. It is no uncommon sight to see the males retreating at a fast trot while the hunter is still a long way off. While doing so they habitually stretch out their noses, holding the head below the level of the back, with the long, lyrate horns brushing the shoulders on either side. Seen thus, there is a suggestion of furtiveness in their actions, and, indeed, they do endeavour to slink away unobserved. When fired at, or otherwise alarmed, they break into a speedy gallop; and may sometimes be seen bounding high into the air, as do impala.

When in flight, lechwe always make for the nearest water: causing a great deal of noise when splashing through the shallows. Though they are powerful swimmers, they resort to this form of locomotion only when their feet are no longer able to touch bottom. Anyone who hunts the swamp lands will soon learn how frequently lechwe advertise their presence — even when completely hidden by papyrus, reeds, rushes, etc., — by the noisy racket of their passage as they flee from real or imagined danger. I do not believe that they enter the water at night except under compulsion.

I have slept in the swamplands many scores of times, frequently almost at the water's edge, but never once have I heard lechwe crossing the water during the hours of darkness. Often in the late evening and again at dawn they may be heard wandering about the shallows or crossing narrow streams.

The weather was extremely hot, and the sooner I could get the specimen to camp the better. Getting a stout pole cut, and lashing the buck to it, I ordered two of the men to return to camp with it. With the remaining man I made a round through the veld in the hope of picking up something else. There was a long, broad belt of rather open fringing forest somewhat northeast of the camp, and I decided to investigate this and see what water lay beyond it. I had not proceeded very far when I was confronted with a belt of Bowstring hemp (*Sansevieria deserti*), which is a sisal-like plant from two to four feet in height, which usually occurs in dense masses.

This belt was of unknown width, and though disinclined to turn back, I yet stood to consider the matter. This Mogotsi (as the natives call it) is a difficult type of vegetation through which to force one's way, as each stem ends in a spear-like point. To trip and fall in such a thicket would be dangerous, as it might well result in the loss of an eye. My boy, however, was familiar with the area, and he assured me that the belt was but a narrow one, so we proceeded carefully.

I had merely walked on for a few yards when some animal broke away in front of me, affording me but the briefest glimpse of it, though I could hear it crashing along for some time. It was a magnificent specimen of a male Chobe bushbuck. There was no time for the quickest of snap shots, but I had clearly glimpsed the massive horns, the white underside of its bushy tail, and the striped and spotted flank during that brief vision.

Realising the futility of trying to pursue it in that sort of cover, I simply stood and gazed in the direction in which it had gone, thinking, unhappily, what a splendid museum specimen I had lost. Though I knew that these bushbuck were to be found in the vast sansevieria patches which occur in several parts of the country, I never again obtained the opportunity of a shot at one. Years previously, I did shoot a young doe, but the pack of native dogs which ran it down so mutilated it that it was useless as a specimen. I saw numerous skins, however, during the period of my work with the T.F.C., and made many enquiries concerning the animal. As I shall not again have occasion to refer to it, let me add a few further observations.

Approximating closely in size to the southern dark Cape bushbuck, the Chobe bushbuck is quite different in colour. These loveliest of antelope are a rich dark red in colour, with six or seven white stripes on the sides. There are white spots on the shoulders, as well as a large number of the same on the hindquarters, with a crest of long white hairs along the dorsal line. I have seen no heads carrying horns over fourteen inches, but doubtless larger ones do occur. I frequently picked up skulls of males which had probably been killed by either wild dogs or the greater cats, but as already stated the horns averaged much the same as those in the south. Whether the Chobe bushbuck is as aggressive when wounded or bayed as the Cape type I had no means of judging, as dogs cannot exist in the fly areas. Although the sansevieria belts are undoubtedly the main stronghold of the Chobe bushbuck in Ngamiland, a few of these antelope occur along some of the rivers. These latter are, however, extremely wary, and are just about as difficult to bag as sitatunga.

I questioned my head boy, Xwedina, about the possibilities for procuring sitatunga in the area, and he replied: "Moreno, the only place I know where there are any *Naakoe* is in the big reeds near Gadimang's Kraal. A few days before I came to work for you Gadimang shot one there, but there are more, and they always remain at that place." He informed me that it would take about three hours fast walking to reach the locality, which was situated on the same molapo (river) on which we were encamped. As I was fearful that my foot might become so painful that I would be unable to do any walking in a few days time, I decided to take the opportunity now. I therefore arranged that he, Gadimang (who was one of my boys), and a couple of carriers should accompany me at dawn next morning, and that they should come prepared to sleep out.

In due course, with Gadimang at the lead, we set off. We held to the margin of the Karanamoxgee Molapo: and the further we proceeded, the less the water became, until at length a chain of widely separated, quickly drying pools was all that remained.

After a couple of hours of walking we noticed a small herd of Lechwe in a very green-looking marsh away to our right. While we were yet a long way off they began to run, and Gadimang said that, as they had constantly been hunted by local people and dogs, we would never be able to approach them. We had now been walking for much over three hours, the sun was cruelly hot, and I began to long for the end of the journey, and for a drink of water. However we had not far to go. Presently a wispy column of smoke became visible above a few thin trees and scrubby bush about half a mile ahead. Gadimang informed me that this marked his kraal. For some time previously I had noticed the enormous reed beds in the distance, wondering vaguely what they held for me.

There were a few scraggly trees near the kraal, which consisted of a couple of tiny huts — more or less in ruins. I wondered what induced these people to choose such a site for a dwelling place. They could hardly have chosen a more desolate and lonely spot. A woman and two potbellied children greeted our arrival with stares, but their lord and master soon sent them off to fetch a supply of water from the molapo. I was pleased enough to rest for an hour, and sat in what shade I could find beneath a sparsely-leafed, twisted tree, partaking of a little food.

I noticed a tiny patch of cultivated ground over which lay scattered some small, withered calabashes and dried up corn stalks. These, in addition to the well-trodden footpath and the tumble down huts, provided the only evidence of human habitation. Presently the woman brought in a clay pot full of horribly stagnant water, but for want of any other we had to make the best of it. I was now sorry that I had decided against bringing a kettle, and a supply of tea and sugar.

The obviously miserable conditions under which Gadimang existed in this place led me to infer that he probably largely depended upon game (he possessed quite a decent magazine rifle) and such fish as he was able to trap, to keep the wolf from the door. He seemed quite satisfied with his pitch however, and remained standing a long while talking to his wife.

After a while, Gadimang came over and, squatting near by, informed me (quite needlessly I thought) that though there were a good many naakoe about in the extensive reed beds, they were difficult to find. He explained that whenever he had been successful in procuring one, it had been during the hottest time of the day: at which time, he averred, the animals came out and fed on the grass and herbs at the edge of the reeds. I found it difficult to believe this, though as the afternoon advanced his assertions appeared to a certain extent to be confirmed.

If plenty of heat was a desirable factor in stalking sitatunga, then the conditions must have been just about ideal when, with the boys at my heels, I finally set out for the reeds. It was stiflingly hot with barely a breath of wind, and I confess I had but scant hopes of seeing anything at all. Where stalking is concerned I much prefer to be quite alone: so, on reaching the reeds and having a look round, I told the boys to move up near the margin and to meet me a mile or two further ahead. Gadimang had his rifle, and I promised him a handsome reward if he bagged a good ram.

Finding a narrow gap, I crossed to the western fringe which here was not distant, for at this lower end the great bed tapered to a wedge. Hugging its margin, I moved forward with care, and had proceeded but a short distance when traces of the game became visible. The long, open "V"s of sitatunga tracks could be seen here and there in exposed patches of moist earth, and some were fresh.

Twice, within an hour and a half, I heard a heavy animal crash into that almost incredible thickness of massed reeds, and could see the violent agitation of their tops, but nothing more; though the sound of splashing within indicated that some water still remained in the brake. I had soon plenty of proof that it was indeed sitatunga that I heard, as the wide open imprints of the immensely long hooves, and freshly turned moist soil, identified them beyond doubt.

Stalking in such surroundings formed a considerable strain. It was a real difficulty to advance without creating any sound. Indeed, this was practically impossible because, apart from the dry stems and leaves of reeds being scattered everywhere, there were stools of semi-dry grass which had to be avoided all the while. An occasional puff of wind — just sufficient to set the fuzzy heads of the reeds swaying lazily or to bear to an alert animal the taint of an enemy — made me realise how true it was that the element of luck counted for much in one's chance of a shot at sitatunga. The ground was perfectly flat with no slight eminence where one might sit and wait for a buck to appear, and I soon realised that more time than was at my disposal would be necessary to collect specimens at this place.

After I had been stalking for rather more than two hours, I saw the boys coming towards me on my side of the reeds. I shook my head to Gadimang's unspoken enquiry, but told him that I had heard naakoe breaking away. He grinned, and said that if I were to try often I would get one. As we sat down to rest, Xwedina informed me that they had found spoor in several places but that none of it was quite fresh. Also that they had come across the remains of a young naakoe: fragments of skin and bone more or less crushed to splinters by hyenas, but that they could find no evidence of what had killed the creature. He thought that it had been destroyed several days before, and that it must have been completely devoured at the time, for no vultures had troubled to settle at the remains.

According to Gadimang it is very rarely that remains of sitatunga are found. This he attributed to the fact that the buck never wander any distance from the reeds, and that no creature on four legs could catch them when once in their favourite cover. I believe that he is probably quite correct about this, though occasional ones must be killed by lions and leopards, and no doubt cheetahs, with their terrific turn of speed, find opportunities to overtake one before it can regain cover.

As there was no object to be gained by traversing the ground over which the men had now come (and there was no time to try for the main reed beds) I decided that we should spread out and walk through the grass and rushes to the pools lower down and almost opposite the camp. Gadimang, however, suggested that we should cross over the molapo which, some distance to the west of where we were, again became an unbroken reach of deep water, choked up with *Kama* (Papyrus). He said that he knew of a good crossing place, and that beyond this was a deep pool near which he thought we might find a crocodile's "nest", but that in any case we might thereabouts also find lechwe or reedbuck. This sounded interesting, so I allowed him to take the lead. As we trudged along towards the molapo (indicated by a line of papyrus about half a mile distant) I noticed a skull which proved to be that of a male sitatunga. With the exception of the long white tips, the horns were hopelessly riddled by horn-borers. I measured them roughly and found that they were approximately twenty-two inches in a straight line. They were spiralled very like those of a kudu bull. Not much more than a hundred yards further on we found another sitatunga skull, with similar sized horns, and equally worm-eaten. Gadimang could tell me nothing of their history, saying that they were lying there when he first came to live at the place. He thought they had been killed by leopards, of which there were plenty thereabouts.

When we reached the Koma, we followed up its margin for a short distance until, arriving at an indistinct path leading diagonally into it, Gadimang followed the latter — carefully picking his way between the tall stems. The other boys were immediately behind me, and as I moved forward I saw here and there a glimmer of water in small gaps of the packed root system of the floating growth, and knew that we were already over deep water, but there was not a movement in the apparently solid decking. This was my first experience of crossing water on papyrus, and I soon learnt the absolute necessity of meticulously following in the footsteps of the guide. At first, fascinated by the novelty of the experience, I blundered along after him and soon stepped into a hole concealed by fallen papyrus heads and other trash. In a twinkling I was up to my armpits in water without touching bottom. The boys dragged me out ere I realised the narrow escape I had had, for, as they pointed out, crocodiles lurk beneath the platforms: waiting for the lechwe, and other game, to pass by the openings.

We were soon safely across, and Gadimang whispered to me that we should now proceed very silently as there was a deep, detached pool near by, close to which he had seen several times recently a large crocodile lying in open ground some distance from the water. Notwithstanding our care, the horrible reptile sensed our approach, and I caught but a glimpse of it scurrying through the low reeds towards the pool some forty yards away. A few minutes later I heard it enter the water. I walked straight there, and found that all the grasses and rushes near the water had been flattened, obviously by the crocodile's continuous passage to and fro over them.

The boys had walked to where the crocodile had been startled, and two of them were carefully digging with sticks into the sunbaked silt. That the crocodile haunted this place habitually was evident, particularly where the boys were digging, so I joined them there and we carefully and laboriously removed the earth. About six inches below the surface a portion of a white egg was

seen, and during the next few moments several dozen were exposed to the light of day. Carefully lifting them out, and placing them to one side, Gadimang declared that there should be more eggs deeper down, and continued to dig. Sure enough, a few inches deeper another layer was uncovered. In all, that nest contained sixty-seven eggs; but both Gadimang and Xwedina assured me that they had seen over one hundred taken from one nest. Martinus Drotsky told me at a later date that he himself had removed seventy two from a site, and a local missionary mentioned having found a like number. Be that as it may, it seemed to me that this effort of Gadimang's crocodile — the one which we had just robbed — was quite an achievement.

In camp next day I measured several of the eggs, and found that they averaged three and three-eighths inches by two inches. The shells — pointed at both ends and rather stronger than hen's eggs — were snowy white and attractive in appearance. I retained eighteen of these, and took real pleasure in smashing the others against the remains of a tree stump.

As we had nothing in which to carry the fragile things, I had to resort, to removing my undervest and packing them in that, between layers of grass. The plan worked well enough and they were all safely conveyed to camp.

I was greatly interested by the finding of this crocodile's nest. In connection with it, however, were aspects of which I have never yet been able to get any enlightenment, either from local natives (who are generally very observant) or from scientific sources. There seems to be no mystery about the method by which the excavations to accommodate the eggs are made. Surely this can only be accomplished by the paws of the creature — probably by a hind foot, as in the tortoises. What puzzled me was the manner in which the eggs were deposited. Are they laid singly, or in small batches? Or is the entire clutch evacuated on a single occasion? On this point native opinion differed, and I received no satisfactory information from Europeans who have spent many years in and about the marshlands. Likewise, a well-known scientist and authority on natural history informed me that he had no information on the matter.

For reasons which will be given hereafter, I am of opinion that all the eggs are laid at one time. If this is not so, the following questions require to be answered:

(1). As exposed eggs are never seen, it is reasonable to deduce that if eggs are laid singly, or in small lots, they must be carefully covered after each laying. This would involve re-opening for each successive installment: an operation which surely would greatly imperil those already placed.

(2). At least half the eggs found were lying side by side at the bottom of the hole, a position one would hardly expect had they been produced on successive occasions.

(3). If laid over a period of days, or weeks, how is the incubation of the first laid eggs — of necessity in the lower layer — delayed?

The sixty odd eggs removed from that site all exhibited the same stage of incubation: large bloodvessels formed, but no recognisable embryo yet evident. Whether crocodiles breed in captivity I know not, but possibly the full life history of these creatures may now be well known.

Gadimang informed me that mother crocodiles spend most of their time lying on, or near, the nests. This, he thought, was in order to protect the eggs from leguaans (large monitor lizards) which are among the crocodile's worst enemies as they can smell out the buried hoard which, with the eggs of other creatures, form their favourite food.

Other native information was to the effect that the mother hangs around in order to devour the hatchlings as they emerge, before they have the strength and opportunity to scurry away to the water where they are comparatively safe! The River Bushmen are adept at finding the nests, and they regard the eggs as great delicacies.

CHOBE BUSHBUCK

Chapter 8

PLAGUE MOST FOUL!

ELSEWHERE in these pages I have indicated the indescribable horror which assails the lonely traveller or Government official when the dread plague rears its loathsome head. The following account of such an incidence is typical of many, and may not be without grim interest.

On the twenty-eighth of November we camped down at a place called Kakanaga, eighteen miles from my former Boayankwe camp. During the cutting of the large clearing at Kakanaga, Drotsky had left no nice trees to shelter a camping site. As I walked about, searching for as pleasant a site as possible for my tent, I saw something which, somehow, acted like an evil premonition. This was the sight of a dead mouse which immediately aroused thoughts of those anxious, trying days on the Thamalukane, just a year previous. Apart from sending in a report, and selecting my camping site as far as possible away from the spot, there was nothing to be done about it, and I tried to stifle my sense of foreboding. Actually, it finally transpired that — through an oversight — my report was never actually passed on to the M.O. (Medical Officer).

It befell, therefore, that on the first Saturday afternoon (after three and a half days at the new camp) I took the small rifle and went for a long tramp up river. After I had walked about a mile, I happened to glance behind and was surprised to see Dick Morambo's small son — a lad of about ten years of age — following me. Thinking that his father might have sent him with a message, I waited for him to reach me, but on doing so he immediately shyly asked if he might accompany me. Rather pleased, I readily assented, and he at once fell in behind me. He was a pleasant, intelligent little chap who sometimes followed me to my work, or round the camp. On previous occasions he had followed me along the river, and though generally too shy to utter a word, he would point excitedly at any goose or duck, and if my shot was successful he would make a wild rush for the bird.

That afternoon my bag consisted of a fine spur-winged goose and two yellow-billed duck, and as I obtained these with three consecutive shots at ranges of fifty to one hundred yards, I was well pleased. The lad insisted on carrying the goose, so letting him have his way, I took the duck and we made our way campwards. We arrived there at sundown, and the youngster's joy was complete when I told him that he could share the goose with his father. My last glimpse was of him fairly racing for their shelter, with the heavy bird dangling from his shoulder. On the following Saturday afternoon I again walked up river carrying the .22 rifle. My small companion (whose real name was such a mouthful that I named him "Tommy" instead) awaited no invitation this time, but fell in behind me with appropriate dignity, which failed to conceal his obvious excitement.

We had not proceeded far before I shot a spur-wing, its mate rising and circling around three or four times during which I tried two flying shots, both of which missed. Hiding the dead goose, which the boy had collected, we walked on again for some distance before another spur-wing was added to my bag. This one was carried by my small companion. A little later I shot two yellow-bills: and now having made a nice bag, I turned and set off back to camp. After some time I became aware that the boy was lagging behind, so sat down to wait for him. He was walking very slowly, and I felt sorry that I had allowed him to carry the weighty goose. As he reached me, he squatted down, and I lit a cigarette while he rested. I asked him whether he found the bird too heavy,

89

but beyond a faint smile he made no reply; and after a few minutes I arose, and taking up the goose handed him the two duck which were barely half the weight.

However, before we reached the place where the first goose had been hidden, the boy was lagging far back again, and when he finally caught up I noticed, for the first time, that he was ailing. His eyes were dull and bloodshot, and the usually cheery little fellow looked very ill indeed. I felt his hands, and found them burning hot, and began to wish that the camp was a good deal nearer. I took the birds from him, and walked on very slowly, keeping him close to me. Having yet another goose to carry, I was well loaded, but managed very well after tying their necks together, and suspending the lot over the rifle barrel on my shoulder.

That the boy might be suffering from an attack of malaria seemed improbable, and I became increasingly worried. On reaching camp I took him straight to his father, explaining his sudden sickness. His temperature registered 102°: he was suffering from a consuming thirst, drinking frequently, and enjoyed a mug of tea I brought him. In fact he begged for more, so I left a supply of tea, sugar, and milk with his father. His breathing was rapid, and I felt really anxious as I sat down to my own supper. An hour later he was still asleep, but I turned in with an uneasy mind.

At earliest dawn I went straight to Dick's shelter. I found him up but the poor fellow looked broken with anxiety. As I entered the hut, I was shocked by the lad's condition. He was jabbering incoherently, tossing from side to side, and his eyes looked dreadful. It took a little while to take his temperature, but the reading of 105° did not surprise me. His body was afire, and when I felt the glands in his groin, my worst fears were confirmed. They were much enlarged, and that the poor little fellow was nearing his end was very obvious. On emerging from the hut, I perceived that Dick shared my conclusion. Plague is endemic in the country, and most natives know something about it.

Alas! Apart from the pitiful aspirins, I had nothing with which to allay the little patient's suffering. I hastened back to my tent where I penned a note to Mr. Wright: reporting the suspected case of plague, and begging him to use every endeavour to contact Maun. This I sent off with one of the labourers who owned a bicycle, instructing him to travel with all speed.

THE REWARD of OUR ALLIES AGAINST PLAGUE!

Apart from instructing the boys to hang out all their belongings in the hot sun, and to change their sleeping places, there was nothing else I could do, and the suspense was well-nigh unbearable. I gave Dick more aspirins, but he, poor fellow, merely shook his dead. I do not think that he was at all concerned for himself, though he must have been well aware how improbable it was that he could himself now escape the dreaded disease.

Up to that time I had, strangely enough, not noticed the almost complete absence of all rodents. With this outbreak of plague, however, it suddenly occurred to me that the local rodents must have died out practically to the last one; and I believe that to be the case, because there were enough small carnivorous creatures and raptorial birds in evidence to have effectually cleaned up any corpses which may have been lying about.

It now appeared that we had camped down in the midst of rife infestation. Whither to flee was an insoluble problem, as there was no means of discriminating between clean and infested areas. Indeed, in any case we had no possible means of shifting a large quantity of equipment and grain. I felt that I could no longer endure the atmosphere of the camp, so swallowing some food, and taking up the light rifle, I set out for the veld across the river.

In the course of my wanderings trees have always fascinated me, and on this particular occasion I came across a particularly fine specimen of the Fig family. Its native name is *Moomo*, and I have heard it called Livingstone's tree. Botanically I believe it is called *Ficus ingens*. This tree is an epiphyte, and, no doubt due to the birds which propagate it through their droppings, being attracted by the luscious fruits of the Mokuchon *(Diospyros mespilliformis)*, one has the impression that it has a strong predilection for the latter. At any rate, Mokuchons are more frequently, in my experience, encumbered and destroyed by its deadly embrace than other trees. The Moomo attains a large size and is of great beauty.

I have seen its murderous work on numbers of Mokuchons in various stages of development. Some with bunches of streamers attached to — or just dangling against — their trunks. Others with huge, serpent-like bands slowly but ruthlessly strangling the life out of them; and yet others entirely enfolded, with perhaps a foot or two of the dead hardwood visible between the constricting bands. In such case was the tree I now reached, and I was fascinated by the amazing manner in which the Moomo had spread its pale, green, soft growth over the huge trunk which it had engulfed. It looked just as if molten green wax had been poured over the trunk and branches of the host until nearly the whole of it had been absorbed. I was as much impressed by the ruthless manner in which this extraordinary vegetable parasite had smothered and killed its unfortunate host as by the way it had usurped its position in an exquisite piece of woodland.

I returned to the camp after being absent for about three hours, and found the boys digging a grave. My poor little friend had breathed his last shortly after I had left camp.

I at once sent off another letter to Mr. Wright by runner: reporting the boy's death, and my conviction that he had died of plague. I knew that the messenger could not possibly reach Nokaneng until late the next morning because natives will not travel by night in lion country. As it happened, the unfortunate man sickened and died of plague on the way, though I only learnt this several days afterwards.

On the previous day one of the men had applied for special leave to visit a distant kraal, but on the grounds that he had had the previous weekend off I refused this. In fairness to all, I could not grant leave of absence to any of my staff on consecutive weekends, a rule which was always strictly observed. This man, however, chose to ignore my refusal, and he paid dearly for his disobedience, as he, too, succumbed to the plague on the way, and was never seen alive again.

Sezumba and Dick Morambo were now the only men I had in camp, and I lived in constant fear that either one or both would contract the disease. My greatest concern, of course, was for Dick. All through he had shared his bed with his little departed son, and it seemed highly unlikely that he could have escaped being bitten by the same flea, or fleas, that had transmitted the malady to the boy.

When I finally received news from Mr. Wright, nothing could have been more depressing. His note informed me that, owing to a general strike of the African operatives in charge of the numerous trucks belonging to the recruiting organisation, no convoys would be running for an indefinite period. The only hope he could offer me of contacting Maun lay in the possibility of a casual traveller calling in.

I was now utterly without transport of any description, and with the nearest help one hundred and twenty miles away, the unpleasantness of my situation may well be imagined.

The boys refused to work and spent much of their time away, and I made no attempt to compel them. Indeed my one personal desire was to get away from the gloom which enshrouded the camp.

However, some form of activity is the only panacea for worry, so I decided to set out for a long day in the veld. Firstly I wanted to get away from the camp, and secondly I wanted to ascertain exactly what the Tsetse fly position was a long distance away from the river. As I started out, two of the absent boys arrived in camp, and one man, named Isaac, asked to accompany me.

Within half an hour we reached unfamiliar ground and were greatly pestered by the detestable Tsetse flies, but these occurred in a narrow belt only, and it was not long thereafter before their attacks had ceased. Over the huge distance traversed that day I encountered no more of the pest until we again reached the riverine forest in the late evening.

After we had walked for about two hours and skirted a thick strip of thorny scrub, a small troop of buffalo went crashing and snorting away through the bush. I immediately sat down, for experience has taught me that buffalo, unless they have sighted a man will not usually run for any great distance. I hoped that, by delaying a while and then making a wide detour, we might again encounter the herd. There was little wind, and what there was of it veered in a manner that made stalking difficult.

After a wait of about twenty minutes I again set off — walking away diagonally from my original course, and slowly swinging round in a big half circle towards the scrub again. We cautiously advanced towards an opening of some extent which was dotted with a number of taller trees, the shade provided by which offered a typical halting place for buffalo when on the alert. My cast around was successful, for Isaac suddenly dropped down: whispering that he had seen a movement in the shade of one of the trees. We were in good cover, and in a direction well away from that in which the animals might have expected us.

As we very cautiously moved forwards, I now saw the object to which he had referred. It was a buffalo standing in dense shade, but I was astonished to see two more much closer; and I was at a loss to understand how we had failed to notice these latter previously, as they were in much more exposed surroundings than the first one observed. The range was not over one hundred yards, and as usual I fired with one knee resting on the ground. The great beast collapsed with a grunt, and its companion behaved in the oddest manner. It trotted up to its fallen, kicking comrade, sniffing at it and uttering short, deep bellows as I had never previously heard these animals emit. It waltzed around the fallen one, scraping the ground and behaving generally in a manner unique to me!

I stood watching the scene for a few moments, waiting for the bull to remain still enough for me to attempt a shot, but it had worked itself into an awesome state of fury and excitement. Its tail swung and whipped wildly from side to side as it grunted and bellowed: flinging up clouds of dust with its front hooves. The smell of blood had evidently maddened the brute, and for a while it did not remain still for an instant.

Keeping the sight on it, I finally squeezed the trigger at the first brief halt in its excitable performance. It also crashed down, falling partly on the other. Not expecting it to rise again, I walked forwards: but to my surprise it quickly stumbled to its feet and, without more ado, came straight for me, uttering hoarse grunts. A second shot, which nearly knocked it down again and evidently shook it badly, caused it to swerve away to the left; and this strangely acting buffalo went off at a heavy gallop in the exact direction from which the herd had come. Soon afterwards I heard the crash as it fell, and it began to bellow - a fairly certain indication that a buffalo is dying. While all this was taking place, four buffalo coming from the same direction went galloping across my front over a small plain, making for a north-west direction. The hindmost of these was a huge beast and, unlike its almost hairless companions, blacker than any buffalo I had hitherto seen. Its massive hindquarters were as round as those of a dray horse, and its great gleaming horns were magnificent. It was evidently in the prime of life, and was probably the master bull. In an instant I had my sights on his shoulder, off which I saw the dust fly to the shot even before the "clop" of the bullet reached my ears. He merely accelerated on receiving the bullet, but a second shot slowed him down, and soon he was walking in the wake of the others. These had halted in a small patch of low scrub, where they turned to face me - revealing little other than their massive, helmeted heads.

Isaac had fled precipitately when the second bull had charged me, and was still nowhere to be seen. I walked on alone to the first one killed, and found it to be an old, but not large, bull in low condition. Looking decidedly sheepish, Isaac now came up as I was examining the animal, and begged me to leave the second bull alone — averring that it was certainly out for blood! I told him rather impatiently to stay behind, and made a detour so as to arrive at the point whence the last bellow had sounded from behind. I caught sight of the poor brute in the same instant that it became aware of my presence. It was lying awkwardly with one foreleg outstretched in front. All its fury and pugnacity had vanished, a feature in which it differed also from the average buffalo; and a merciful bullet ceased its suffering.

This bull was fat, and it had large, though not outstanding horns.

I was very anxious to obtain the third — big — buffalo bull, and, as I expected to find it dead in the scrub where the others had awaited it, I returned to where I had left Isaac, and we went after it. All we found, however, was a patch of blood covering a couple of square feet of ground as well as bloody froth on the grass and twigs of scrubby bushes. Obviously this had been coughed up, as the result of a lungshot, but there was no other sign of the buffalo. All four had apparently gone off from this point at their usual heavy gallop, and for the next half hour we could have run on the spoor — so plainly did it show. Thereafter, things became really difficult! The tracks led right into thick bush, mostly of the thorny acacia type which played havoc with my shirt, shorts, and skin. The tracking had become dangerous also, and frequently we had to slacken up and make certain that the wounded buffalo was still with the others. This cautious sort of progress continued for the best part of an hour when the bush thinned out before finally ceasing altogether. Here, on the edge of a considerable open plain, the buffaloes must have halted awhile — probably listening. At any rate there was quite a considerable patch of blood, but about ten yards away from the other spoor. It seemed likely that the wounded beast might turn away from the others at this place, so we very carefully followed its tracks. However, its spoor soon rejoined that of the others about one hundred yards ahead. All the spoor led into the open country for several hundred yards, when, for some inexplicable reason, the leaders had suddenly swerved sharply to the right; and within about a quarter of a mile the beasts had re-entered the thorn belt. They were travelling near the edge of the bush, however, and the spoor was more easily followed as the buffalo were again running.

There was now not a breath of wind and the heat was so terrific that I decided, unless we came up with the buffalo within half an hour to abandon the hunt as our thirst was becoming overpowering. When more than that space of time had elapsed, and the spoor indicated that the four animals were still together and going strongly, the necessity of our reaching camp before dark further decided me to "throw up the sponge" - which I did with sincere regret!

With the intention of taking home the tongues, I told Isaac to lead me straight back to where the two dead "buffs" lay. African natives are usually very reliable guides in the bush, but on this occasion Isaac completely lost his sense of direction, and to cut a long story short we had in the end to leave the dead bulls and concentrate on getting back to camp, relying entirely on my own observation of the country. Twilight had already set in before we finally reached our quarters. I was more than tired, but the day's adventures had acted as a soothing balm to my frayed nerves, and a blessed, though temporary, respite from the past few days of anxiety.

That night a hyena entered the camp and dragged away the sundried hide of a buffalo which had been shot on the evening of my arrival at Kakanaga. On the following morning I paced the distance that the hide had been lying from my tent and found it to be exactly twelve yards! A buffalo hide is a heavy object and, when dry, as stiff and hard as an oak board: yet that hyena had contrived to drag it for 250 yards through bush so thick that the two boys whom I sent to retrieve it found no little difficulty in bringing it back - notwithstanding that several square feet of it had been chewed away!

Following the drag marks, I soon found the brute's spoor. I had the hide placed in its former position, and before darkness again set in, I attached to it a length of baling wire — the other end of which was fastened to the frame of my stretcher. With the knowledge that the slightest tug on the hide would now awaken me, I retired in the full expectation of giving the sneaking thief the surprise of its life. Whether, however, that hyena expected reprisals, or had found something to eat involving less risk — or whether, perhaps it had not thought much of the hide — it failed to return so all my trouble was in vain.

By December the eleventh there had been no fresh cases of plague. The boys, with the exception of Dick and Sezumba, kept away from the camp: sleeping at one or other of the widely scattered huts of the local inhabitants. Poor Dick strolled around like a man half dazed and seldom uttered a word; but Sezumba was cheerful enough, regularly performing his duties; the most arduous of which consisted of keeping the camp supplied with drinkable water.

The following morning my early morning tea was not brought to me, and I wondered sleepily why Sezumba was late. A few minutes later I was mystified by a curious shuffling sound near the entrance of my tent. As I raised myself on my elbow to peer out, a horrifying spectacle became visible to me. Sezumba was crawling on hands and knees, and as he entered the tent he began to call out: *"Thusa Marena, thusa!"* (Help me). I leapt out of bed and attempted to lift him, but he waved me aside, continuing to cry: "Help me Sir, I am dying"! There was no doubt that he had been stricken by the plague, and I summoned Dick and Isaac. They rushed up, almost naked, and gently lifted and placed him on a seat, but he could not endure the upright position, and begged to be laid down again. On Dick's suggestion they carried him to his own shelter, where he was made as comfortable as possible.

I, meanwhile, made a pot of tea, and with a mug of this I forced Sezumba to swallow several aspirin tablets, though it seemed like offering a drug to a man under sentence of death, and I had not the heart to assure him that they would bring relief and help. He continued to cry out *"thusa, Morena!"* Dick gently ushered me out of the shelter, assuring me that it was no use staying there as there was nothing more we could do for him.

The sense of despair and complete abandonment which assailed me at this new outbreak can better be imagined than described. Suddenly my attention was attracted by a small cloud of dust which seemed to be moving along in the direction of the track. I scrambled on to a stump to watch the dust. Yes! Unquestionably it was moving, and rapidly too in our direction! Only a motor vehicle could be approaching at such speed: but hardly daring to express the relief which surged up within me I remained watching it. Presently I caught a glint of metal between the trees, then the sound of an engine, and finally, to my indescribable joy, a large truck loomed in view, rapidly approaching. Thank God! Relief at last! I yelled out the joyful news that help was at hand, and then hurried to the road which passed some little distance from my tent. In the truck, as it finally drew up, were two good friends, in the persons of Mr. Cairns, D.C., and Dr. Gemmell - our M.D. at Maun.

I do not think that I have ever experienced greater relief and joy than was afforded me by the arrival of these gentlemen, and my feelings must have been patent to them. They had left Maun purely on the strength of a vague report, which had somehow filtered through, of a suspected outbreak of plague somewhere beyond Nokaneng. When they had reached the trading station,

Andrew Wright at once advised them to "forget about suspected outbreaks and to proceed as quickly as possible to Wilmot's camp, where there was plenty of trouble!"

Within a matter of minutes Sezumba had received a maximum injection of serum, and, indeed, his life was saved by the miraculously timely arrival of these officers. He was in no fit state to travel, of course, and in any case as the next few hours would decide life or death, to move him at once would have been an unnecessary risk. His chances of recovery were about fifty-fifty, but when we left I felt that I had not seen the last of him, and so it proved. The boys' shelters were changed to another site, and all refuse was burnt. While this was taking place, I attended to my own packing of equipment. With Dick's able assistance everything was soon ready, and within a couple of hours we were on our way to Maun.

Not long after leaving Toteng (where the native lorry staff prepared an excellent supper for us) a hyena suddenly appeared in the road ahead of us. Bewildered by the tall grass brilliantly illuminated by the headlights which seemed to hedge it in on either side, the hyena tore along the sandy track at its greatest speed, bouncing along with the ugly shambling gait so characteristic of these ungainly creatures. The District Commissioner, who was driving, contrived to keep the bumper of the truck in almost continuous contact with the creature's short, bushy tail. It was a comical sight, and I imagine that no hyena was ever in a greater state of terror than that one! The chase continued for perhaps a quarter of a mile, when an open gap in the tamboekie grass afforded the quarry a means of escape. We finally reached Maun near midnight on December 13th.

Early on the morning of the seventeenth, I awakened with a splitting headache: feeling generally wretched, disinclined to move, and thirsty. While awaiting the arrival of my tea, an unpleasant thought occurred to me, and automatically I felt the glands in the groin. There was no doubt about it! They were enlarged and painful to touch. So after all, I had not escaped the attentions of the Kakanaga fleas! I was very soon in hospital, where — Dr. Gemmell being absent on field work — my old friend, Matron Murch, admitted me and at once gave me an injection of 20.c.c. of serum.

No doubt that serum was good, and it prevented the pestilence from obtaining a proper grip. Beyond that I am not prepared to say a word in its favour, for it brought on an irritation such as I had never suffered before. Urticaria began at my feet, from whence it spread at an incredible rate until every square inch of my skin was covered with lumps. These in turn slowly merged into each other until they were no longer visible as bumps of concentrated, maddening itch; but as an unbroken surface of fiery torture. Indeed I fancy it must have driven me nearly off my head, as the Matron long afterwards told me that she had found me in the grounds, completely naked, and wringing my arms and hands like a being demented! I shall never forget those hours of exasperating aggravation which will remain my one and only vivid recollection of that dose of plague.

If it is possible to associate any virtue with bubonic plague, such must lie in the fact that either one dies very quickly from its effects or else makes an equally rapid recovery. That was the case with me, and I know of many similar cases. On December the twenty-second I was discharged from hospital: ready and equal to any Christmas fare and festivities in the offing!

Chapter 9

TSETSE FLY CONTROL WORK, AND GAME AT CHUCHUBEGHO

MOPANI BUSH

AFTER the events just related, I had a term of several months at Headquarters, when my time was divided between office work and supervising the erection of a residence for the Tsetse Fly Control Officer. It was during this period that the District Commissioner was transferred from Maun, and on his departure he presented me with a young sitatunga doe, which had been given to him by a headman somewhere in the Nokaneng area.

I was delighted with the gift, and kept the doe in George Scholtz's grounds. The beautiful creature was as tame as a pet lamb. It followed us all around, often entering the house where it instantly got into trouble by slipping on the polished cement floors. We often laughed at the astonishing "splits" it achieved; and its subsequent frantic endeavours to regain a firm footing always reminded one of the initial efforts of a boy on roller skates! However well-adapted its long, narrow, awkward-looking hooves might have been for negotiating the marshlands to which it was native, they were entirely unsuited to its new surroundings. The poor, lovely creature suffered numerous falls, and it took a long time to learn to walk on cement at even the slowest pace. It managed tolerably well on the surrounding sandy areas, but whenever possible avoided hard surfaces.

The sitatunga often followed me to the hotel, loitering on the way to nibble at aromatic shrubs, when — finding herself alone — she would come galloping after me in her awkward, ungainly manner. Of all places she loved the river best; and she spent most of her nights there. Un-happily she was not long in discovering the neighbours' flower and vegetable gardens, and her periodic raids on these led to a well-deserved unpopularity! I was asked to restrain her move-ments, but this was rendered difficult by the fact that she reso-lutely refused any green provender which I gathered for her. In the end I sadly contacted several institutions with a view to find-ing a home for her.

The Director of the National Zoological Gardens, Pretoria, was anxious to have the sitatunga: but much delay occurred through various formalities having to be complied with before the Union Veterinary Department would furnish an import permit. Eventu-ally a huge cage was dispatched from Pretoria, but through fur-ther delays in transit it only reached Maun a month later, and sad to relate the lovely, rare specimen had vanished on the day pre-ceding its arrival.

I did not enjoy my work at Maun, but occasional pay trips in-volving a round of the various camps in the "fly" area provided a respite from the hated office work. Parties were as numerous as ever in the settlement, and not many of these were missed by either George or myself; yet I longed ceaselessly for the outdoor life to which I had so long been accustomed. Weekend fishing or shooting trips up or down river formed welcome breaks, but they never completely satisfied my restlessness.

My work was seldom uninteresting, but the knowledge of being a misfit at the office had a depressing effect on me which added greatly to my state of mind. Then, towards the end of April, 1946, and coincident with the arrival of the Resident Commissioner of the Bechuanaland Protectorate, I was one day informed that my services would no longer be required. Although I realised that the post I held was redundant, and that I possessed neither the ex-perience nor the ability for wholly efficient service in the office, my dismissal nevertheless came as a severe shock. Thinking the matter over for a few minutes, I requested to be given a trial on permanent field work. I knew that a vacancy existed for another ranger, and I had only refrained from previously applying for the post because I had been engaged periodically in work of a similar nature, though with added responsibilities.

My request was immediately granted, with the proviso that the scale of pay would be reduced to a level applicable to the post. Knowing that my greatly lowered living expenses on full time field work would very nearly balance the difference, I gladly accepted the conditions.

My first camp, in my new assignment, was at a place called Chuchubegho which, though only sixteen miles west of Maun, is within the swamps area. The site I chose, beneath splendid mokuchon and other trees, was a magnificent one, and it lay only about fifty yards from the molapo from which the place derives its name.

My quarters consisted of a small, screened structure, measuring approximately fourteen feet by six feet. A tarpaulin stretched across the top, and reaching some three feet beyond the sides, afforded protection from rain: while the screening barred the entrance of such pests as mosquitoes, Tsetse and gad flies generally, snakes, mice, etc. A comfortable bed, a minimum of camp furniture, and a rack containing my books — together with some fly materials and a few army steel trunks, constituted the whole of my equipment, and I was less cramped for space than I had been in my tent.

After all the undergrowth had been cleared away beneath the numerous fine trees, and the whole area raked and swept, the camp became a place of beauty. As I settled in comfortably, it seemed as if years of trouble and boredom had fallen from my existence. Fresh joys and interests entered my life, and looking back now I cannot recall so happy a period, nor the finding of so much contentment, since the passing of a beloved wife thirteen years previously, as I enjoyed at that place.

The only lack at the time of my arrival was that of open, running water. Naturally I looked forward to the coming of the annual inundations when all the innumerable water courses would fill to overflowing with sweet, unmuddied water — bringing with it also the multitudes of waterfowl for which this country is so justly famous.

A fellow ranger, Mr. D. J. Odendaal, came along with a large squad of boys and constructed, in a few days, a fine causeway across the molapo, without which the camp would — on the arrival of the first water — have been cut off, so far as vehicular traffic was concerned, from Headquarters.

One of my first duties was to cut "fly rounds", of which fairly accurate compass surveys and maps had to be made. I was started on this work by Major Miller, who arrived at Chuchubegho at the same time as I, and who remained four or five days. The preliminary work on the lines occupied but a week or two, but much had to follow, and months were actually spent on the task which entailed a great amount of walking. My staff consisted of half a dozen fly boys, a few labourers, one hunter, a cook, my personal servant, and - whenever I had a lorry - the two men in charge of that.

By arrangement, all rangers were entitled to use their trucks for the purpose of fetching supplies and seeing the weekly "Flick" in Maun; but never during the remaining two years of my stay in the country did I take advantage of this concession: finding far greater entertainment in hunting or just exploring the beautiful woodlands surrounding my camp. Periods of a month to six weeks often elapsed without my visiting the settlement. I was supremely happy at Chuchubegho, and loneliness was a condition of mind from which I never suffered.

There were finer trees in the Chuchubegho area than I had observed anywhere else in Ngamiland. Certainly at Shakowe on the Okavango, and again at Kasane on the Chobe, magnificent trees enhance the scenery: but there the fine timber is confined to the river banks. At Chuchubegho, an area intercrossed by numerous periodic waterways, and having large tracts regularly flooded, the fringing forests which contain the noblest trees are more widely spread. Here the lofty *Acacia galpinii*, the wellknown "Aapiesdoorn", towers to over sixty feet. *Acacia burkei*, and *Acacia nigrescens* ("Knob thorn") attain exceptional dimensions, an achievement shared by many lesser members of the family. Other arboreal giants here are *Combretum imberbe* (Motswiri); *Diospyros mespilliformis* (Mokuchon); *Ficus sycamorus* (Mochaba); *Colophospermum mopane* (Mopani). Of the latter usually gregarious tree I have found isolated specimens attaining a height of fifty feet, with trunks upwards of four feet in diameter. Common also, and growing larger than elsewhere, were *Lonchocarpus capassa* (Appelblaar, Mopororo); *L. Nelsii* (Moporota); and *Garcinia livingstonei* (Motsaudi) — a strikingly beautiful evergreen. *Albizzi-*

as, Cretans, Combretums, and a multitude of others, abound in the local bush.

The area was equally well-stocked with game in extraordinary variety, and it was a veritable naturalist's paradise. With the advent of the annual inundations, all the water-dependent animals would regularly appear. Every species of mammal native to the Protectorate, with the exception of rhinoceros, eland, and rhebuck, was represented. Elephant seldom came, though a few passed through during my sojourn there. I often saw, and always enjoyed watching, a mixed herd of sixteen giraffe which habitually browsed loftily in a belt of acacia jungle.

This seasonal influx of game (particularly buffalo) was always reflected in the tally sheets by an upward trend of the number of Tsetse flies captured during the tri-weekly patrols of the established rounds. Unfortunately incessant war had to be declared on the animals, which are largely responsible for carrying and maintaining the pest. *Glossina morsitans* can neither exist nor multiply without blood, and on this account the elimination of warmblooded animals in fly-infested areas has always been regarded as an important factor in the system of control.

When the terrible Rinderpest epizootic of 1896 ravaged the country, it virtually wiped out all the game. Apparently as a result of this, the Tsetse flies also vanished from areas of their greatest density. Consequently, in Ngamiland at any rate, livestock waxed fat and multiplied exceedingly in regions where previously they had been unable to exist. Of this I had abundant visual proof because in the very area where I was stationed there are to be seen the remains of many large cattle kraals. One of my own employees pointed out such a site to me: declaring that, as a young man, he had been posted there with others to be in charge of a local headman's cattle.

Such game, however, as survived the Rinderpest slowly recovered in numbers, and in time the old haunts were again well stocked. In due course the Tsetse re-appeared, and finding in abundant supply all its food and breeding requirements, multiplied rapidly. Inevitable losses of livestock from Ngana ensued in increasing numbers; and this finally led to the complete human evacuation of the splendid pastoral region of the Xnaraga valley and neighbouring parts of the fly belt, which reverted to the game and to the tormenting, killing Tsetse fly. Indeed, the trouble did not end there, because the original "clean" areas to which the stock had been withdrawn also became endangered by a steady, if not rapid, encroachment of the pest. It may therefore be understood that what Nature had accomplished in one gigantic swoop had to be artificially repeated. This resulted in the Tsetse Fly Control Scheme, for which a considerable sum had been voted from the Colonial Development Fund.

I am well aware of the great conflict of opinion as to the justifiableness or otherwise of large scale destruction of game as a factor in Tsetse Fly Control, and, beyond stating emphatically that I have always opposed this measure in principle, I do not consider myself competent to enter the lists of argument on this vexed question. One of the objects of this narrative is simply to offer the reader a straightforward account of our activities under the present Scheme: leaving all controversy to those better qualified to take part! The measures for control were threefold:

1. Destruction of game.
2. Erection of fences capable of excluding game from "clean"areas.
3. Clearing of bush and undergrowth.

During a period of nearly two years, a great deal of my time was occupied on work appertaining to the breeding habits of Tsetse flies. No species other than *Glossina morsitans* had so far been reported from Ngamiland, but the possibility of one or more of the several other known types occurring there was never excluded by the authorities. This necessitated a careful record of all flies caught. As there is some variation in the breeding habits of the various species of Tsetse, my work was extended to the search for pupation sites. In this connection, types of vegetation covering fringing forests, savanna woodlands, belts of Acacia, isolated clumps of trees, mixed scrub, clusters of scrubby *Hyphaene* palms, and even Mokudi *pluchea* shrubs and tall grass, had all to be searched exhaustively in turn. With few exceptions, however, all the breeding places found by myself and staff were confined to the riverine or fringing forests. Here we collected many thousands of pupae.

The exceptions mentioned were found respectively in Mopani woodland and beneath thick patches of young *Hyphaene* palms. As, in each case, such sites were adjacent to fringing forests, we deemed them of no special significance — being in all probability merely "accidentals".

I am no longer in possession of records kept, but am reasonably correct in stating that many thousands of sites were located: a percentage of which were numbered and visited periodically. In the pursuit of these duties, I believe that I fossicked through practically every square rood of the local fringing forests. Much fruitless searching in the open woodlands of the vast sand belts was also involved, and I came to know the area very intimately indeed.

Where *Glossina morsitans* occurs, one has only to enter a belt of fringing forest and to search diligently beneath fallen trunks; in hollow stumps; or under sharply reclining trees in shady situations; to find the oval, black (without any gloss) pupae. These are easily recognisable, as they have two minute projections at one end. During the search for such, shells of those previously hatched will always be found in greater numbers: and on very rare occasions, if one is lucky and knows what to look for, freshly deposited larvae (which are creamy-white and rather fatter than when in the pupal stage) may also be discovered.

Tsetse flies do not lay eggs. The first stage of development occurs within the body of the parent. The fecundity of this fly, therefore, is fortunately in no way comparable with that of many other types of flies which produce bunches of eggs. Among the Tsetses caught during the routine rounds a few pregnant females were generally to be numbered: and the larva could generally be ejected by gentle pressure, or - if not sufficiently developed - by dissection.

All the collected pupae were preserved in small glass tubes, stoppered with a wad of cotton wool; and of these occasional specimens metamorphosed within the tubes. As the latter were examined daily, the emerged, perfect Tsetses were always found alive.

One morning, as I was examining the specimens, I was delighted to note an unfamiliar living fly in one of the tubes. This led to a most careful scrutiny of the discarded pupal case. Using a powerful magnifying glass (supplied especially for this work) I soon realised that the empty shell was identical with hundreds of others I had on hand. The strange fly was a parasite on, and therefore a deadly foe to, Tsetses; and, as such, was of very special interest.

Most unfortunately, however, the fly was inadvertently destroyed before it had been properly identified, and no similar specimens again came under my notice. As only about two per cent of collected pupae hatched out, there may well have been similar instances had it been possible to store daily collections under more natural conditions. The episode was a most disappointing one.

To my personal knowledge there is very little definite information about other natural enemies of the Tsetse Fly. It is probable that drongos, rollers, and other birds with similar hawking habits may account for some fly. In any case, in view of its naturally slow reproductive system, there is not great difficulty to turn the balance against this pest; and if it were possible to introduce parasitic enemies, Tsetse might soon be exterminated. Such a solution would save the millions of pounds spent in control schemes over various parts of Africa, let alone the tens of thousands of the magnificent African fauna.

In addition to the supervision and personal participation in the daily "fly" work, shooting, and the control of the native hunters, were included in my manifold duties. At the end of each month a day was devoted to the writing up of returns which had to be submitted to Headquarters, otherwise I was rarely in camp except for meals: often not troubling even to return for lunch. At the end of patrol days, every fly caught had to be examined under a lens, and as a good light was essential for this purpose my Tilly Pressure lamp came in very useful. All details concerning the day's capture had to be recorded. There were always a few specimens which required dissection, and one to two hours were occupied in this way. This work was interesting, and it became trying only during windy winter nights, when my open-sided shelter became intensely cold. With a kaross wrapped round my legs and feet, I managed well enough.

When I first arrived at Chuchubegho there was no trace of roads or footpaths. The camp was near a stream passing through terrain composed of forests, bushveld, grassy downs, swamps, and large alluvial flats: probably in much the same condition as it was hundreds of

years before. Although it teemed with wild life, the nights were strangely silent. This is a strange, indescribable feature which I have also experienced elsewhere in the Protectorate. I can only attempt to describe it very vaguely thus: "Listen for sounds, and none will be heard: listen again and you will 'hear' the silence!"

Of course certain sounds were audible from time to time. When water was flowing in the molapo, the splash of a fish, or the distant croaking of passing waterfowl were typical. Lions and leopards were rarely seen at Chuchubegho, though numerous tracks testified to their presence in the surrounding bush. Certainly this was the case with leopards, which are not so inclined to wander as lions; and though I never sighted them by day, evidence of their presence was never lacking. Their harsh, grating calls were only occasionally heard; but spoor and the drag marks of captured prey were so frequently observed that there could be no doubt of their presence in fair numbers.

The periodical roars, yells, and frantic screams of a colony of baboons which nightly slept in the upper branches of a grove of giant Acacias furnished further evidence of the activities of leopards. During my searches for pupation sites I visited the place on a number of occasions and found remains of baboons which had failed to evade the leopards. A lot of noise from baboons does not necessarily mean an attack or kill, and the mere sight of their arch enemy will set them off until the leopard gets out of view. When a kill does occur, pandemonium will reign for an hour or more. This colony of baboons — quite the largest I have ever encountered — ranged over a vast extent of country. Their daily wanderings were extended when the mokuchons were in fruit, but they always returned to the same roosting place at night. I sometimes passed the spot at dusk, and on moonlight nights, and noticed that generally they slept in the topmost branchlets of trees towering to sixty feet. Doubtless this was a precautionary custom in that area, but their quarters cannot have been comfortable.

Very occasionally lions would roar on several consecutive nights, though no doubt they were more often in the neighbourhood than one suspected.

I have made passing mention of warthogs and have given some indication of their prodigious numbers in the swamp country. Probably there are not so many remaining there nowadays because these ugliest of nature's children are always much sought after. Not only do they afford good shooting, but their flesh is less dry and far more palatable than that of most species of buck. I have on several occasions had to stop a charge from a wounded one, but warthog are far less aggressive and dangerous than the smaller-tusked Bush pig. Where the latter will not disdain carrion, I have never known warthog to partake of any food other than that of a vegetable nature.

When scampering away, warthog have a droll habit of keeping an eye on you over their backs; and, trotting along with their tails stiffly erect, they form always a mirth-provoking sight. Then: natural pace is an exceedingly fast trot, but when startled they break into a gallop and crash through the thickest bush. When hard-pressed they never hesitate to enter any hole large enough to accommodate their stocky bodies, and it is laughable to see them whisk their bodies round and enter the hole backwards — as is their invariable custom. On such occasions it is a foolish practice to stand either in front of, or to kneel down and peer into, such a hole, for if it happens to be shallow they not infrequently charge out, inflicting dangerous wounds on anyone in their way.

On one of many occasions when a warthog had thus gone to ground, I stretched out flat on the top side of the burrow and peeped in. As I did so, my helmet slipped off and rolled down the sharp incline. Much noise and dust immediately issued from the hole, and when this had ceased I poked down a hooked stick, fishing for my prized old headgear. The first attempt brought forth fragments of ripped khaki cloth attached to a round of cork!

CARACAL.

I swore vengeance on that pig, but, what with the heat and the lack of suitable digging tools I was eventually compelled to give up in despair, and was reduced to using the tail of my shirt against the sun's scorching rays!

A friend, after shooting the mother, once captured three very young warthog piglets. In a few days they became very tame and affectionate, following their master all over the place, squealing and romping round his feet. He kept them until they were almost adult and they remained constantly friendly and faithful, though their "beauty" deteriorated rapidly with the passing of the months.

In country where dogs cannot be used it is rarely indeed that a sportsman will obtain a shot at either caracal or serval. Both these beautiful wild cats lie up in the densest cover and they slink off silently when their lairs are approached. I have seen both taken in native traps, and for implacability and sheer ferocity they equal their large spotted relative — the leopard. Both furnish lovely pelts which are always in good demand, but happily, owing to their secretive habits, neither are in much danger of extinction. Each play a useful part in the balance of nature. A most interesting, but locally rather rare small wild feline, is the *Sebulabulakwana*, or Black-footed Cat. This is the smallest of the African wild cats: but what it lacks in size is fully compensated for by its extreme ferocity. Though its weight is only about a quarter of that of a small sheep, this little feline readily attacks those animals. It fastens on to the neck and hangs on until the jugular is pierced. This I have not seen myself, but have so frequently been told the same story by old reliable natives that I cannot doubt the assertion.

These Black-footed cats have heavy and broad skulls and almost disproportionately large and strong canine teeth. All Masarwa Bushmen will tell you the absurd story that these little cats will fasten on to the neck of a giraffe, just as they do with a sheep or a goat!

In Ngamiland, in fact, the *Felidae* are particularly well represented. Most South African species occur there, and

BLACK-FOOTED CAT.

111

even the more nocturnal types — such as civets, serval, caracal, and all the lesser cats, which are seen rarely indeed, were trapped from time to time by our men. Skins were usually obtainable, either from the natives themselves, or at the widely scattered trading stations. Perhaps because they were more generally sought after than any of the others, skins of lion, leopard, and cheetah were the most easily acquired: the former (during my time) being the cheapest of all. Africans have offered me lion skins at ten shillings each, but I was never sufficiently interested to buy.

The dog tribe was always in evidence. Both species of hyenas, wild Hunting dogs (no longer plentiful), jackals, and foxes — two species each of the latter. There was always a plenitude of ratels; but mongooses, genets, and all the smaller carnivorous and insectivorous mammals were less numerous than in other parts of the Protectorate through which I have hunted.

Wherever lion are plentiful, there also are to be found vultures, marabou storks, and carrion crows. Raptorial birds occur in truly amazing variety: themselves forming a fine field for study.

Of the greater cats, the lion is by far the most plentiful — or at any rate the most frequently seen; and the majority of the old residents have had affairs with these magnificent creatures at one time or another. This is so to such an extent, in fact, that tales of stirring adventure with lions arouse less attention than the details of the previous night's party or singsong. Nevertheless, the bagging of a lion will probably always form the young sportsman's chief ambition, while older hands are always conscious of a quickening of the pulse when in pursuit of these majestic beasts. More, surely, has been written about their habits than about those of any other of the large and dangerous game, so that little remains for a hunter to recount than his own, personal experiences.

Leopards are more strictly nocturnal in the swamps region than in mountainous or rocky country, where on several occasions I have seen and shot them in daylight. During the first year of my stay at Chuchubegho I found that a pair of leopards undoubtedly had cubs in a belt of really heavy fringing forest. I first became aware of this fact early one morning when I was out on one of my weekend jaunts. The fresh spoor of a large male, with drag marks beside it, attracted my attention, and having nothing particular to do, I followed it. The spoor was less easy to hold, where it entered the timber, but with care, and as silently as possible, I held on until I was led to a perfect labyrinth of huge fallen trees. These were covered with climbing plants, with coppices of *Gymnosporia* and scrub palms in the gaps between the prostrate giants. Owing to the obstructions on all sides, it was a thoroughly difficult area to hunt. Advancing with all my senses on the alert, I presently found the remains of an impala which had been devoured during the night. Chewed bones, fragments of skin, the shank bones with hooves attached, and the head from which the nose and tongue were missing, were, with the contents of the stomach, all that remained. The cubs must have been young then, as there was no sign of their presence at the repast, though on the following weekend the imprints of their neat little feet showed that they had mingled freely with their parents.

On my second visit, I approached the place stealthily from the opposite side, upwind: but apart from abundant spoor and fresh excreta, as well as both shrivelled and perfectly fresh remains of baboons, there was no sign of the leopards. It was several weeks before I could visit the place again, and then no fresh signs of leopard were visible anywhere, and I believe that the sagacious beasts had become suspicious, and had removed their young to safer surroundings.

Years before, in the Tati Concessions, I found a similar site beneath a huge overhanging granite boulder in thick bush. In this case also I found a lot of bones scattered around, including which were the skulls of duiker and young warthog. Scattered about also were bunches of fur — obviously that of hares — and a quantity of guineafowl feathers: indicating the varied diet of leopards.

The finding of these sombre relics raised some interesting speculations. Why, I wondered, were all those decaying bones lying around in a country full of scavenging hyenas? I have never had the question satisfactorily answered. Possibly, by some instinctive arrangement, the breeding places of leopards are taboo to hyenas which, normally after a night or two, leave hardly a smell to bones with which they have finished. It is also possible, of course, that hyenas have learnt from painful experience that it is wiser to steer well clear of leopards with cubs. But the facts, as observed, are likely to remain yet another veld mystery.

Dogs, unfortunately, could not be kept alive in Tsetse areas, or good sport might have been obtained with the leopards.

Cheetahs were not uncommon, but less frequently seen than lions. I was once hunting up the margin of a considerable stream which, at intervals, opened into broad, shallow lagoons. I was actually in search of warthog for the larder when I perceived a small round object on the far side of the lagoon. It resembled a calabash floating on the surface, but thinking that I had observed a movement, I sat down on the slope of a termite hill to watch it. The distance was about three hundred yards, and as I watched, the object made another slight movement, then a steady advance right towards me.

For the life of me, I could not make the thing out, but remained quite still. In a short while the creature reached shallower water, when the shoulders, and top of the head, could just be seen. Once again it got into deeper water, and I could see now that it was obviously swimming quite fast, and when it was about only one hundred yards away it reached very shallow water through which it now walked at a fair pace. It looked to me like a half-grown lion, but I could not positively determine the species of the beast, which, on reaching some thinly scattered sedges, stood with its body well out of the water, staring fixedly at me. I was puzzled, and quite unable to identify the animal. It presented a fine target, however, and taking steady aim, I squeezed the trigger.

The shot was followed by snarling grunts and a terrific splashing as a great cat-like creature came bounding out of the water and into the tall grass growing at its edge, where it immediately vanished from my view. I rushed up the antheap, expecting to see the animal passing through the grass, but no movement was perceptible. Having gained the impression that the animal might be a young lion, I did not much fancy walking into such cover; so after a minute's delay I knocked off some clods from the top of the antheap and flung them into the grass where I had last seen the beast. There was no response, so I made my way to the water's edge and found several streaks of blood on the wet grass where it had emerged. With rifle fully cocked, I followed the tracks, and within thirty yards or so came on the body of a magnificent male cheetah. It was dead, and had turned head over heels in falling, as its tail was pointing in the direction in which it had been running.

The whole episode was a curious one. I had never previously seen a cheetah in the water, and the fact that this one was heading straight toward me suggested that it had been quite ignorant of my presence on the antheap. My own eyesight is very indifferent else I might earlier have determined the identity of the animal.

Probably owing to its being wet, the coat was unnaturally dark and that helped to deceive me. I believe that the cheetah had merely wished to cross over the water to new ground, and had risked the presence of crocodiles of which, I think, all wild creatures are well aware.

I had to walk about five miles in order to fetch a couple of boys to carry home the cheetah, but the distance seemed shortened by my good fortune to bag two warthog on the way.

I dropped the first one standing at about one hundred and fifty yards, and its companion — which was busy grubbing quite near it — at not less than two hundred yards while it was running at full speed. Owing to my usual bad performance at running shots, this last effort pleased me greatly. I had thus procured three fine head of game at the expenditure of only three shots.

On another occasion I was travelling to Headquarters on a good half ton truck. Along one part the track traversed a narrow strip of bush bordering an extensive, smooth plain. As we cruised merrily along, we nearly ran over a brace of young warthogs which rounded a corner at full speed. The cause of their flight was evident as a large cheetah halted suddenly in a cloud of dust, and turning about made off for the open plain. I slowed down, searching for an opening between the trees, losing perhaps a minute before reaching clear ground where not one but two cheetahs came into view. They were some distance away, standing about seventy yards apart. Stopping quickly, I jumped out and was about to fire at the largest when I noticed two nearly half-grown cubs between them, slinking through a patch of tussocky grass. With a hope of capturing the youngsters, I desisted from firing and leapt back into the truck, giving instant chase. But could those little creatures run! Except for occasional antbear holes — easily enough located by the earths — I had no reason to fear to "step on the juice"; but, with their characteristic looping bounds, the cheetah family easily outdistanced me, and presently they reached another belt of bush and so I was beaten. However I was exhilarated by the run, and not ill-pleased by the escape of the family.

Cheetahs are sometimes very destructive where farming with small stock is carried on. In 1910, in Southern Bechuanaland I saw five sheep and goats killed by a similar family to the one just described, and very little of the victims was eaten. On the whole, however, they are rather harmless and certainly beautiful animals which should receive a measure of protection. They are taller than leopards, though much more lightly built, and they are not true cats for they lack fully retractable claws: theirs being blunt like those of a dog, and only partially retractable. Moreover, unlike their distant implacable cousins they do not habitually stalk their prey, but run it down in fair chase. When brought to bay, they sometimes show fight, but they cannot be termed dangerous game, and when caught young become affectionate pets.

Chapter 10

TIGER FISHING AND A
SWAMPLANDS STORM

TIGER FISH
CAUGHT
AT
MOHEMBO

ABOUT the middle of 1946, as all the work was proceeding well, I decided to apply for my occasional leave earlier than usual. I had always wished to see the Okavango where it is yet a great waterway confined to a single channel, and I was keen to make the acquaintance of the Ngamiland Tiger fish. Hitherto I had seen none in this country, though I had previously enjoyed much sport with the species in many of the tributaries of the Zambezi, as well as in that great river itself. I therefore decided to plan a collecting trip to Mohembo.

Apart from an occasional possible shot at a crocodile, I intended to do little shooting. It was to be mainly a fishing expedition, and I took with me only one personal servant to attend to the cooking and washing.

On the following day we travelled through to Shakowe — one of the most beautiful places in Ngamiland. At this place the Labour Recruiting organisation has a large and well founded depot, of which a friend of mine was in charge. Other friends of mine also in residence there were Mr. Jack Lord, whom I first met some

MAMBOKUSH
·WOMEN.

MOHEMBO.

thirty years earlier, and Mrs. Lord. Although I had intended to trav-el right through to Mohembo (eight miles further along the river) I now learnt that the convoy was, in fact, not proceeding beyond Sha-kowe. However, Mr. Matthias ("C. J." to all his friends) kindly sug-gested that I should stay a few days with him, after which he would run me to my planned destination. He had to transport some re-turning natives a few miles within the South West African border; and since Mohembo is on the way, it would be no inconvenience for him to take me along. I was delighted to take advantage of his invitation, and my few days spent at Shakowe were full of interest.

There is a large native population in the neighbourhood, mostly Mambukush; and I found this tribe, and its culture, most interesting. The Mambukush are an industrious race. They are, I believe, the largest producers of grain in Ngamiland. In the Namasere valley immense tracts of land are cultivated — the main crop grown being *lebelebele* (sorghum). As is generally the case with native races, the most arduous field labour is undertaken by the women. However they, poor things, having known no other conditions seem to be happy enough; and in the cultivation season wield their heavy, primitive hoes in the manner of those born to the job.

Much else is of interest about these dusky ladies. For instance they wear their hair long: fine fibres being twisted into the locks which dangle down their backs, and which are kept in a perpetual state of saturation with crude castor oil. This commodity they themselves produce from the beans of indigenous plants which flourish along the rivers. On the top of the head the hair is woven into a sort of crown of which they are very proud.

I was anxious to obtain one of the latter as a museum specimen, so I offered three pounds to any woman willing to part with hers. However, as the mere suggestion appeared to be offensive to them, I had to desist. I examined their mode of hairdressing carefully, and made many notes. Unfortunately the latter have been lost, and I can no longer remember details sufficiently well to render an accurate description. What impressed me most — if unpleasantly — was the horrible mess of castor oil which fairly oozed from their heads whenever the sun was hot.

The Mambukush are skillful craftsmen, manufacturing, among other things, finely made large wooden bowls capable of holding up to four gallons of liquid (generally, in their case, native beer). Some of these wooden bowls were shaped exactly like the conventional native clay pots, and they were hardly any thicker. These, and similar vessels, were well finished and symmetrical. They were as smooth internally as externally.

Another interesting item was a small metal tool of their own manufacture. This is called a *dekora*: and it is with the aid of these instruments that the hollowing out, and finishing, of vessels of all kinds are executed. The one I procured was about six inches in length, curved into a shape closely resembling that of a question mark (?). The curved portion is flattened out and ground to a fine edge. The opposite end is left round, and it forms the tang which is inserted and fixed in a strong wooden handle from two to four feet in length — depending on the nature of the work in hand. A lengthy handle, for instance, would be used in the creation of one of their long, wooden drums; while a shorter one would be required for a bowl or platter. The dekora, which is used with both hands, is of course a type of scraper, and in the hands of an experienced native craftsman, it is a most efficient tool.

The Mambukush make very fine hunting knives in their primitive forges. These knives are fitted with carved wooden handles, and beautifully made; carved and sometimes fretted sheaths contain each knife. The knives, which are dagger-shaped and exceedingly sharp, are in great demand among other tribes. I also managed to acquire (for a mere matter of four shillings and sixpence) a pair of beautifully wrought and handled ceremonial knives. Wooden platters, dishes, milking pails, a large drum, baskets and sleeping mats occur among other articles which I obtained from the Mambukush. Spears and Bushman bow arid arrows I purchased from one of the local traders.

The major portion of my time at Shakowe was spent on the river. The area of the camp sloped down to the grand, swiftly flowing Okavango, and C. J. put his boat — a small steel barge - at my disposal. I obtained some quite good tiger fishing, but special efforts to secure other species of fish were unavailing.

It was pleasant to troll downstream, but real hard work for a couple of paddlers to return up current. Spillways from the main channel of the river first occur a few miles beyond Mohembo: which place may be said to mark the beginning of the delta, which rapidly widens with recurrencies of the same nature. At Shakowe the main channel of the Okavango is on the west bank; but the spillways higher up have already drawn largely on the volume of the stream, and swamps and lagoons reach away for a mile or more eastwards.

With a couple of paddlers to perform this heavy work, I entered one of the lagoons from the river and proceeded a long distance without viewing its end. The water was deep: completely calm; and walled in by papyrus and reeds. Though not unattractive, a suggestion of something sinister seemed to pervade that secluded backwater! I cannot exactly explain this impression produced

by the environment, though the presence of crocodiles (I saw five heads in a quarter of an hour) no doubt had much to do with it.

My mind was jerked abruptly to actualities when the spoon I was trolling behind was taken with a sudden, mighty jolt which thumped the rod against the steel gunwale and almost out of my hands. A fairly large tiger fish, breaching magnificently, freed itself from the triple hook and was gone almost before I had time to recover my thoughts. Quickly I reeled in, and finding all in order, let the line run out again: alert and ready for the next strike. But indeed there was no waiting, for I had struck a shoal, and the glittering silver and red spoon was immediately taken. A short, sharp fight ensued. This fish - a seven pounder — was successfully boated, and moments later I was again engaged.

This second fish surfaced several times without actually leaving the water, and it fought with tremendous courage. Two long diagonal runs, followed by deep boring directly towards the boat, caused me to suspect its escape; but in an instant it was off again, this time on its longest run which ended in a clean, neat leap many feet above the water. I could hear the rattle of the spoon as the fish furiously jerked its head to regain freedom. This was the final effort of a great fighter. A minute later I had it alongside — still struggling gamely. It bored down repeatedly, but utterly spent at last it came to the surface, belly up, and I lifted it into the boat. This tiger was no larger than the first, but what a fighter! What a gallant fish!

Ordering the paddlers to turn about in a wide circle, we again crossed the same area. A single pounder snapped at the five inch spoon, and bagging this one I tried again. However, the shoal had now moved away, and only "squeakers" appeared to be interested in what bait I had. Near the margin, lotus discs and blooms dappled the surface, and a more likely spot for bream could hardly be imagined. Either the fish were not present, or they despised my offerings, and I gave the word to return to camp.

On the way back, more crocodiles were sighted, and I had two shots. Nothing, however, is more unsatisfactory than shooting at these brutes from water level. Two small projections, marking

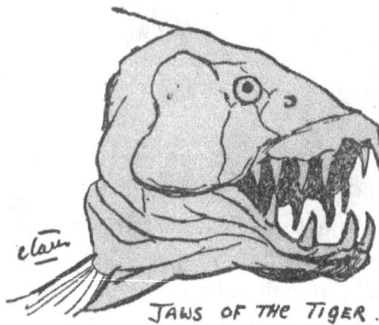
JAWS OF THE TIGER.

the snout and eyes, and little else are visible. I have repeatedly heard my bullets striking loudly against solid bone: but of many scores of shots I have had in this way, not a single croc has been secured, though some have, unquestionably, been killed outright.

Over "sundowners" that evening my friend and I discussed many things, fishing in particular. He mentioned that the local record weight for tiger fish was fourteen and a half pounds: though there can be little doubt that heavier specimens are there for the taking. My own record for tiger fish (Zambezi River), taken only two years ago, is twelve pounds. That was a grand fish, and a great fighter, but in Southern Rhodesia, at any rate, the idea that eight or ten pounders are more sporting prevails. My own experience confirms this.

The Ngamiland Tiger fish lack the beautiful pink striping present in their Rhodesian relatives. Apart from this colour variation, I could detect no difference in the respective types. In habits they are identical.

Spinning and trolling are the usual methods of taking tiger fish: yet, on the Zambezi and a few of its larger tributaries, I obtained my best specimens and most exciting sport by bottom fishing. A big fillet of their own flesh was used as bait. This method has several advantages over spoon fishing: for instance it can be done from small gaps in the waterside vegetation where spinning would be impossible. Also, visitors to rivers like the Okavango and Zambezi are not always able to procure craft for trolling purposes.

During the hot summer months, spinning (where it is possible) from the bank becomes very exhausting; whereas the bottom fishing angler can usually find some shade, and when he has a filleted hook in the water his sport is not confined only to tiger. In Ngamiland, huge barbel which fight well (and perhaps other species not yet known) may be taken. This applies, also, to Southern Rhodesia.

During my last trip to the Zambezi — at a place called Sinagatenka — I caught, in a few hours and in the order mentioned:

1 Tiger fish	(12 lbs).
1 " "	(3 lbs).
1 Vundu	(50 lbs).
1 "	(56 lbs).
1 Barbel	(4 lbs).
2 "	(3 lbs each).

And I lost two more good tiger fish. On that trip, during which I trolled nearly two hundred miles of the river, all my best sport was obtained with bottom fishing on fillet bait. The many vundu taken (the smallest was ten pounds) were chiefly responsible for the weight, but tiger fish from ten pounds downwards also contributed to the total.

Vundu, which to some extent resemble barbel but possess two dorsal fins and tremendously long "feelers", are probably the most sporting of all the cat fish. A twenty pounder has been known to run off a hundred yards of line in a few seconds, and these fish put up a marvellously sustained fight. One of the two largest I took on the Zambezi left on the drum no more than half a dozen coils of the two hundred yards of nylon I had on my reel. My cast was about forty five yards, so that at least the initial run could not have been less than one hundred and fifty yards, but several not much shorter ones followed. Save for the fact that there was no impeding obstacle along my side — enabling me to follow the fish downstream — I would most certainly have been broken. Even, when towards the end of the fight which lasted seventeen minutes, I had the vundu within a couple of feet of the edge, it made repeated plunges into the depths: and minutes passed before a Batonka villager who accompanied me was able to drive his long-handled spear into the game fellow. The fifty six pounder fought in exactly the same way and my tactics were no different to those employed on the other, but this larger fish was speared thirteen and a half minutes after the strike. I got a lot of others up to thirty four pounds weight, and not one of them failed to put up a good battle. One of ten pounds took seven minutes to subdue and gaff. Thus it will be seen that, from a sporting point of view these fish are not to be despised.

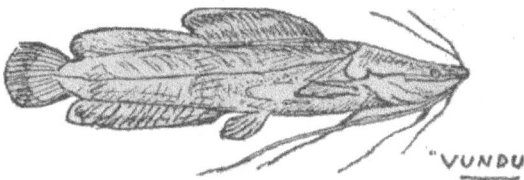

"VUNDU

Vundu have salmon-pink flesh which, if somewhat coarse, is well-flavoured, wholesome and almost free of small bones. The largest taken by myself were midgets compared with some monsters I have been informed of, and these catfish certainly attain a weight of well over one hundred pounds.

To return to my trip. On the following afternoon I set off with C.J. on his short trip into South West Africa. Leaving my servant and kit at Mohembo, I accompanied C. J. to where the men and their brightly painted boxes were to be deposited: thereby gaining my one and only glimpse of the territory of South West Africa. Finally my good friend put me down at Mohembo again on his way home. Sufficient daylight then remained to permit me to settle myself in at the vacant European Police quarters, which consisted of a fair-sized dwelling house that still contained a little furniture and a case full of books. Prior to my arrival, I had not known of the existence of this place, and the accommodation was a pleasant surprise. I had originally planned to sleep out and, not having brought a tent, some unseasonable rain which fell during my stay there would have made things unpleasant; so the old house proved to be very useful.

A couple of African police had their quarters a few hundred yards from the house, and these men were obliging and useful to me. It was owing to their efforts that I was able to secure the use of a fairly large, if somewhat leaky and battered, dugout.

Spinning for tiger fish proved unsatisfactory at this place. One only was tempted by the spoon, and this was a small thing which should have been filleted for bait. Instead, I spent most of the day skinning and mounting the specimen, which looked quite well when finished. Tiger fish have rather loose scales, and I found them among the most difficult of fish to mount.

The following morning I had just finished breakfast when one of the policemen came to say that the promised dugout was at the landing stage, and that two paddlers were busy bailing and cleaning the craft. I thanked and rewarded the man for his trouble, and was about to collect my fishing tackle, camera, and rifle, when he asked whether I would be interested to visit a small Bushman village which was situated a few miles upstream.

This was certainly an interesting suggestion, and I learnt that I could get right to the site by water: and that the place could hardly be missed.

Hooking a TIGER FISH IN THE /GOSHA CHANNEL
OKAVANGO DELTA

At the riverside I found the paddlers awaiting me. Having been scooped out of a curved tree, the dugout was by no means all that one could desire — especially as a small trickle of water was pouring continuously into it! Nonetheless, since no other was available, I was grateful enough for the use of it. With an armful of freshly cut papyrus stems as a cushion to sit on, I managed to keep dry: and periodically one of the men bailed put the accumulating water with a half-calabash brought specially for the purpose.

We were soon making rather heavy way against the swift current. I left the matter of our progress entirely to the stalwart and experienced paddlers, and busied myself with the rod. As soon as the spoon was out, I loaded my rifle and kept a sharp look-out for crocs.

The low banks were reed-lined, with here and there partly submerged trees full of driftwood, leaning in the direction of the current. A large flock of black herons rose from one of these, and the birds flapped along to another tree some hundreds of yards ahead, whereon they alighted — squawking and squabbling over perching places. Black herons are rather rare birds, and I hoped for a nearer view, but this they would not permit: always moving on well ahead of us as we approached. Other interesting birds were the bee-eaters which repeatedly swooped simultaneously to the water; causing quite a splash as they breasted the surface together; finally rising soaringly in a big half-moon curve. This performance was repeated over and over again. Unfortunately these were as shy as the herons, and I was unable to determine their

125

species. When we returned in the afternoon, when the water was pretty rough, these bee-eaters were engaged in the same manner.

I noticed, as we proceeded, that the river was broadening rapidly into a considerable lagoon. After a while we reached a portion where there was no perceptible current — its own force carrying the rapid flow against the curving west bank. The unstable craft made shooting very difficult, and I missed two shots at crocodiles. The heads of several more surfaced in the usual sinister fashion as we passed, but a fierce strike from a tiger fish caused me hastily to lay down the rifle and grab my rod. An instant later the fish struck again, and this time I hooked it. This tiger, which proved to be an eight and three-quarter pounder, fought toughly, making no fewer than four huge leaps out of the water — rattling the spoon loudly as it battled to free itself. It was well hooked, however, and slowly coaxed into gaffing range. The lagoon was alive with these fish, which attacked the lure as quickly as I could return it to the water.

Unfortunately my line was old and quite unequal to the power of many of the fish. In a short while I had lost five spoons, and, judging by the size of the leaping fish seen, this was not surprising! The stiff, short rod I was using was quite unsuitable for such formidable breaching, otherwise a record bag might have crowned my efforts that day. Still, I was well satisfied. Nine good tiger fish, of which the two largest weighed eight and three-quarter pounds each, were flapping in the bottom of the boat.

It was at this point that I noticed — a short distance ahead — several grass hovels which, one of the men informed me, comprised the Bushman village. A long, narrow strip of papyrus in the only shallow part of lagoon and river stood tall and thick between us and the dry land. The men paddled to the far end of this, where lay a narrow channel of very deep water. The huts were opposite, and the craft was drawn up on the steeply shelving margin, so that I was able to jump out without having to wade some yards as is often the case in the swamp lands.

In a few minutes we had arrived at the village: if a small cluster of ill-made, grassy bowers could be termed such! This little community consisted of sixteen individuals — none of which seemed in the least surprised or even interested in my arrival! A middle-aged man was engaged in stitching some skins together: in fact he was making a kaross of a mixture of pelts, among which I recognised lechwe and reedbuck. He used a very fine awl and short threads of sinew, but no needle. His fine, even stitching proclaimed him a craftsman, and notwithstanding his primitive methods the work was not slow.

This Bushman understood a little Tswana, and I asked him where the best fishing was obtainable. He pointed upstream, insinuating that there were plenty of tiger fish in another lagoon a few miles ahead. He insisted, however, that it would be unwise to venture there at present as a school of hippopotami, among which were two cows with young calves, had recently been making fierce demonstrations against passing craft, and that the river folk were keeping well clear of the place.

The man was a Maxanaxwe or black River Bushman — as indeed were the whole tribe. For a Bushman he was exceptionally well built and well nurtured, but a most taciturn individual who never opened his mouth or looked up from his work unless spoken to. I tried him with the few words of Sesarwa I still remembered, but he merely shook his head and continued with his stitching. When, however, I used the word *"Tshoerie"* (tobacco), his face lit up, and, almost imploringly he begged: *"Tshete tshoerie, M'bai!"* ("give me tobacco, friend!"), so proving that he could indeed understand some of my scanty Sesarwa! He clutched the handful of cigarettes I gave him with both hands. Clicking a few unintelligible words, a young girl brought to him a glowing brand from the communal fire; but I took this from her hand and tossed it back towards the fire, drawing from my pocket a lighter which I flicked rather near his nose to give him a light. Thoroughly startled, he edged to one side, blinking his astonishment, and I think he only realised that I had been offering him a light when he saw me light my own cigarette. He now held out his cigarette to me, but, shaking my head, I told him to draw, and nervously he returned the cigarette to his mouth. A wild shriek of laughter from the watching females greeted the backward jerk of his head as the lighter flashed a second time and the cigarette fell to the ground.

With a scowling glance at the others, he turned back to his work, though I noticed that he betrayed a lively interest when an elderly woman wished to try. She took the cigarette and resolutely faced the terrifying lighter, puffing away with obvious pride and satisfaction — if not very skilfully. Whereupon all the others, including the children, clamoured for cigarettes, and by the time their demands had been satisfied, few cigarettes remained in my packet! Excepting the man, every member of the party was now puffing like a steam engine, jabbering and giggling gleefully. The man still refused the lighter, however, and insisted on another firestick. Truly, he let his sex down badly.

I managed to purchase a few attractively woven fibre bangles from the women for a few pence, and a finely made fishing net, hanging beneath a small tree, interested me greatly. The usual netting knot had been employed by the maker: the work had been evenly executed, and the fine brown (tanned) corded line might have been machine-made. I was informed that this net was made from the fibre of the *Magotsi (Sansevieria)*. The owner of the net would not sell it to me for any price, and of course it was probably the surest means of a regular food supply possessed by these people.

As in the case of the Masarwa, the people of this little clan had few possessions. Apart from a neat two-man dugout — used for attending their nets: a few clay pots, calabashes, tortoise-shells, and some skins; nothing was visible about the place. As already stated, these Bushmen were black, or at least very dark brown in colour. Their language sounded similar to Sesarwa, though I was unable to understand it. My knowledge of Sesarwa is so slight that possibly theirs is a dialect of that language. While no Bantu "clicks" have ever caused me much difficulty, several in Sesarwa have completely baffled me. The Bushman language is frequently described as a hideous jargon, but in my opinion it is rather picturesque. It is certainly one of the most difficult tongues in the world for the European to master.

I took a few photographs of these people and their shelters, arid then walked a few hundred yards down the margin of the deep channel in the hope of getting a shot at a crocodile. My idea probably originated from a remark passed by a Mokoba native, to the effect that, where there are no Europeans to shoot them, crocodiles are careless of the presence of natives: permitting the latter to approach them closely, without taking alarm. I told one of the paddlers to lead the way; and, walking quietly, we kept the far edge of the water in view.

We had proceeded barely more than one hundred yards, when the man suddenly crouched — gesturing to me to do the same. There, on a sloping papyrus platform across the stream, and not more than twenty yards away, lay a huge, basking crocodile. It must surely have been aware of our presence but was too indif-

ferent to move, and as my .303 bullet crashed through its neck, its head dropped and quivered. It was killed outright, and the man called to his companion to bring along the canoe. We had just embarked when I noticed the reptile slowly slipping backwards off the steep slope, and though we hurried across, it sank from sight just as we reached the place. I ordered one of the paddlers to hold on to the papyrus and steady the craft while I pushed down a ten foot paddle to probe for the carcass. However, even with the full length of my arm thrust down, I was unable to reach the bottom.

In my bag was a very heavy hand line, almost a quarter of an inch in thickness. I required but a few minutes to attach this to a large three pronged hook — one of several purchased for just such a contingency. I fished with this for several minutes before it became transfixed to something solid, when I used so much power while hauling that the craft heeled over dangerously to the alarmed protests of the men! However, I maintained a steady pull, and presently some of the line was slowly recovered: bringing with it the object to which the hooks were attached. Peering over the edge, I finally saw the crocodile's tail, still deep down in the clear water. At last, I thought, I had procured a good specimen of a croc, when suddenly the line slackened once more and down sank the carcass again. I persevered for half an hour, but, alas, was unable again to strike the hook into the body, which, having been raised tail first, had probably now glided at an angle to the bottom, possibly resting on any side several yards from its former position.

In any case the search had to be abandoned at this point, as a strong wind, preceding the threatening mutterings of an unseasonable thunderstorm, had arisen. Though sheltered by the dense growth, I could now see and hear the papyrus heads bowing and swaying wildly, and it was clear that the storm would be soon upon us. The men became very anxious, insisting that we would be swamped unless we hurried across the lagoon before the water became rough. As we emerged from the sheltered channel and rounded the corner we drove into the teeth of a rapidly increasing gale, and it became clear that we were in for a rough passage. Our immediate object was to get into the lee of the high western banks which were nearly half a mile away, and although the swells were as yet not bad, it was clear that they would soon become dangerous for the crazy craft with its few inches of free board. The paddlers, one at each end, stood poised against the blast. They worked grimly and silently but rapidly as they watched the water. Not a stroke was lost, but in no time the full fury of the storm was upon us, and rain in pelting sheets completely obscured from view our distant, tree-lined objective.

I feared for the camera which, though well wrapped in canvass and a big leather bag, was difficult to keep out of the water we shipped at every few yards. I was at length obliged to sling the bag over my shoulder and get to work at high speed with the bailer; but as every third or fourth swell gushed over the weather side the water flowed in more rapidly than I could bail, and presently I was sitting in several inches of it.

The stalwart fellows at the paddles stood unwaveringly to their heavy task: neither slackening nor increasing the power of their strokes, maintaining a constantly even poise. Had there been no rain, sweat would have been pouring from their glistening bodies, and they seemed oblivious of everything but attaining the shelter of the now invisible banks. I wondered if they could swim: natives in crocodile-infested areas seldom can! For my own part, swimming held no terrors, but I shuddered as I remembered the many crocs I had seen during that morning.

With a veering wind, the men slightly altered course, and instantly we shipped a large quantity of water which brought us perilously near to foundering. The water so filled the craft by now that it was possible to push it out with the halved calabash, and how I blessed that gourd! Without it we would have been long since struggling for our lives in the water. Many of the swells were now breaking in creamy, gurgling foam; a sure indication that we had passed into swifter water flowing against the driving wind. Then, as suddenly as it had begun — after the manner of tropical storms — the rain stopped; leaving clearly defined before our eyes the waving trees and bush, only a couple of hundred yards ahead. The waves became larger, but having taken the bend we were able to meet them head on, and we were now taking in less water. The wind dropped spasmodically, becoming gusty until, presently, it ceased altogether: and the swift current soon becalmed. A few moments later we drew into the bank, where I told the men to clutch on to the vegetation and to rest awhile. I lit cigarettes for each of them, and as we sat thankfully enjoying these, the sun emerged from the clouds, and the amazing transformation from the terrifying turmoil of but a few minutes before was miraculous and wonderful to behold!

The great and lovely waterway, lashed to sudden anger and power by the unexpected storm, had revealed an ugly side of its nature which will always remind me that precautions must be observed against the allurements of such places.

Chapter 11

"IN THE CLUTCHES OF A LION"

ONE brisk August morning, the camp being without meat, I set out in the truck, with a native driver and four boys, for Goboxlo, where I hoped to find buffalo. We cruised around that area for an hour or so, and then, finding no fresh signs of those creatures, decided to try for a couple of blue wildebeests; a small troop of which we surprised rolling and gambolling in an open space dotted here and there with flat-topped Moshu trees.

The beasts were exceedingly wild, but as meat had to be secured I instructed the driver to follow them, and eventually I managed two quick shots. Both missed, but the second had the effect of knocking up a cloud of dust which fortunately confused the wildebeests. They turned right about, and careered off in the opposite direction with wildly lashing tails and characteristic capers. I got in several more shots, with the last of which I knocked over a heavy bull which turned a complete somersault. Driving up to it, I found that it needed no further attention than disembowelling and loading; so leaving the boys to attend to this, and hoping for fresh buffalo spoor, I walked to an adjacent waterway screened from view by tall fringing forest. Although there were plenty of old tracks, there was nothing sufficiently fresh, so I returned to the truck and, everything being ready, started back for camp on a roundabout route, hoping for something more.

After we had proceeded for a couple of miles, there was a rapid tapping on the canopy, and as we drew up, one of the boys shouted excitedly: "*Detau, Morena, detau!*" ("Lions, Sir, lions!"), but I had already noticed a big male lion looking at the truck from behind a broad, low antheap. From the ground little more than its great shaggy head was visible, but I chanced a shot, and heard the bullet clip against a distant tree trunk. The old male was instantly off, running obliquely away from me. My second shot, at two hundred yards, rolled him over beautifully; and just then I saw a fine lioness galloping off to the right at much the same distance. She was running through mixed bush with openings here and there, and as she crossed one such gap I took a snapshot, but felt, even as I pulled trigger, that I had shot past her front. She disappeared from view, and I saw no more of her.

One of the boys now shouted that the lion had got up and running forward had entered a thick Sitshe bush some hundreds of yards further ahead. So instructing the driver to proceed as though he intended to pass the bush at a distance of thirty or forty yards on the right side, we moved on, and presently we were stopped by more urgent tapping on the roof. I jumped out, but the strong glare from the whitened grass prevented my making anything out in the dark shadows. The boys on the back of the truck affirmed that they could distinctly see the lion from their position, so I climbed up behind, but even then could make out nothing even remotely resembling a lion. The driver now suggested that we should move round the bush and try with the sun at our backs. The idea seemed good enough, but on making the turn he pulled

out further from the tree, and we were now fifty or sixty yards away. However, one of the boys, trembling with excitement, pointed at a small object in the deep shade and declared positively that it was the lion. To me it seemed like a small "Blind" antheap, but as nothing else was visible I determined to try a shot — a risk which should never have been taken.

In order that the reader may better understand the situation, I should first explain that the rear of the truck was facing almost directly towards the lion: that three boys were crowded against its canopy; one kneeling on the carcass of the wildebeest which all but filled the remaining space. I found standing room between its legs, right against the back flap.

From this position, then, I took careful aim. The shot was acknowledged by horrible grating snarls, and the great brute rushed out full of fiery hatred, and with stiffly erected tail charged straight for the van. It was a matter of seconds for him to come up, but it takes a while to tell all that occurred in that brief space of time. The three boys at the canopy contrived to scramble over it and somehow to squeeze into the cabin. Their shaking of the truck of course rendered it utterly impossible to get a sight on the maddened brute, but I pulled the trigger when he was within a few yards. No shot followed! I was certain that he would bound right on to my chest in the next instant, but Providence saved me because, instead of making the leap, the lion swerved violently — flinging a heap of fine dust in my eyes — at the same time banging the end of the van with the swing of its tail. It galloped on for about forty yards and then stood, growling. I again pulled the trigger, but again no report followed. Opening the breech, I found that not a single cartridge remained! That was my second piece of folly that day.

I was now in a quandary. There stood as grand a specimen of a lion as one could wish to see, and there was just nothing that I could do about it. One of the boys had a single-barrelled shotgun with just one No. 5 cartridge — utterly useless under the circumstances. Not certain of the lion's intentions, I remained standing on the back of the truck, watching him. He stood quite still, half sideways to the truck, and utterly indifferent now to our presence. After a few minutes he lay down, but arose again in a very short while and began to walk away without a backward glance. He was obviously very sick now, and that charge proved to be his last great effort. Certainly he looked appallingly grand during that awe-inspiring rush, and I imagine that the only reason why he had not beaten me down was that he was incapable of the great leap required. Perhaps more experienced old hands can suggest a better reason, but I can think of none other, and I have described the episode exactly as it occurred.

Grateful for my lucky escape, I now set off for camp for breakfast, and a fresh supply of ammunition.

After breakfast I called up the boys, but only the driver and the one who had remained with me in the back of the truck turned out. The rest flatly refused to go near lions again! Four others, including one of the regular hunters who was an excellent tracker but an atrocious shot, and three fly boys, volunteered to come. Having arrived back at the scene of our adventure, we left the track and began to spoor the wounded lion. Only an odd spot of blood was visible because the lion had bled internally as I learnt later, but the spoor was easy enough to follow at first. Later it became mingled with that of another large male and two lionesses, and it then took the tracker and the rest of us some little time to puzzle things out. Eventually, by casting ahead, I found a smudge of blood on a grass stem, and thereafter, having only a single track to follow, we were never at fault again.

Ten minutes later I saw the poor beast standing with its mouth near the ground, seemingly near its end. To my annoyance the hunter fired hastily, and I saw his bullet strike up dust one hundred yards or more ahead. I quickly fired for its shoulder, and the lion collapsed on its belly — hardly moving again. However, as the darkness of death descended on him, he twice emitted a deep, low roar, and so the breath left him. With a feeling akin to regret, I looked down at the magnificent beast, but, remembering my own narrow escape, I knelt down at its head and, drawing my fingers through the long dark mane, could not sufficiently admire my splendid prize. I still have the skin and the monstrous skull: the latter with canines measuring two and a half inches from the jaw to their points. It was truly a magnificent beast with a rich brown hide and short heavy limbs. As I felt the splendid proportions and strength of the colossal forearms, it was not difficult to understand how the great buffalo bulls so often got their necks broken in the manner previously described.

I believe that I had a mild adventure with the same lion about six weeks earlier. At any rate the animal looked very similar and the episode occurred near the same locality. On this occasion I was again on my way to Goboxolo in the truck, with a couple of boys on the back. This time, however, I was driving myself, and was some six miles out when the sun rose. At this point the road was over hardish black turf with a thin layer of fine stuff on its surface on which the smallest tracks showed plainly. I was travelling as slowly as possible, watching keenly for spoor as we passed, when I came to where a lion had been rolling. His departing tracks followed straight along the road. Instructing the boys to look out carefully, and doing the same myself, we presently saw the lion trotting away slowly through low Mopani scrub, and knowing the ground well, I put on a spurt; hoping to approach near enough to enable me to jump out and get a shot. But the lion, exactly resembling the great cat that he was, now ran at full speed towards a belt of tall, closely growing Mopanis, which he managed to enter before I could catch up with him in the truck. Halting the latter at the edge of the forest, I jumped out of the van and ran after him as fast as I could go, with the fly boy at my heels.

I caught several glimpses of the lion between the trees as there was no undergrowth whatever, but these were all of far too fleeting a nature to afford even a snapshot, and eventually we lost sight of the lion altogether. His tracks led us to another open space covered with very sparsely growing scrub. This opening was of great length but only about six hundred yards across, and the tracks we were on seemed to lead on beyond to another belt of tall Mopani. Feeling certain that the lion was indeed heading for this, I ran on again, leaving the boy to follow the spoor. I soon found, however, that I was mistaken, and that the lion must have stopped in light cover or else had turned up or down the valley.

Retracing my steps to where the boy was slowly advancing along the spoor, I came presently to a small patch of Moselesele - a spiky acacia-like shrub — which here covered an area roughly thirty yards by thirty yards. I had run past this previously but now began to walk into it, never dreaming that the lion would have stopped in such leafless cover. I had only penetrated a few yards into the coppice, when I was halted abruptly by a deep, rumbling growl. Feeling certain that he was about to charge, I slipped down the safety catch: feeling rather perturbed about the thickness of the prickly growth as I raised the rifle. However there was no further sound, neither could I see the slightest movement. Not daring to move, I waited with the blood tingling to my fingertips. I remained thus for about a minute and a half, when I heard the boy shouting that the lion was making off across the flat. As I rushed out of the Moselesele, the boy ran up, pointing across the valley, and there was the old brute loping at full speed through the scrub: already so far off that it was useless to fire at him.

This lion was very near when he growled, and I cannot account for the way in which he got out of the thorny thicket without my hearing him. However, he was gone; but not without having provided some minutes of very pleasurable excitement.

A few months after killing the big lion and within a couple of miles of the same spot I had another adventure with these beasts. This, however, was an affair which terminated in something rather more than mere excitement, though there was sufficient of that as well.

A friend who had just previously joined the Tsetse Control Department called at my camp and remained to chat for a while. On leaving, he asked whether I could arrange an outing for him as he was most anxious to make the acquaintance of the local buffalo. I suggested that he should come over for a weekend, then we could go out together. He duly turned up on the evening of the following Saturday, so making all arrangements before turning in and having told off half a dozen boys to be ready for an early start, we were able to leave at dawn, making for Goboxlo. As we neared the favoured spot, and just after sunrise, there sounded the usual rapping on the roof of the van, and at the same time we spotted five buffalo a few hundred yards from the road.

Leaping out, we began to stalk the animals which had trotted on a little further, and my friend made a couple of ineffectual shots. Convinced of one of these being a hit, he ran forward, while I followed on behind. Not being much scared, the buffalo stopped every few hundred yards, standing always in mixed cover and dappling shadows; never once offering a favourable opportunity for another shot. Realising the futility of proceeding further, for the buffalo were now thoroughly on the alert, I managed to persuade him to return to the truck which was now at least half a mile away.

As we walked back, lions could be heard roaring in three different directions: seemingly voicing maledictions on rival forces, for answering roars followed quickly and regularly. Twenty minutes later, once again in the van, more and very urgent roof rappings

brought us to a halt, and on jumping out we saw a large lioness and two rather more than three-quarter grown cubs with her. The lioness dropped to my shot with a bullet through the back, emitting grating snarls as she bit at the wound, struggling desperately but futilely to regain her feet.

My friend continued to fire at the others while I ran at full speed towards the stricken beast which, seeing my approach, ceased her struggles. Rising on to her forelegs, she watched my advance through the grass with anything but an amiable look, growling most menacingly. My boys called out loudly, advising me not to approach the lioness; but I was already within fifty yards, and a moment later I put a bullet into the heavy, exposed shoulder. The game beast, fearless to the end, collapsed without a sound: and when I reached her side a minute later she was stretched out full length and had ceased to breathe.

My first bullet, I found, had broken her back just in front of the hindquarters. The beast was in fine condition, and she was as large a lioness as I have ever seen. I examined her long white and clean canines, and unsheathed the deadly claws of a mighty forepaw. She was fully adult, and though not old, had probably produced several litters of cubs beside the two, now almost fully grown, which had accompanied her.

I rejoined my friend, who had hurried across a drying swamp to where the young male had stood when he had fired his last shot. He informed me that he had knocked it down, so we searched the hard ground, pierced by numerous old buffalo footprints, for blood. Though we found none, I had little doubt that he had registered a hit since, with small bore rifles, blood is not always quickly found.

The third animal, a young lioness, had meanwhile entered the thick scrub some distance to our right. We again took up the spoor, advancing into the worst type of cover imaginable: short, thorny

scrub with occasional larger trees, mostly Camel thorns; but still we failed to find any blood. I warned my companion of the danger of entering such jungle after a wounded lion, but he was red hot on the hunt; suggesting that we should follow the track for a short distance and then, after marking the spot, return for the truck, and driving a little further, continue to do the same. To please him, but against my better judgment, I agreed to this plan.

After a while the tracks became difficult to follow, so that while casting ahead we got several hundred yards away from the truck before I again picked them up. My friend went back to fetch up the truck, while I remained behind to mark the place, and a boy who carried a single-barrelled shotgun remained with me.

Having waited a few minutes, I wearied of the inaction.

I had advanced only a few paces along the spoor again when, without any previous warning at all, the lion suddenly came straight for me, uttering rasping snarls. The boy fled precipitately as I hurriedly raised my rifle. I could see but a few yards ahead and could see the bushes shaking as the lion crashed through them, but nothing else.

It was a thoroughly nasty situation, yet, perhaps owing to constant practice, my nerves stood the test, and I felt quite calm as I waited for the enraged brute to come into view, and quite confident in my ability to kill him. In the next moment he was out of the scrub, and I pulled the trigger point blank in his snarling face. But, to my utter mortification, only a dull snap resulted from a misfire, and it flashed through my mind that nothing now could save me. The lion did not leap, but rushed straight at me along the ground. Jumping sideways at the same moment, I dodged him for a few seconds round the thorns, and then felt an agonising pain as his powerful fangs fastened in the calf of my left leg. He bit right through the muscles, cracking the shin bone — as the doctor afterwards told me. I crashed down into a small Camel thorn, the rifle being knocked out of my hand. I was up in the next instant, only to be pulled down again. One moment I was on my stomach, the next on my back: yet I succeeded in regaining my feet once more before I came down again. I now received several bites on the side of my right hip and the top portion of the buttock, and was shaken as a terrier shakes a rat! Squirming like a snake I was next on my back again, and as the lion came for my face I flung my right arm against my throat; and as a last resort thrust my left hand into his mouth, suffering severe pain as the hand was pierced in two places.

Presently I was astonished to find that the brute had left me; and on looking up saw that he was running back whence he had come. I got up, frantically searching for my rifle which I soon found covered with sand. Flinging open the bolt, I ejected the worthless cartridge, and having inserted another, limped after the lion. I can honestly state that my blood was now so well up that, had there been several wounded lions about, I should still have been bent on revenge!

I heard the lorry coming as I hobbled along in pursuit of the lion, and presently saw the latter crouched in some longish grass under a bush. His ears were flattened, and he was growling in a most threatening manner. I managed to give him a shot (with the rifle over my left wrist) which caused him to collapse, but I fired another shot into the moving grass as my friend and a couple of native hunters ran up. They fired a few more rounds into the grass, and I sat down suddenly with a queer feeling of bleariness about my vision, and a swimming sensation in my head.

All the excitement was now over, and the kettle and water which had been brought for coffee was soon heating on the fire in order to produce hot water to wash my wounds. While we were waiting for this, we frequently heard the young lioness, who was still in the vicinity, making the low, moaning call characteristic of these animals when they become separated: and I feel convinced that, but for my mishap, we should have accounted for her also.

Two hours later we were back in my camp where we took some photographs, and then, after gathering some clothing, we set out again. Within another two hours I was in the hospital at Maun. Here the unremitting kindness and skill of the young Medical Officer and the sisters in charge aided me to a splendid recovery in a few weeks. The wounds in the buttock became slightly septic after a week, but that was quickly rectified. I had twenty-three wounds over my body and limbs; only five of which, oddly enough, were claw marks — and these were superficial. The hand remained rather painful for several months; but, apart from some weakness and stiffness of the fingers, it causes me no pain now. This affair occurred on November the second, 1947.

It is inexplicable why the lion left me when I was approaching exhaustion, but I believe that my life was saved by the animal's inexperience. No human being could have prevailed against him for any length of time, indeed he was quite large enough to have accounted for the biggest of bullocks.

When shooting at a wildebeest on the day previous to this affair, I had a misfire. The cartridge which let me down so badly now was from the same packet. I mention this to show what a source of danger faulty ammunition can be.

Chapter 12

A LONG-SUFFERING LION, AND A DISCOMFITED WITCHDOCTOR

WHEN over a number of years, a man's occupation has led him in almost daily contact with wild animals, he will almost certainly become aware of wide differences in temperament among individuals of any one species. By degrees he will become convinced that there is no great distinction between the idiosyncrasies of animal and human kind. This is a fact, I think, of which all students of nature are aware. But even the average man - not very observant, perhaps, nor particularly interested in nature — can hardly fail to notice it.

For instance, one is approaching, say, a flock of starlings. The majority take to flight while you are still some distance away, but a few are sure to remain on the ground. One might safely conclude then that the more timid had sought safety in flight, while the remainder had failed to find cause for hasty retirement.

When a troop of baboons is surprised: emotions indicative of caution, fear, anger, and noisy, swaggering impudence are all revealed. Patient observation on such lines adds greatly to the fascination of rambles in wild places, and to a discerning hunter in quest of dangerous game it provides also an additional measure of safety. He would learn, for instance, that a bullet striking one fleeing lion may merely cause an acceleration of speed, with no more dangerous reaction than grunts of resentment: while similar treatment to another may raise its ire to white-hot fury resulting in an impetuous charge at incredible speed, accompanied by nerve-shattering snarls. Another, again, may merely crouch, with rumbling growls and flattened ears, awaiting the next move from its enemy.

Failure to take into account the often widely divergent individual temperament of any one species of the more dangerous game has led to numerous tragedies in the hunting field. When a hunter accepts previous experiences as a criterion to the reactions of dangerous animals to any form of illtreatment or annoyance, he is looking for trouble. There are no certain rules governing this aspect of animal nature, and it is seldom that a sequence of manifestations of ferocity, patience, or just sheer disinclination to fight, will occur.

It is well, in my experience, at all times to be prepared for the unexpected to happen, and the greater security lies in regarding dangerous beasts as highly dangerous. Circumstances, nevertheless, not infrequently impel a man to take grave risks.

There is a compelling fascination in the danger involved when following a stricken beast into difficult cover; and as no sportsman willingly gives up a fine specimen he has hit, he is usually prepared to accept the risk. Recognising the danger, his faculties and bushcraft are keyed to their highest, and, if his nerves hold, the odds are in his favour provided he does not underestimate the danger or lapse into moments of inattention. The major peril lies in being unprepared for a charge.

In an earlier chapter I gave some account of the hunting of a mild-natured, well-fed lion. As further proof of the annoyance these animals will sometimes submit to without active resentment I shall here relate a quite extraordinary adventure I had with a large male in January 1934.

I was a temporary stock inspector at the time, operating along the Nata River — not far above its junction with the Great Makarikari Salt pan. One morning I received a note, carried in a cleft stick, by a runner, from an old friend — Lieutenant Bob Hurndall, O.C. of the Foot and Mouth Cordon Police, whose headquarters was situated on the wellknown Tsehuba pool some three miles up and across the river. The "chit" requested that I should accompany my friend to a place called Mampsi, just off the northern edge of the Makarikari. Having made two previous visits to the locality,

I readily agreed, because, in addition to the cattle there having caused me some anxiety, I knew that the country was interesting and that we should get some good shooting.

I arrived opposite the Tsehuba camp early next morning, and I had to strip to cross the river for the water was running strongly. Bob was at breakfast when I walked in, but as he was thoroughly prepared we got away soon after. The journey of about twenty five miles, though over a rough track, was delightful in other respects. Copious rains had fallen a few weeks previously, and all the pans — around the sedgy margins of which large numbers of waterfowl had gathered — were full, resembling in the distance flashing gems in a setting of soft, velvety green. We had little time to admire the birds though, as by the time we had finished our work and bagged a couple of springbuck, heavy thunder clouds had gathered. We had to rush back to camp in order to avoid being caught in the treacherous black soil, which becomes a quagmire when wet, into which your vehicle will sink up to its axles. We reached the Nata, just beating a heavy shower across that perilous surface, as the sun was dipping to the horizon.

My friend offered me a "sundowner" while one of the buck (a leg of which I was to take with me) was being skinned. Twenty minutes later, when the sun had already set, I was on my way back to my camp. As already stated, there was a fair amount of water in the river and I decided not to cross until I got opposite my camp, where at one broad sandy stretch I knew the depth would not be more than a few feet. I rather foolishly followed the course of the river, which hereabouts winds a good deal, and as I was much hampered by having to force my way through thickets of hook-thorned Acacia, darkness had set in before I reached the place where I intended to cross. Walking became thoroughly unpleasant; for apart from the clutching, thorny scrub, I had continually to guard against falling into innumerable eroded gullies winding their way down the sloping banks, and the heavy rifle and the venison did not improve the situation. Overhead black clouds obscured most of the stars, and only a foot or two ahead was visible at a time. Everything appeared strangely different in the darkness, and eventually to my dismay I discovered that I had overshot my mark by a considerable distance.

Hoping fervently that I would strike a crossing, I made for the channel which I only reached after struggling through dongas and very rough ground. I could hear the purling of the stream and soon caught a glimpse of the water itself, but though a fairly strong swimmer I admit frankly that I little fancied facing the river that night.

However, with the alternative of spending a night out in lion-infested country (not to mention the mosquitos) without a fire, the river, which fortunately is free of crocodiles, seemed the lesser evil, so I was not long in stripping. Fastening the clothing in a bundle with my boots inside it, and leaving the venison and rifle, I entered the water. By good luck I had chosen as good a crossing as any I could have chosen by daylight, and but a few minutes sufficed for me to return for the gun and the meat. Ten minutes later I was able to proceed once more, experiencing some difficulty in trying to penetrate, in the prevailing darkness, the rather dense bush bordering the river. Had I been aware that two hungry lions were then somewhere in the vicinity - perhaps even within a few yards of me - I should certainly have wasted less time trying to disentangle my clothes and person from the clinging attentions of surrounding thorny twigs.

Not having lions in mind, however, I threaded my way along quietly, and presently emerged in a small glade. As I reached this I became aware of the cheerful sounds of croaking frogs a short distance ahead, and at once I realised that these proceeded from a little pan of muddy water in the middle of a clearing through which I had passed while out for a stroll with my gun on the previous afternoon. I had evidently overshot my camp by at least a mile. However from here on it was easy going, and within a few minutes I caught occasional glimpses through the trees of the distant camp fire, and a little later I received the usual delighted welcome from my terrier. I did full justice to the meal which my cook, a Baralong named Fox, set before me. During my long tramp downriver I had longed for a smoke, but as I had left my matches at Bob's camp I had to do without it. Now, after supper, how I enjoyed that pipe! However, I was soon in bed, having issued instructions for an early start on the morrow when I was to inspect a mob of cattle.

By dawn the wagon was in motion, and before the sun had beamingly appeared high above the horizon we were approaching the native kraal where the inspection was to take place. As we arrived, the Bushman in charge of the post appeared, and in a very excitable manner delivered a lengthy tirade on the evil propensities of wild animals generally and of lions in particular: winding up with the information that all the cattle had been stampeded by a couple of these marauders. Thinking that he had failed to collect the stock, and that the lion story was a mere fabrication, I was about to give voice to all the hard words I could think of when the fellow forestalled me by suggesting that I would accompany him to the kraal where a fat cow had been killed and partly devoured. I was soon beside the carcass.

Within thirty yards of the kraal it lay, and no greater distance separated it from the little grass shelter wherein the Bushman and his anxious family had lain listening to the feasting brutes. Awakened by the crashing of the bolting cattle, the man had peeped out but dared not show himself, though by the faint light of dawn he was able to make out the shadowy forms of the lions as they were tearing at the carcass. The intervention of daylight had prevented the lions from eating their fill, but nevertheless, having consumed most of the flesh on the inner sides of the hind legs as well as some of the internal organs, they had not fared badly. Feeling the carcass, I found it still slightly warm and flaccid, and certainly it was the freshest kill I had hitherto examined.

Turning to the Bushman, I enquired how long he thought it would take to collect the cattle, to which he replied that there was little hope of finding them that day. I was inclined to agree with him, and after some consideration I decided to attend to the herd on my return journey. Only another five miles had to be covered — downriver — in this section to complete my round, and it would not really matter whether I saw the stock that day, or a few days hence. All that was needful was to warn the Bushmen at the kraals lower down that I would see their stock on the following day, and the man immediately sent off a young lad with the message. I then began to examine the lion tracks, and noticed the Bushman's spoor beside them. He had earlier puzzled them out, and now showed me exactly what had happened.

Proving his statements with the spoor of the lions which had approached the kraal upwind, he pointed out to me where one had crouched, while the other, without fuss or bother, had quietly circled the kraal which was very much of a tumbled down thorn bush structure. As soon as the cattle caught the wind of this fellow they, with wild accord, rushed to the other side, bursting through

the dried-up, rotting branches and, of course, right on to the waiting lion. The latter had at once pounced on and broken the neck of cow at the spot where I had seen her.

I determined to try for these lions (both adult males), and I informed the Bushman of my plans and asked what men he could collect. He replied that, besides himself, there was only one man and a youth available. Moreover he considered that ii would be a waste of time following the brutes, as on previous occasions after similar raids on local kraals many hunting parties had failed to get the lions, which had always successfully evaded their pursuers in the scrub across the river. Speaking in Tswana he added that he knew these lions well, and that they were "*viry-viry*" but what that mysterious term indicated I have never been able to discover! Telling him to collect the others and be ready to follow me in a few minutes, I walked over to the wagon where Fox had already cooked my porridge. It did not take long to satisfy the "inner man", and having filled the magazine of my rifle I was ready. Fox was keen to take part in the hunt, so he followed me to the kraal where the Bushmen were waiting with a couple of shockingly lean dogs — mere caricatures of dogs — as Bushmen curs usually are, though many of them are wondrously plucky and faithful too.

Taking up the departing tracks of the lions, the Bushmen walked at speed on the spoor, which held in a direction cutting diagonally towards the river and below where we had spent the night. I noticed, as we proceeded, that the lions had followed their own tracks of the forward journey and that they had never broken from a walk. Obviously, the old fellows were in no way fearful of being

caught away from their haunts in daylight. They must certainly have heard the approach of my wagon.

In rather more than half an hour we reached the river and, standing on its bank to collect my bearings, I presently made out the spot where I had crossed on my way back from the O.C.'s camp: it was a few hundred yards above where we now stood. The channel had swung across to our side, and the water rushed with considerable force below a sheer bank of some eight feet in height.

Clearly impressed on the sandy edge below, we could see the pug marks where the lions had landed after jumping off the bank. They had probably had a drink, but there was no sign that they had loitered otherwise. The tracks led straight into the water, which they could not possibly have crossed without swimming, for I found it to be shoulder deep.

We were all soon across, but were delayed a few minutes on the slope of the far bank where the ground was hard and much eroded. But, like bloodhounds, the Bushmen soon picked up the trail again, and, once over the crest, we were in sand once more. Here it was possible to run along the spoor so plainly did it show, and now we were traversing ground with which I was familiar, for the tracks held parallel to and up the river — now about half a mile away — and the cordon road holding the direction of the stream was only a few hundred yards to our left. For several miles Motlopi, Grewia, Mopani and thorny scrub in thick clusters covers the ancient alluvial flats, the soil of which is loose sand and silt, and the tracking could hardly have been easier. Nowhere was it necessary to force one's way through the vegetation as small open spaces between the thickly dotted bushes were always visible. As we remained in exactly the same sort of veld for nearly the whole of that day, these details should be remembered.

With the dogs ranging ahead, we pushed on for perhaps a mile when the spoor veered riverwards, and small clumps of trees were passed. Ahead there was a stand of tallish but young Mopani growing rather thickly, and as we approached this we heard a faint rumble, at which the dogs bolted past us as though the devil was after them! In a few moments they halted, and, with bristling hair, let off a few sharp barks.

We had of course all come to a standstill, listening intently, but not a sound reached our ears. The thicker cover was still some sixty or seventy yards ahead.

Taking the lead, the Bushman now walked silently in that direction, but had not gone ten yards when, with a beckoning wave of his hand, he shot off towards the right, running as only a Bushman can run in the sand. We all sprinted after him, but I had not the slightest notion what it was all about. What with heavy boots, a heavier rifle, and forty odd years at the back of me, I was soon a long distance in the rear and, though I was doing my best, quickly lost sight of the men. Obviously the senior Bushman, who had so far always taken the lead, must have had reason for his haste; so I continued running, keeping an eye on their spoor, and presently I saw them waiting for me some distance ahead. By that time my lungs were just about bursting, but as I came up with them the leading Bushman calmly requested me to hurry! Asking him what the blazes he thought I had been doing, I sat down to recover my breath. The man insisted that we would never get the lion unless we were quick. I told him that from thence onwards he would hunt my way or not at all; so, with a shrug of his shoulders he also sat down, with the others, and, mollified by a few cigarettes I handed round, they were presently chattering happily enough. Only then did I realise that I was sitting on the fresh spoor of a lion, so I enquired what had happened. The Bushman replied that he heard the lions breaking cover and had seen the tops of the scrub move as the animals passed by, thus getting the direction they were holding, and he ran ahead. Repeating that he knew these lions well, he emphatically stated that unless we followed quickly I would never catch sight of them, let alone get a shot. Telling him that I could not shoot after running, I enquired

cordon road - just beyond which was a man - obviously a Bushman - gazing at the ground. It was of course the lion spoor which interested the stranger who, at our approach, clicked off a few questions to which his compatriots replied. A little talk ensued, and they all stooped down and began to clear and smooth a patch of sand, while the old man - who proved to be a Bushman witchdoctor - produced a small leather bag (the dressed scrotum of one or other of the larger buck) and loosened a sinew thong by which the bag was closed. The old fellow then emptied the bag, which contained an assortment of small bones, the hoof of a duiker, an eagle's claw, and a few other odds and ends, on to the prepared sand.

Selecting five items (which included the hoof and the claw) from these, he returned the remainder to the pouch which, duly fastened, was slipped under the cord to which his *moesieto* (loin cloth) was attached. The magic bones were then rattled between the hands, and with something of a flourish cast on the smooth space. Greatly impressed, and uttering in softened tones a series of weird clicks, the other Bushmen closely watched every movement.

After a careful scrutiny of the position of each piece, the learned one gathered them up and, after further rattling, again cast them to the ground. No comments followed this throw. The same performance was repeated for the third time, and then the rogue rose to his feet remarking something to the effect that it would be folly to follow the lion further without good dogs.

Realising what this performance was about, and that, so far as the Bushmen were concerned, this statement was tantamount to vetoing the hunt, I unostentatiously clinked some silver in my pocket and stooping suddenly, pointed to one of the pieces, saying: "Look! This one is the wrong way about!" and quickly flipped it over; whereupon the old rogue hurriedly knelt beside me, muttering: "Yes! The White man is right — that one is lying wrongly." He gathered them all up, and after vigorously shaking them in his hands, flung the lot to the ground with a picturesque flourish. He then carefully fingered all the pieces, and mumbling a long rigmarole in a queer mixture of Sesarwa and Tswana, of which I understood exactly two words: Ghaam (lion — Sesarwa) and Makoewa (White man - Tswana): he quickly scraped together the "all-powerful" instruments of his profession. Jumping up, he repeated: "The White man is right!" Then, in impressive tones, he declared: "We will pursue and the lion will be killed, but it will be by me, and not by the White man that the lion will be killed!" At any rate I was pleased by the success of my intervention, and in no way perturbed by the doctor's verdict, so I smilingly handed him a shilling which was immediately accepted by the old villain. Everybody was now satisfied, so we resumed the hunt.

Those who know the Nata valley will tell you how tremendously hot it becomes on a midsummer's day, when not a breath of wind is available. The sand is deep and loose, excepting after rains; and the thunder showers had, up to the time of my story, missed this area. Every small pan revealed only dry, cracked floors; and no water, other than that flowing in the river, was obtainable.

After walking for about half an hour, the Bushman in the lead stopped suddenly and pointed to a lion track which crossed our route at right angles. It was certainly fresh, but otherwise of no particular interest to me. Both he, and his companions, however, insisted that it was "our" lion: declaring that always, when they had been after this pair of lions, the same thing had occurred. I was unconvinced, however, and ordered them to stick to the spoor of the beast which we had hitherto been following. With another shrug, the leader obeyed. A quarter of an hour later we were confronted by our own tracks once more; and the Bushman, looking round with the flicker of a smile on his face, pointed to the marks on the ground. On reflection, it seemed to me that this continuous harrying must finally exasperate the lion into turning to fight, and I told Fox to explain this to the men. Shortly after this there was a repetition of the same experience, and the Bushman again stopped, with a look which clearly conveyed the question: "What now?"

We had now got into rather thinner and more scattered scrub, and I told the men to spread out into skirmishing order — the tracker holding the spoor and myself on the extreme left. With the others lined out on the further flank we moved slowly forward in that formation. Within five minutes this plan bore some result. From the man on the extreme right came an indistinct shout, and in an instant my rifle was up to my shoulder. A movement in the vegetation was immediately followed by a glimpse of the bounding form of a lion, and though the vision was but a fleeting one, I was ready, and took a split-second shot. This was acknowledged by a short sharp grunt, and one of the men shouted: "It is hit!" There had been no time to aim, but I felt that I had indeed scored a hit. The lion however made no sound, though we heard it crashing through short stuff some distance ahead. The sight of the magnificent beast — which, brief though it had been, reminded me of a great yellow bull — made me keener than ever to bag it. The general opinion was that, if really wounded, the beast would come to bay before much longer: otherwise it might maintain its original tactics for the remainder of the day.

With their marvellously developed bush craft and ultra-acute senses, there can be few people in Africa who can excel the Masarwa Bushmen for work of this description. I think, too, that on the whole they are rather more courageous than other native races with which I have had anything to do. Little indeed escapes their observant eyes or ears, even while engaged in spooring, and this is of utmost advantage to a white hunter who needs to concentrate

on little more than doing his own stuff. When walking over featureless country nothing is easier than to move in a circle, so that within half an hour of resuming our tracking I was shocked to find myself once again crossing my own tracks. I am not certain whether I should then have observed the fact had I not seen the Bushman draw my attention to it, without looking round, by flicking up the thumb of his left hand — a common method among the Masarwa of signalling the sight of followed footprints. Without stopping, but with undiminished care, he carried on in the lead. Some minutes later all the Bushmen halted suddenly, with their heads slightly turned, listening. Presently I also heard a movement in the scrub, and when we finally reached the place, there, sure enough, was the lion's spoor, but once again he had quietly eluded us.

This lion's forbearance and patience astonished me, particularly as these creatures become lethargic during the heat of the day: invariably seeking cool spots in which to lie up, where they are untroubled by strong light — so generally disliked by the cat tribe.

Water had become a pressing need, for the sun had long since passed the meridian, and the heat rose from the baked sand in quivering waves. There were no trees about, and the scrub casts no shade that affords any protection from the scorching rays of the sun. Fearful that the witchdoctor would influence the rest of my retainers to give up the hunt altogether, I showed him a shilling and remarked that it would be his if he fetched us some water from the river, now about three miles distant. He set off without a word, evidently pleased to be rid of the arduous tracking. Hoping that if left alone for a while the lion might settle sufficiently to allow us a nearer approach, I decided to rest for an hour. We were all tired and the men were pleased enough to squat down, and in spite of our thirst we each enjoyed a cigarette. I was glad when it was time to move on again, but with the completion of two more rounds, with the same discouraging results, the men became dissatisfied They grumbled that this sort of thing would continue until darkness set in, and we might just as well give up the hunt. Finally I had to bribe them with five shillings each to make one more round on their own, while I climbed into the tallest bush I could find in order to get a more extended view. If this also proved a failure, I would give up the hunt.

Fox put the scheme to them, and to my delight they assented, so I looked around for a suitable bush. There was little choice, and the best I could find was a Mothopi, but it had no horizontal branches and none more than an inch and a half in thickness. Handing the rifle to Fox to pass up to me when I had got into a suitable position, I began to climb. It was a most uncomfortable perch, but eventually, with my legs spread and a small branch for each foot, and another between my legs to steady my balance, I achieved a position which I felt I could endure for a quarter of an hour! The soft Mothopi wood gave so much under my weight that, by the time I was settled, my feet were only six feet above the ground. However, I could certainly see a great deal further from that slight elevation.

Taking the rifle, I bade the boys move on and concentrated my gaze over the surrounding bush. If the lion showed itself to my front, well and good: otherwise shooting was going to be very difficult.

The boys were hardly out of sight when, distant about several hundred yards, I saw the witchdoctor approaching with something in his hand. He must also have seen me, as he was walking directly towards me. After that my attention was otherwise engaged, for I had heard a sound away to my left front, just where I could see a round-topped thorny Acacia. Though I could not precisely define this noise, it sounded most like a human cough. For an instant it occurred to me that the men might have decided against the risk and were returning to me, but the direction was wrong. I caught a couple of glimpses of the old Bushman picking his way along the openings, and with eyes and ears well open I carefully covered the surrounding bush.

All of a sudden, the deadly quiet was broken by a fearful commotion! Frantic yells emitted by the approaching Bushman were mingled with the horrible grating snarls of an enraged lion, but I could see nothing of what was taking place. I aimed in the direction of the alarming sounds (which had now ceased), and this was only possible by twisting my body round. I had not long to wait, however, as in the next moment the lion appeared. It entered a small open space about twenty five yards away and, on seeing me (which it instantly did), it crouched low with outstretched wrinkled muzzle and a display of shining white canines, while deep growls rumbled in rapid succession from its great heaving chest.

The lion's body was not directly in my line of fire, which, perhaps, was fortunate as I aimed for its nose, but missing this was lucky enough (owing to the elevation from which I fired) to strike it fairly in the small of the back. The shot was followed by a terrific noise: not roars, but the deepest, throatiest snarls I had ever heard. As it uttered these, the stricken beast was dragging itself round and round by its forepaws, and biting at the wound. I fired another shot, which seemed to have no effect, and before I could get in a third the lion's struggles had carried it behind a bush and I could see it no more.

At this moment, one of Bob's African police, who happened to be in the vicinity and had heard the shooting, came on the scene from the opposite side. I handed him my rifle and half scrambled, half fell out of the bush — of which I had already had far too much!

Together, we slowly circled the spot where the lion had vanished. A complete round afforded no glimpse, but as we had found no spoor, and as one of the dogs was barking persistently near the place, we knew that the brute was still in hiding there. I was about to approach nearer when the man touched my back, whispering that he could see the lion. Looking in the direction in which he was pointing, I made out first its mane; then, slowly, the outline of its forequarters came into view. Just a few wisps of tallish grass had camouflaged it in an amazing manner; but once made out, I wondered how I had failed to see it sooner!

Only twelve yards away, it rolled over to my shot, but as it expired it gave utterance to several deep-toned half roars, scraping the ground simultaneously with its upper forepaw. It's eyes were glazing as I walked up to it, and with a few spasmodic shudders it died.

It was only now, at the close of those tense minutes of the final scene, did I recall — to my shame — the poor old witchdoctor's disquieting encounter with the lion. Filled with anxiety on his account I mentioned the incident to the policeman, but he, having approached from a different direction, had of course seen nothing of him. The other boys, hearing my shots and the noise made by the lion, had absconded, fearing that a wounded lion might be among them. In response to our shouts they now came up, and with them, very greatly to my relief, was the witchdoctor.

Examination of the dead lion revealed that, apart from the snap shot earlier in the day which had merely cut the skin on a hind foot (which wound had dried during the long hunt), only two bullets, both inflicting mortal wounds, had struck it.

I asked the witchdoctor what had occurred when he screamed. He replied that he had come face to face with the lion and it had charged him, and had it not been for a thorn bush (the very one I had noticed) he would have been dead. Now that he was safe we could all laugh, which we did, but, as providing further evidence of the tolerant nature of this lion — which could have clawed him from beneath the bush without the least trouble — his experience was interesting. "And where is the water?" I asked, but of course I knew that he had dropped the pail on being charged; and though the very thought of the precious fluid being wasted in the sand was maddening I could not blame him. So terrible had become my thirst, that I felt that I had never previously known the meaning of the word.

Handing the men their rewards, I told the witchdoctor that he would also receive a like amount when he delivered the lion's skin at my wagon. Poor old fellow! Apart from the promised "windfall" which was more than the average Bushman earns in a year, it had been an unfortunate day for him. Besides the loss of his professional prestige, he informed us that on his way to fetch the water he had walked right on to the second lion which, jumping away from him with a nasty snarl, had scared him greatly.

Before leaving the wagon that morning I had given instructions for it to be taken on to my next camp, five miles downriver, to await my arrival there, so there was still a long, wearisome walk ahead of us. However, water was now the first consideration for all of us, and we strode rapidly towards the river. We drank our fill from the fine, long and deep reach called by the Bushmen Ghaam-tsaa (Lions' water) and after a short rest and smoke Fox and I walked along the Cordon road to the Motsiara drift where the wagon was waiting. Here an old friend and Tati neighbour who was also doing a turn at cordon duty was stationed. We reached the camp in not much over an hour, though darkness overtook us on the way. Never did a "spot" taste so good! My friend, with whom I had supper, had already learnt of my success with the lion from the police boy who had gone back to camp after the incident, and he congratulated me heartily. We chatted for a while, but I was not long in leaving for the wagon which was outspanned on the far side of the river, about a quarter of a mile away. I crossed at the old drift, where today a fine low-level concrete bridge spans the stream.

The adventure just related will ever be a memorable one to me as this was the first lion I had ever killed.

Chapter 13

MORE EXPERIENCES WITH BUFFALO

WHENEVER I ran out of meat at my main camp, and time was available from more important duties, I would collect a few boys and drive in the truck to the Goboxlo area. It was seldom that buffalo could not be located in that vicinity. Other game also, including wildebeest, kudu, sassaby, impala and pig abounded, and it was rare indeed that at least something for the pot was unobtainable there.

Much of the track, which had been worn into a passable motor road, skirted open downs and natural clearings which divided the forests from the more open savanna woodlands of the sandbelts. By travelling at dawn, buffalo, wending their way towards their uncongenial but comparatively safe retreats in the sun-scorched, sandy scrub-covered wastes, would often be seen on or near the road. These buffalo were usually in small parties of from four to a dozen individuals. Only once did I find thereabouts as many as fifty in a mob; and, as shown, they only passed through the forests (where occasionally they could not resist the temptation to loiter) for the purpose of drinking: clearing off again at dawn.

During those early morning trips in that area I shot more buffalo than anything else; and as the incursions of the beasts kept the surroundings pretty heavily stocked with Tsetse flies, I experienced less compunction in taking a heavy toll of the "buffs" than I might otherwise have felt.

One morning, about three miles short of Goboxlo, my driver suddenly jammed on the brakes, and I at once noticed four or five buffalo in some scrub about one hundred yards away to our right front. I fired from the cab, and saw a huge beast topple over on to its side as if pole-axed, but instantly it was on to its feet again — running heavily in the wake of the others. I jumped out of the cab, and was about to give it a second shot when it fell once more, and I spurted on after those ahead, with the driver and three boys after me.

Unknown to me, the little troop had halted in a patch of young Mopani. As we approached, however, they went galloping away again, and I took a hasty shot at about one hundred and fifty yards — the bullet clapping loudly. A few seconds later the buffalo entered a belt of tall, scattered Mopani with some dense brush which obscured them from view. Entering the forest we followed the spoor, searching for blood. We had moved thus slowly for about seventy five yards when there was a loud crashing ahead of us and at the same instant I saw a buffalo coming straight for me at a terrific speed.

I was about a dozen yards ahead of the boys, and owing to several thick, intervening trunks could not, for the life of me, get a sight on the brute. Only just in time did I manage to jump round the trunk of a big tree to avoid the determined rush of the big beast as it charged up and — fortunately — past! Ready for instant action, I contrived to plant a bullet behind its short ribs as it sped forwards. The range could not have been more than five yards, and it later transpired that my bullet had pierced the heart, for within half a minute we heard the familiar dying bellows.

Turning towards the men, who, at the sudden charge of the buffalo had been unable to select places of safety, I saw three of them some distance up the trunk of a tall, straight Mopani - the lowest branches of which were at least fourteen feet from the ground. They were clinging like monkeys, and the lowest man, "who was badly scared, was but a short distance up; and had the buffalo turned to fight he might well have been battered to death! Between the first indication of the buffalo's charge and its passing, very few seconds

had elapsed, and it struck me that getting as far up that tree as they had succeeded in doing was a remarkable feat of agility. Needless to say, their hurried contact with the exceedingly rough Mopani bark had resulted in severe abrasions on the inner sides of their legs: otherwise, apart from their terror, they were safe and whole. As they slid from the tree, the fourth man (who had taken refuge under a small bush some twenty yards away) joined them, and the glances exchanged were eloquent of all that had happened, or might have happened, within those few breathless seconds!

Together, we walked to where the bull had been bellowing, and we found it lying dead on a patch of green sward near the margin of a dried-up swamp. A careful all round examination revealed no bullet wound other than the one I had given it slantwise from behind, so obviously the wounded bull was still with the others. Before following this, we returned to the buffalo first shot. As I had run past it, in pursuit of the others, I felt certain that it was dying. It was still alive, however, as we now came up with it, and I gave it a final brain shot.

The boys, among whom were the cook, Disho, who had no use for living buffalo, and the regular hunter (he who, complete with rifle, had a few minutes before sought the shelter of the little bush) were all of opinion that we now had sufficient meat. Naturally, however, I was averse to leaving the wounded bull, which might in any case by now be dead, so I told them to follow me.

Back among the mopanis, we scouted around for blood, and who but Disho, who had an appalling squint and was carrying my shotgun, should see the first splashes found? The beasts had bypassed the scrub, and had galloped right through the belt and across open ground towards another similar one. Here we found that the animals had joined quite a herd of fresh buffalo, of which the ones we were following were probably only a remnant which had wandered ahead. The ground was much trodden, and after a time no more blood could be found, and, to cut a long story short, I finally decided that it was a waste of time to continue the hunt.

As two buffalo had to be skinned and quartered, we took a short cut back to the carcasses. On the way, the hunter pointed out a patch of thorns where, he averred, he had been afraid to follow a buffalo which he had wounded two days previously.

As the thorn patch was not far out of our way, I told him to lead me to the place. Having arrived at the hedge-like border of the thick stuff, we searched for blood and spoor, and it was presently the squint-eyed Disho who first found blood again.

It was old and dry, but in bountiful evidence. The trail led us to two places where the unfortunate brute had lain down, but neither was fresh. Traces of scraping on the ground and among the leaves indicated that the beast had not been using its off front foot, and that it probably had a broken leg, or shoulder. A few hundred yards ahead we came to a place from which the buffalo had moved only a few hours before, and thence its spoor led towards the water in a molapo (river) not very far away.

Presently one of the boys sat down so suddenly in front of me that I nearly fell over him, and I realised that he had seen the buffalo. I scanned the veld beyond, and soon spotted the animal in some sparsely growing tamboekie grass about sixty yards away. It collapsed to my bullet, and I walked up to where it lay. Disho, who was in the rear, became suddenly imbued with unusual valour, and equally unusual concern for my safety. He rushed up, shouting: "My Master — my Master will be killed by the *Nyari*!" He then loosed off my shotgun presumably at the buffalo — from a few yards behind me, and must have come very near to peppering me with a charge of birdshot as I felt the blast of the pellets passing my bare legs! I have no idea where the pellets went, but certainly not one of them touched the buffalo.

Uncertain whether the buffalo would again rise, the men, watching it intently, stood well clear. However the poor old brute was so far gone that it did not even utter the usual dying bellows, and no finishing shot was required. It had fallen on its injured side, and I had it turned over to examine the old wound. The knob of the big bone at the point of the shoulder had been shattered, and my bullet must have saved it months of dreadful suffering.

While collecting thatching grass in the Goboxlo area for my shack, I had two affairs with buffalo which I think are worth relating.

On the way to work, early one morning, we walked on to a small herd of buffalo grazing in an open vlei. One of the men, the regular hunter stationed at Chuchubegho, fired before the troop started to run, and I heard the clap of the bullet.

A cloud of dust was immediately raised by the hooves of the stampeding animals, obscuring our view, but, cutting in diagonally from the left towards the herd, and much closer, I saw three other buffalo pelting along at a hard gallop. The range was only about two hundred yards, and I at once fired at a good bull.

The buffalo, breaking from its gallop into a trot, turned sharply towards the forest on the left — not very far from the spot where Disho had sought the safety of an antbear hole.

It was obviously severely wounded, reducing its pace to a slow walk, and I began to run towards it. Unfortunately I tripped over a stump hidden in the grass and came down heavily right into a small Kameeldoorn bush a step or two ahead of me.

The result of this was that a spiky thorn which had entered and broken off just below my kneecap had to be removed before I could proceed, and the few seconds required for this were sufficient for the disappearance from my view of both the boys and the buffalo. After a moment's consideration, I decided to follow the former. This turned out to be a fortunate decision: resulting, as it did, in some minutes of thrilling excitement which otherwise I would have missed

Walking rapidly along, I eventually struck the spoor where it had crossed the road, and while following this I caught a glimpse of the men nearly half a mile ahead. They were much to the right of the direction the herd had taken, and I concluded that the wounded beast had turned that way. I was about to follow, when a small splash of blood on a dry, whitened leaf induced me to hold to the spoor I was on. This led straight to the margin of the heavy riverine forest lining the upper reaches of the Chuchubegho channel, and as I was about to enter this, a young, unattached lad who had been spending a few days with the boys, and who had turned back from the hunt, joined me. As he came up, I found more blood — just a small smear on a grass stem — and pointing this out, I beckoned to him to fall in behind me. However, on reaching really thick cover only a few yards further on, there was no sign of him again, and I decided that it was better that he was out of the way.

The buffalo had chosen its cover with characteristic cunning. With a thumping heart, and keyed up for an instantaneous shot, I advanced a step at a time: stopping frequently to listen for the slightest sound and to peer into the almost impenetrable thicket; but all was deadly still, with a silence charged with suspense.

I had covered perhaps thirty yards in this way when, with a nerve-wracking crash, the buffalo charged suddenly from behind some taller and thicker undergrowth, further in than I expected. Beyond the violently agitated scrub I could see absolutely nothing, and realising my peril I dashed up the side of a nearby and much overgrown antheap, where I got down on my right knee: waiting and aiming at the spot where I expected the beast would emerge. For several seconds the dense, twining thorny growth impeded the efforts of the maddened beast, but at length it forced a passage, and, having my wind, it was in the act of coming at me when I fired into the exposed chest at a range which I later found to be just seven yards.

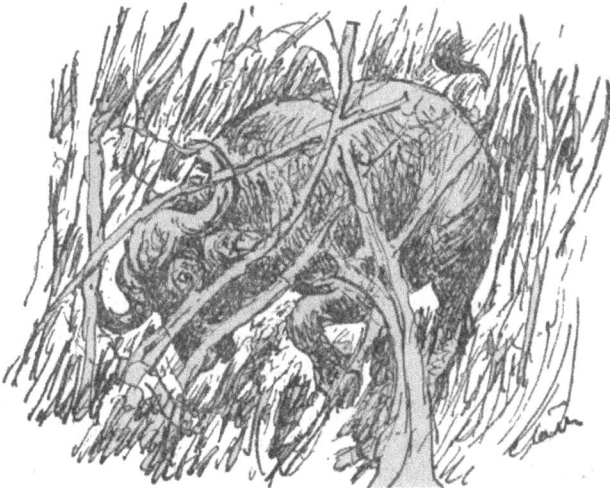

The impact of the bullet knocked the buffalo to its knees; but it struggled up again instantly, and seemingly having lost all interest in me swung round so quickly and sharply to the left that it was out of sight before I could manage another shot, if, indeed, such was necessary. In a few moments all the noise had ceased, and I was not certain whether the beast was dead, or whether it was again waiting in ambush. From the summit of my antheap I could see even less than from my original position, so descending again I walked to where the boy had so mysteriously vanished, and found him trying to free himself from the grappling branches of a hook-thorned bush, beneath which he had obviously dived at the first alarm. How he had contrived to get under it I do not know: certainly he was unable to extricate himself without my assistance. Shiveringly he asked if the Nyari was dead, to which I replied that I was not certain. He promptly began again to force his way into the completely unsafe place, but I laughingly suggested that he should rather climb a tree instead, which he did with alacrity.

As this lad was only about fourteen years old, and had doubtless listened to countless tales about the cunning and ferocity of the buffalo, I held nothing against him for his natural fear. How often have I not seen adult kindred equally ready, even when well armed, to seek cover when little danger of a charge by buffalo threatened. Only the older, experienced hunters could be relied upon to stand by one in a real emergency.

Though I little fancied doing so in that nasty cover, I turned to take up the spoor. It took but a minute to reach the spot where the buffalo had been turned, and from here on the dense, low scrub was gory with blood which must have been fairly spouting from the small bullet wound. Soon both my shorts and bare calves were streaming with it. I was certain that the beast was either dead, or at the point of death, and yet on account of the terribly thick, thorny cover - worse than anything I had ever hitherto threaded after buffalo — and the almost complete lack of visibility, it must have taken me a quarter of an hour to cover the first twenty yards. Feeling certain that, whatever happened, I would be able to get in at least one more shot, my nerves — as happens in such circumstances — steadied up, and I rather enjoyed the few tense minutes which followed. The end of it was that I almost stumbled over the brute lying stone dead in a patch of tall, stiff, nettle-like shrubs.

The excitement being over, I shouted to the boy to come down from his perch; and he presently rejoined me as I was examining the carcass for bullet marks. I could find only my own chest shot, but the lad remarked that the foot was broken. Examining this I found that the inner hoof of the near hind foot was shattered, but no other damage was discernible. So much for the shooting of the African hunter! The pity of it is that the same sort of thing happens continuously where native hunters are employed.

While I was still examining the smashed hoof, a terrific commotion broke out in the heavy vegetation about forty yards away. The terrified boy crouched down against the dead bull's belly, and I knelt beside him: my rifle ready for a quick shot. However, as the sounds receded towards the river I ran quickly in that direction. The dense bush so impeded my progress that before I had caught up with the author of the disturbance, a tremendous splashing announced that the buffalo (for such it proved to be) was already making for the opposite side where I finally caught but a glimpse of it vanishing between the trees. That buffalo, which had remained near its wounded comrade, could never have been more than fifty yards away from us while we were in the forest. It had obviously been totally indifferent to either the sound of our voices or the shot fired, and this was not the first occasion when I have known buffalo to remain in hiding close by.

The dead bull was an aged specimen. Several inches had been worn off the points of its old rugged horns, but it was in good condition — despite the fact that its teeth were level with the gums. Leaving two men to attend to the skinning and cutting up of the carcass, I returned with the others to where I had last seen the bull which I had wounded.

This buffalo also had retreated into unpleasant cover, and it took me some time to puzzle out the correct spoor from a perfect maze of tracks everywhere. Guided by occasional splashes of blood, we held on: presently reaching the water in which, standing belly deep we saw the wounded bull — about one hundred yards away. I was surprised to find the poor brute still alive, seemingly trying to cool its burning wound. It was standing with its broad, rounded stern directly toward me — an unfavourable position for an effective shot; but fearing that it would go further into deep water, or perhaps right across into the marshes beyond, I felt obliged to risk the shot. The immediate effect of the bullet was to send the bull plunging wildly forward, causing a splashing through which it was difficult to see anything. Fortunately it turned toward a projecting spit of land which lay on the near side but across the narrow opening of a wide bay, and I had to make a wide detour through thick bush again to come within range.

As I forced myself through a strip of small trees and small, dense bushes, I saw the buffalo lying in the water about thirty yards away. On my appearance the bull leapt to its feet and at once came straight for me, uttering a series of ferocious grunts. A chest shot knocked it flat, but the game animal made frantic efforts to regain its feet: bellowing very loudly and viciously the while. My next shot put an end to its sufferings, and the boys soon gathered around.

This bull was in prime condition, and it carried an exceptionally beautiful pair of horns which I determined to save. Unfortunately, when I finally left the country the veterinary restrictions then in force obliged me to leave the trophy behind. As the beast was being skinned, I traced the course of each of the first three bullets, and found that each would have, in time, been mortal. This is a fair indication of the tenacity of the buffalo.

To indicate how these beasts vary in temperament, I may perhaps briefly relate another experience which occurred a few days after the above. I had fired at one of a troop of eight buffalo at full gallop towards a belt of timber. My shot was taken at three hundred yards, and the bull ploughed the ground in an astonishing cropper. It stumbled up quickly, however, and made off after its companions at a heavy canter. My next hurried shot was a miss, and before a third was possible, my quarry had vanished into the cover. We soon reached the place, and at once took up the spoor. After we had proceeded a short distance, the buffalo broke cover and, without any attempt at a charge, tore round in a wide half circle: the thickness of the vegetation eliminating all hope of a shot.

Eventually, after much difficult tracking, the hunter (who was in the lead) jumped round past my back, whispering that he could see the animal lying in a clump of weeds. With straining eyes I searched the patch of twining plants indicated; and although I advanced close, moving from side to side, I simply could not see the buffalo, and final- ly I told the man to try a shot himself. He stepped forward - obviously very nervously - and took a wavering aim: firing, so it seemed to me, only in the general direction. After the shot he instantly flew past me, screening him- self behind a thick tree. Simultaneously the buffalo plunged from the very spot at which I had been staring, and without any attempt at vengeance rushed wildly away. I examined the shrubbery where it had been lying and found only - a trace of blood, so I judged that, in view of the manner in which the beast had dropped to my first shot, the bullet had simply grazed the spinal column, probably just beyond the root of the tail. This seemed to be confirmed by a smudge of blood I had noted high up on the trunk of a sapling, against which the buffalo had brushed in passing.

Here, closing my tales of adventure with these game beasts, I would add that none, in my experience, has ever exhibited less resentment to injury than the last beast described. Unwounded, I have found buffalo rather timid than otherwise, but when injured they are full of cunning and truculence, and rank certainly among the most dangerous of game.

If some of the foregoing accounts indicate the awe with which buffalo were regarded by some of the local tribesmen, it would be incorrect to assume that such applies to all Africans. So far as the Department's regular hunters were concerned, the contrary was in fact nearer the truth, because the majority were men of wide experience, often fearless to a fault, and generally prepared to follow up and finish off wounded game. Moreover, many were capital shots. Unfortunately a minority existed who were both cowardly and poor performers with the rifle. These were weed- ed out as replacements became available, but many had to be maintained on the roll for too long a period. The fact was that the rangers had neither the time nor the opportunity of gaining a personal knowledge of the ability of individual hunters, whose camps were dotted along one hundred miles or more of the Fly belt. The only check on many lay in the number of tails — the only proofs of their performances — brought in as compared with the quantity of ammunition expended. This was not entirely satisfactory for many maintained a fair average without producing one buffalo tail! This was an important and significant fact. Important, because buffalo, which habitually indulge in partial seasonal migrations, are unquestionably the chief carriers of Tsetse (though other species of fauna play their part); and significant, because on account of their fear of these animals a not inconsiderable percentage of hunters — to my certain knowledge - avoided shooting at buffalo. When they happened to do so, it was invariably a case of long range shooting: resulting only too often in the beasts being wounded and permitted to escape, thus becoming a source of grave danger to other men operating in the area.

The following account concerns an instance which resulted in the death of a fearless and excellent hunter. This man, who was hunting alone, was passing through some heavy cover when he walked practically on to the horns of a buffalo which, in his opinion, had been wounded weeks before. He had no time to evade the charge, and the poor fellow, before he realised what was happening, was tossed high into the branches of a bush. There he must have hung unconscious for a while; but, on regaining his senses, contrived to reach the ground by falling through the branches.

The man's abdomen had been ripped open and the intestines were protruding. These he pushed back and held in position by stuffing the front of his shirt into the ghastly wound. With amazing fortitude he then began to crawl in the direction of the camp. According to native report he must have swooned several times during that dreadful ordeal, but he was still full of courage when found by comrades who were searching for him on the following morning. That he had escaped being attacked by hyenas, which will boldly attack a disabled man during the hours of darkness, was almost as great a miracle as the fact that he was alive and conscious when brought into camp. It was late in the afternoon before the truck, which had been sent for him, reached the hospital. On the following day he was flown to Francistown Hospital. For a week he seemed to be making excellent progress, and then a deterioration set in quite suddenly, and he died that evening.

The above was not the only instance to come under my notice, but I think sufficient reason has been given for the necessity of employing hunters of proved ability.

I have heard and read about incidents where unprovoked attacks have been made by bulls, which, if apparently uninjured in body, were possessed of savage, irritable or vengeful natures. Such instances are not common, and they are more likely to be met with during the emotional period of the rutting season.

With cows, the case is somewhat different. Those without young are both inquisitive and timid: but a mother suckling a small calf is a devil; and anybody either designedly or inadvertently approaching one closely will be almost certain to be charged.

Chapter 14

SOME BECHUANALAND SNAKES

BIBRON'S ADDER

IN the course of regular engagement in field work, one can hardly fail to have periodic encounters with various species of local snakes. I feel that some of my experiences with these universally dreaded reptiles may be of interest: particularly, perhaps, as reference will be made to the habits of several species of snakes seldom or never met with in the more closely settled areas.

Ngamiland, abounding as it does in vegetation of great variety, numerous rivers, vast areas of swamp lands, and an immensely heavy rodent population as well as a subtropical climate, should be suited ideally for the requirements of snakes. Curiously enough I did not find this to be the case.

Over a period of four years when most of my time was spent in field duties and hunting, I encountered fewer snakes than I had ever done over a similar period in any other locality in which I had lived. Thus when, after a sojourn of thirty two years in Northern Bechuanaland Protectorate (of which Ngamiland is the most northern district) I was eagerly questioned about the varieties and prevalence of snakes — particularly the dreaded Mamba — I have always had mainly to draw upon my pre-Ngamiland experiences which were gained chiefly in the Tati Territory of Northern Bechuanaland Protectorate.

In the following brief account I shall have to resort to the same procedure.

So many well-authenticated accounts about unprovoked attacks by mambas are current, and linger in my mind, that I cannot doubt the truth of these as applying to certain areas particularly in the eastern seaboard, and the Lowveld of the northern and eastern Transvaal. I believe, however, that such accounts can only apply to a relatively small percentage of the reptiles. It is possible, though, that differences in climate, and possibly the existence of little known subspecies may account for such differences in disposition as are recorded from widely separated areas.

Most men who have knocked about in wild country have probably experienced instances where normally mild-natured, or even timid, animals have acquired aggressive habits: and the same no doubt applies to reptiles generally and mambas in particular. Nonetheless, I repeat that unprovoked attacks by these snakes cannot be very common.

It has been stated that a mamba is capable of overtaking a galloping horse! Well, while agreeing as to the exceptional rapidity of movement attainable by this snake, I can only wonder how human beings have been able to survive when living in areas abounding with such monsters! Certainly during many years spent on the Tati — during each of which I killed several mambas — never did I see, or even hear of, unprovoked attacks made by these snakes, and very rarely did I meet one which was not anxious immediately to seek cover.

On one occasion, I killed a seven-footer with a small hand axe. This snake, sprawling across the branches of a small Grewia bush, could hardly have been attacked with a more awkward weapon, and I would not have attempted so foolish an act had I not noticed that a large bulge in its interior would handicap its movements. After its death, the recently swallowed prey was revealed as a young hare. Not long afterwards, another seven foot mamba was killed at my kraals. This one had engulfed a three foot long puff adder. Neither of these mambas was unduly vicious — certainly not more so than any of the cobras would have been under similar circumstances.

I was once travelling down the Ramaquabani River by scotch-cart, when, while passing an abandoned native kraal, I heard the shrill chirpings of a number of drongos, starlings, and other birds in a nearby tree. Suspecting that they were baiting a snake, I took the whip from the driver, and, fastening the *voorslag* to the back end of the thong, I walked to the tree and immediately saw a large mamba in the upper branches. I began to strike the snake, which at first darted from side to side of the tree. After receiving several strokes, it remained in one position, and, at every blow I struck, it flung seven or eight feet of its length towards me in furious but futile strikes: ballooning its throat with each strike in typical mamba manner.

It was an unequal contest, however, and a succession of heavy blows from the doubled whip so disabled it that it continually lost height, falling and slithering to the lower branches and eventually to the ground, where I speedily dispatched it. This snake measured eleven feet eight inches, and was blacker and more glossy than the average mamba: many of which, in the Tati Territory, are of a very dark brown hue. Its long, narrow head and other mamba characteristics left me in no doubt as to its proper identity.

While I was out hunting one morning, and walking through knee-high grass, I saw a really large mamba suddenly raise itself above the grass and immediately come darting straight towards me, raising its forepart higher off the ground as it advanced.

To raise the rifle and to fire required but a second or two, but any experienced person will know how difficult it is to hit a moving snake with a bullet. I missed of course and hardly had time to think what next to do when the creature disappeared down a chimneypot antheap some five yards ahead of me, as I had often seen these brutes do. For a fleeting moment I had thought that I was experiencing an unprovoked attack, but my relief, as the snake vanished down the hole in front of me, can easily be imagined. The whole episode occurred in a matter of about four seconds. Mambas can move at a speed that must be seen to be appreciated.

On another occasion, while out after klipspringer and walking across an immense "*dwaala*" (a

MAMBA

smooth outcrop of perfectly solid granite), I noticed a snake gliding quickly along about one hundred yards ahead of me, and at
right angles to the direction in which I was walking. A gleam from
its glossy skin reflecting the rays of the late afternoon sun had
attracted my attention, and I realised instantly that it was a mamba. It was obviously making for a pile of colossal boulders ranged
fantastically upon one another.

Withdrawing the heavy shot cartridges, and replacing with No.
6, I ran at top speed to prevent the snake from reaching its retreat: reaching the cairn before the snake had become aware of
my presence. It was less than ten yards away when it suddenly
reared up some five feet, at the same time puffing its throat. As
it remained, halted, in this position it formed a fearsome spectacle, but, with a double twelve-bore charged with birdshot in my
hands, I was not much perturbed as I interestedly watched it repeatedly ballooning and deflating its neck: a trick for intimidating
an enemy to which these snakes often resort.

Presently I advanced a few steps towards the mamba, and pro-
vokingly waved my gun in its direction. Apart from the continued
ballooning of its neck, however, it maintained perfectly motionless, and it might have been a model cast in blue-black steel for
any other sign of life displayed. Raising the gun I blew half its head
away and, as soon as the violent writhing had ceased, measured
it. It taped twelve feet seven inches and was the largest mamba I
had seen in life till then, though in the old home at Highlands we
had a skin of a black mamba which was fourteen and a half feet in
length. Of this particular specimen we had no record, other than
that it was collected in Southern Rhodesia during the Matabele
Rebellion.

Just a year after the above described incident, I killed another twelve foot seven inches mamba, and as this was procured under rather curious circumstances perhaps I may describe the adventure in detail.

I was farming at that time, and milking a large number of cows in open kraals. Owing to the improvident habits of the half-wild natives employed there, I found it necessary to dish out their rations daily, and it was the duty of one of the two calf herds to cook the milkers' food during milking hours.

The rations were drawn in the early morning, being weighed off in an old kerosene tin. In this tin, one morning, I noticed a large leguaan (Monitor lizard) which one of the herds had killed — these big lizards being regarded as great delicacies by the men, and frequently brought in. I merely noticed the corpse, and told the lad to remove it while weighing the meal. At the end of the day, when darkness had already set in, I was engaged in supervising the milking when the lad whose turn it was to do the cooking entered the kraal, and I heard him ask a milker whether the leguaan had been eaten during the midday meal. Receiving an affirmative reply, he declared that there was something in the tin which startled him.

Calling the boy, I asked where the can had been left and was told that it was in the hut. Telling him to follow, I walked over to the compound and, guided by a fire outside, approached the hut in question. Pulling a handful of thatch from the roof, I lit this at the fire, and with this homemade torch and armed with a couple of sticks, I entered the hut. The interior was - apart from the can which stood against the far wall, a blanket or two, a few empty sacks and a small three-legged cooking pot - devoid of contents.

As I peeped into the can I was astounded to see a large snake coiled up in it. Recoiling from this unpleasant sight, I dropped the burning grass on to the snake and bolted out of the door — grabbing, en route, another handful of thatch from the roof. Having lit the grass, I returned to the hut and found the snake whirling round and round its interior like a thing demented, even striking viciously at a crumpled blanket. As it passed away from the doorway, I jumped in and aimed several, but quite ineffective, blows at it. These caused it to turn on me with such maddened fury that I once again bolted through the door, expecting to feel its fangs in my back! Strangely enough it made no attempt to pursue me, and I lost no time in flinging in more burning grass. Repeatedly the snake struck at the flickering flames, but as portions of its sinuous length contacted the wisps of burning grass, it went careering off again.

Apart from myself standing prepared with a good stick, just outside, there was nothing to prevent the snake from leaving the hut, but again and again it streaked past the doorway, and I certainly had no further desire to fight it in that confined space and poor light. Eventually, just as I was considering whether to set fire to the place, the snake halted its frantic pace and began to crawl out of a small ventilation hole about four feet above the floor. It was now clearly at a disadvantage; and I rushed round and, with a few good blows of the stick, killed it while the greater portion of its body was yet in the room.

The boy, who had kept me supplied with handfuls of flaming thatch, now informed me that he had actually put his hand on the snake while feeling for the tin in the dark. Recoiling in horror, he had fled at once, and I can but add that his escape had, indeed, been miraculous!

What, I believe, is the largest mamba I have ever seen (though I had no opportunity to measure it) was one which I shot while searching for warthog. Accompanying me on this occasion was a smart Irish terrier. While I was walking along a disused road winding between small koppies, I heard the dog bark a short distance ahead, and rushed forward, feeling certain that it had found a snake. Sure enough, there he was, running and jumping round a great black brute of a mamba! I lost not a second in firing, and blew the monster's head away; but had some trouble in restraining the excited terrier from dashing in and worrying the wildly writhing coils. This was a big snake, but as I was anxious to continue my hunt I decided to return for the skin next day. Unfortunately when I next saw the remains, little more than shreds of skin and the broken up skeleton remained. What a couple of meerkats had been unable to demolish, an eagle must have attended to, because I found indubitable evidence that all these creatures had feasted there, and thus I lost an outsized trophy.

Near the same locality, not long afterwards, I was again after pig. The same terrier, and a smaller companion, chased a warthog past me along the steep slope of a koppie. I was unable to take a shot, as the Irish terrier was snapping at the warthog's ears, and the other dog worried at its tail. As the comic trio passed, I was horrified to see it blunder right over an outstretched mamba. Fortunately the latter was too startled to retaliate, and it darted into a crevice between granite boulders and vanished before I could shoot.

Early one morning I was travelling to a cattle post by motorcycle, and while passing along a somewhat sandy road — but making good time — I was horrified to see a mamba stretched right across the wagon road, not more than ten yards ahead. It was impossible to stop or to turn to either side, so I accelerated, and, lifting my feet as high as possible, passed right over the snake at perhaps forty miles per hour! The road was bad, and I dared not look back, but I feel convinced that the reptile had been as badly scared as I was.

Having arrived at the cattle post, I found the boys busy at breakfast, so I walked towards the sandy river to see how much water remained in the drinking pool. Merely some thirty yards beyond the kraals I perceived another large mamba moving fast towards a low mound. I flung a stone at it, but missed, and before I could find another it had disappeared down an anthole. Later, the herders informed me that they had on several occasions seen that snake, but that it had always eluded their efforts to kill it. Knowing the African's respect for the mamba, however, I had a shrewd notion of what their utmost efforts would have amounted to! The interesting point is that, though upwards of two hundred head of cattle had been posted at that place for two seasons, none was ever bitten. I might add that over the full period of my farming career in those parts, I lost but two head of cattle from snake bite.

I have, however, had the sad experience of seeing two grand dogs — both inveterate snake-killers — die from the bite of a mamba.

The one dog was a pointer bitch — an expert on birds. One morning, while searching for Francolin, as I walked through a bushy patch I heard her utter a single bark about forty yards ahead, and beyond my view. Dashing forwards, I was just in time to see a snake twist round from the dog's jaws, and strike her just above the left eye. Instantly she dropped the mamba, and I shot it a moment later. I usually carried a little Brunton First Aid outfit but unfortunately on this occasion I had forgotten to bring it. The house was half a mile away, and I began to run in that direction but the stricken bitch would not follow me, but simply stood with her nose near the ground, and with drooping tail. Pointers are no light weight, but I grabbed her in my arms, and, alternatively running and walking, made the distance in very quick time. It took but a few moments to gash open the wounds and apply permanganate of potash (my only remedy at the time), but in just under an hour from the time she was bitten she was dead.

The second case was rather similar, occurring in Southern Rhodesia. A fine terrier, belonging to my brother, rushed at a big mamba and, gripping it somewhere about its middle, unsuccessfully tried to shake it: its usual procedure with smaller snakes, squirrels, rats, etc,. I saw the snake bite the dog on the upper lip — an inch or two back from the nose. In this instance also the dog let go instantly, and the snake darted away into the grass where it disappeared.

I had no gun, but in any case my thoughts were only for the dog, which followed me as I began to run towards the house, distant about half a mile as in the last case. I had not, however, covered more than a couple of hundred yards (making rather heavy going of the steep incline) when the terrier fell over on its side. Snatching it up under my arm, I continued to run and arrived back badly blown. The poor little chap was already in the throes of death as I applied the permanganate. It had survived barely a quarter of an hour!

Those are the only deaths I have seen from mamba bites, and they were horrible to behold! I had the impression that death was due to suffocation, so probably the venom has a paralysing effect on the lungs.

All natives (excepting Bushmen) regard mamba bites as being invariably fatal, and I shall here cite a case which, though it did not come under my personal observation, emanates from a reliable source.

At Kalakamati in the Tati, a native who had been bitten by .a mamba ran wildly past several occupied huts, shouting: "*Deshule! Deshule!*" (I am dead! I am dead!), and sure enough he was dead within a minute of being bitten. No known venom can cause death so rapidly, and his passing can only have been caused by heart failure due to terror and shock. Many such cases undoubtedly occur.

On the other hand, animals, which lack the acute human imagination, succumb only to the actual effects of the venom. In the case of mamba bites, they will survive as long as — even sometimes longer than — cases of cobra bite, from one of which I saw a dog die in five minutes.

Mambas are large, heavy snakes: and it is reasonable to suppose that they are capable of injecting far larger amounts of venom than can their smaller relatives. I believe that scientists agree that cobra venom (of at least some species) is more rapid in action than that of mamba. The important factor lies in the volume of venom introduced into the blood stream.

During the 1933-34 Foot and Mouth campaign in Bechuanaland a native was bitten at the back of the neck by a very large mamba, but his life was saved by an injection of antivenin.

Mambas were by no means the only large snakes occurring in the Tati. Pythons were not rare, but three species of other large snakes though not numerous, were seen almost seasonally.

Banded cobras — great slayers of poultry, and more aggressive than mambas; Egyptian cobras; and a large black serpent with an ashy white belly, which, for want of a better name, we always

EGYPTIAN COBRA

called "Lazy Mamba". In size, these latter equalled mambas and could easily, at first sight, be mistaken for them. But the pale underside and much broader and rounder head unmistakably distinguish them. Moreover they are habitually lethargic, never attempting to move out of one's way.

Twice I unwittingly nearly stepped upon these snakes, and in each case I made a startled sideways bound to get beyond possible striking range! They seemed, however, to be completely indifferent to my proximity, neither deigning to hiss nor raise their heads. Not the slightest display of aggressiveness did I ever witness, though I would hesitate to deny that occasional "bad uns" might occur.

Habitually sluggish as they are, "Lazy mambas", when roused into flight through attack, can dispel all illusions one might have as to their torpidity. One such instance came under my notice, and I was not a little impressed by the speed which that snake attained.

That they are very venomous, I have little doubt. At any rate they are armed with two long upper fangs and carry a lot of venom, as I discovered by squeezing the sides of the heads of the only two which I have killed. Unfortunately, in those early days, I was not sufficiently interested to carry the ones I procured for miles back to the house for preservation and ultimate identification and consequently to this day I do not know with which family of venomous snakes they should be classed. A neighbour suggested that they were a species of cobra, but their lethargy and lack of ferocity

179

when attacked argue against that theory. In addition, I never saw one inflate a hood, as do cobras.

Only four years ago, in Southern Bechuanaland Protectorate, I encountered one of the most horrible snakes which I have ever beheld, and though I cannot be certain on the point, believe that it might have been an "outsize" specimen of a "Lazy mamba".

I was hunting for guineafowl one morning. Carrying a .22 rifle, I was walking down a broad, sparsely bushed depression — the upper reaches of the Moselebe valley — when I was attracted by the shrill chattering of one of these birds, some distance to my left. Walking in this direction I presently saw the bird standing on top of a mound covered with short couch grass, about one hundred yards away. I shot from my knee, and the bird fell fluttering to the ground, so after re-loading I proceeded leisurely towards the spot: well pleased at having procured a tasty item for next day's dinner. When I reached the spot I expected to find the bird lying dead at the back of the mound, whither it had vanished during its struggles.

For a few moments I could see nothing, then, about fifteen yards away, a black object came into view. It was not the guinea-fowl, and for a few seconds the dreadful thought flashed through my mind that I had accidentally killed a naked, native child. A moment later, and with almost equal horror, I realised that I was gazing at a monstrous serpent which even then was uncoiling itself and moving towards a clump of thicket to the left of where I stood. It was moving fast when I fired, but I had an idea that I had hit it. Before I could place a second shot it vanished in the covert.

There was no opening where the snake had disappeared, so I had to pass the spot where it had been lying and to make a short detour. Here I managed to make my way through the growth. As can be realised, I was nervously watchful of every bush and tussock of grass as I advanced, step by step. In less than a minute I came right on to the snake suddenly — and at much closer range than I liked! It lay some three yards away, facing me. Its head — raised about three feet above the ground — swayed slightly but continuously from side to side. For the first time I noticed that it was white below, but otherwise jet black. Though its attitude was not vicious, there seemed to be a mesmeric quality about the evil-looking head and glittering black eyes.

I was thoroughly scared of the brute, and cold shivers fled up and down my spine!

However, I aimed at that ugly swaying head, and must have grazed it as the snake flopped suddenly into the grass, and before I realised what was happening its tail had vanished down one of quite a warren of springhare holes. There was nothing to be done now, and feeling still decidedly "creepy" I got out into the open ground as quickly as possible. I estimated the length of that snake to be about fourteen feet, and the thickest part of it was equal to that of the calf of my leg. Having lost my guineafowl, and all further interest in hunting, I made my way back: reaching camp at dusk.

I called the men — among whom were two who lived permanently quite close by — and told them about my adventure, describing the snake. The local men immediately stated that they knew that particular snake quite well. For years past, they said, it had been seen at frequent intervals, but, being regarded as very dangerous, nobody had attempted to kill it. The name they use for the species is *Noga ya megobe* — literally, the snake of fresh water pools or pans. The place is called Moetsentse: area, Bangwaketsi Reserve; distance from Lobatse about forty miles with a fair weather track which I travelled by truck. Any reader desiring to procure a fine specimen is recommended to go there!

Other Bechuanaland snakes which are not widely known are several species of Bird snakes, and the nasty, very venomous adder-like Shield snakes, which burrow readily and emerge at night.

The name "Shield" snake is derived from the fact that these snakes have at the end of the nose a curious scale, shaped like a shield; and as this projects slightly upwards, like the snout of a pig, it is no doubt a useful appendage when the creature desires to dig itself into the ground. The bodies, which bear ill-defined brown and yellow bars, are rather thick. Specimens of three feet in length are rather rare: two feet being the average.

One of these snakes bit my cook on the foot, and the kick he gave it sent it flying about fifteen yards away where it was killed by the man's companion. Only a few minutes after the mishap, I injected a single dose of serum, and the next morning he was back at work. A few years later one of my labourers had a similar experience. He also made a speedy recovery after a serum injection, which as in the first case, was administered within a few minutes after receiving the bite. Had the treatment been delayed, no doubt recovery would also have been prolonged.

Other kinds of snakes, quite unknown to me, were occasionally killed. As there is often considerable variation in the colouration of juveniles, I think it is very easy for the untrained man to be misled, and I am rather ashamed to admit that I have never possessed a book on South African reptiles.

There is one species, however, which I am never likely to forget. It is known as Bibron's Adder. It is an insignificant looking black creature with a white belly, small head, and eyes hardly larger than a pin's head; but it is armed with enormously long fangs. This is another burrowing snake, and the only living ones I have seen were found at night.

In length these little adders hardly exceed twelve inches, and they have a thickness about equalling a lady's small finger. Whatever they may lack in size, let me assure you is fully compensated for by the quantity and the highly toxic nature of the venom which they secrete in their absurdly small heads.

While I was sitting at dinner one night, my wife, entering from the kitchen, announced that there was a small snake at the side of my chair. Glancing down, I perceived what I took to be a young Mole snake, and, remarking that it was a harmless creature, leaned over sideways and grasped it with the intention of throwing it out of the door. The little brute immediately fastened on to the forefinger of my left hand. As I dragged it off, it contrived to jab its fangs into the same finger of the other hand, hanging on like a bulldog. A sharp jerk dislodged it, and I crushed it under my heel. By that time I was already aware that I had been bitten by a venomous snake. Severe pain almost immediately followed the bites, and swelling set in very quickly.

While I sucked the one wounded finger, my wife did the same to the other, and I believe that this speedy first-aid probably saved my life. When you consider the manner in which the snake held on, I must have collected practically all its available venom. Less than an hour later I was in the Francistown hospital. Although no antivenin was at the time available there, the wounds were incised and a mercurial preparation applied. Just four hours after being bitten, however, two doses of antivenin were thoughtfully procured by the Sister in charge from my old friend, then Major Bob Hurndall, who had just come in from field duties. I received both injections simultaneously.

I do not think that I suffered from shock, but never before or since have I suffered such excruciating pain. The hands were so swollen that it seemed they must burst open, and I fairly writhed in agony. This continued for three days and nights, during which time I found it impossible to get any but a few hours of drugged sleep. After a week in hospital I returned home, and was treated by my wife, who was a trained nurse. Three wearisome months, however, elapsed before I was again able to use my hands and to this day the hideously contorted and weakened fingers serve as a reminder that it is wiser to leave unfamiliar snakes alone.

Though having a wide range, and often frequenting quite heavily populated areas, the Spitting Cobra or Ringhals is a snake about which surprisingly little is heard. Yet, in my opinion, it is one of the most aggressive of snakes, and if perhaps less deadly than other members of the cobra family, it is nonetheless dangerously venomous. I saw a medium-sized dog die in fifteen minutes following the bite of a Ringhals.

The Ringhals is, however, highly temperamental, and it is unwise to predict what individual snakes of this species may do. While one will quietly slink away, at the approach of an enemy, if it thinks that it can do so unobserved, another — to all appearances yearning for a scrap — will immediately rise with outspread hood to dispute the way! While a third may, without any provocation at all, send a spray of blinding venom into the intruder's eyes. I have heard of several such attacks, in one case an old friend of mine being the victim. Quite unaware of the presence of a ringhals he suddenly received a charge of "liquid fire" into both eyes, and could only stand in agony, wondering what had happened to him! Much the same thing happened to my youngest son when about four years old, only fortunately his elder brother was with him at the lime. Years later, I had my own turn, receiving a charge of venom in both eyes, and I understood then — as never before — what the little lad had suffered.

In my case, however, I had rather "asked for it", because I was tormenting the snake by hitting it with a damp towel while it was trying to make headway over the polished linoleum of our dining room floor.

As a young man, before my marriage, the differing traits in the ringhals always intrigued me, and I took an impish delight in provoking them in all manner of ways, often taking stupid risks. One day, while crossing a patch of eroded, sunbaked ground — carrying only widely scattered tufts of grass and a thick covering of fine gravel — I came face to face with a large and very black ringhals which immediately reared in a most threatening manner. I had no weapon with me, and stood watching it for a few moments — feeling, I think, all that the snake schemed that its aspect should convey; which, first and foremost, was a plain hint for me "to quit". Admittedly, the snake's attitude and expression was not encouraging of dalliance, but I was fascinated with the idea of teasing it a little. Then, in a flash, I got the idea. The gravel! Yes, by Jove! The very stuff!

Without diverting my eyes from the snake, I took a step or two backwards and, with my feet, soon scraped together quite a heap; while, by dint of slowly sinking to my knees, I filled both shirt and trouser pockets. I must add that the wind was blowing steadily crosswise, thereby considerably reducing the snake's ability to spray venom at me.

My first shower of gravel hit the snake, and its fury was fine to behold. In its initial astonishment at the stinging charge, it deflated its hood momentarily, and then spread it wider than before. It responded to a second charge of grit by rearing higher and hissing — a curious throaty sound; and then, with head held high, it shifted its position by a yard to one side. As it moved, I gave it a third handful with all the force at my disposal. Maddened with rage, the ringhals now darted several feet towards me, still striking stupidly at nothing. This sort of thing continued until my pockets were emptied, and I had to look round for more ammunition. Although the snake had made no more than feigned attempts at coming for me (an exhibition of bluff rather than aggressiveness, in fact), it certainly had yielded no ground, and I began to wonder how I was going to kill it eventually. I could see some useful stones about forty yards away, but I felt sure that as soon as my back was turned the snake would escape. Even as I considered this, I felt moisture spatter my left arm, and realised that the brute had taken a shot at my eyes. Either its aim had been faulty, or the slight breeze had foiled the attempt.

Anyhow, I eventually decided to collect the stones, and of course in the meantime the snake made good its escape. After quite a search I located its hole, almost completely obscured by a tuft of grass. This ringhals had afforded me some diversion, and the study of its actions had been interesting, and I begrudged not its escape.

In 1922 I had an extraordinary adventure with another ringhals, and I think this experience is worth recording.

An old friend, Mr. Lloyd Watkins, who is still farming in the Tati, was with me at the time.

Early one morning, the boy who brought in our tea mentioned that a calf had fallen into the well. Rather surprised, I told him that we would attend to it later on. "But, Moreno,, the calf is bellowing," he replied. This surprised me still more, as I knew the old disused pit to be over sixty feet in depth, and that it contained only about eighteen inches of stale rainwater, and a lot of toads. Anyway, having collected some boys and reims, we were soon quickly dressed and on our way to the scene of the tragedy. The sun was just rising as we reached the place, and we could distinctly hear the bellowing of the distressed little creature at the bottom of the well.

Above the well a crazy, rickety old windlass with a very rusty cable was still standing, so, after manning the handles of the contrivance, I ordered one of the boys to go down and fasten the calf to the kibble. This immediately evoked a cry from all the men, who declared that the rope would not support I he weight of a man. Angrily, I told them that the cable was strong enough to carry the weight of them all put together, but it was no use! They flatly refused to take the risk. There was, of course, some slight risk of the unexpected, so, on further reflection, I decided that I had best make the attempt myself. So, putting a couple of reims into the bucket, and with Watkins (who is a powerful man) on one handle, and a native on the other, I climbed in and was slowly lowered. Only on nearing the bottom did I realise that I still had my boots and socks on, so signalling for them to stop, I got out and removed these, shouting to those above to haul the bucket out of the way. The poor calf — which seemed little the worse for wear after its long fall — was terrified as I tried to fasten the reims, and it moved continually around, stepping again and again on my bare feet in the confined space.

While I was so occupied, I could feel my bare legs being touched by the unhappy toads, whose number was regularly increased by others falling from above, but for a while I took no notice. At length, however, a curious "gripping" sensation becoming increasingly evident on my leg, caused me to glance down. To my unspeakable horror, I saw a largish snake attempting to climb up my leg. I need hardly say that I jumped — and with such vigour that I managed to shake off the reptile: and then followed a merry-go-round comprising the calf, the snake, and myself as the only performers. After the first wild scuffle, I stopped to look for the snake, but in the dim light could see nothing of it. I struck a match, and saw a twelve inch length of "two by three" quartering floating nearby, which I eagerly snatched as a weapon of sorts. Then, near the calf's face, the snake re-appeared. Desperately I tried to strike another match, but the box slipped from my fingers into the water, of course being thus rendered completely useless. I could only stand still, waiting for my eyes to recover from the bright glare of the match, and presently I again made out the snake. It disappeared under the water with the force of the blow I dealt it, but reappearing on the surface it immediately struck at the calf's nose, and I had the impression that it had driven its fangs home. This set the merry-go-round into motion once more, but in a little while the snake emerged for rather more than half of its length upon a little ledge of the jagged, broken granite. I approached it closely, and with the little piece of quartering pinned it tightly against the rocky side. With my left hand I unclipped a heavy clasp knife which always dangled from my belt, and grasping the handle with my teeth, managed to open the blade with which I sliced off the reptile's head. Some idea of the state of panic that I was in may by gauged from the fact that it had never occurred to me, until that moment, to shout for the bucket! When it was lowered, I placed the snake and its severed head inside, and signalled for it to be raised to the surface. The calf was then safely raised, and I got out on the next trip, with a number of rescued toads squatting round my feet. I had various abrasions on my feet and legs, but could find nothing resembling fang marks.

Great patches of naked, bleeding skin showed on various parts of the calf — these must have been sustained during its terrible drop into the well — but it seemed miraculous that it had not a single broken bone. The little animal quickly recovered, and it eventually grew into a fine, fat bullock.

How long the snake had been in the water was impossible to compute: but the fact that both the calf and I had escaped being bitten seems to point to an immersion of several days, as that could have damped all the ire out of it. It was a four feet long ringhals.

Unlike other cobras, the ringhals — *Ipimpe* of the AmaXosa - does not lay eggs, but brings forth its young alive. Also, whereas all true cobras in my experience have smooth, glossy scales, the Ringhals has a ridge, or sort of keel, down the centre of each scale: this produces a rough feel to the skin, as well as preventing the fine gloss observable in true cobras. In other respects this snake has typical cobra attributes.

Just one further anecdote about the spitting cobra, and this is given to show that these creatures are born full of venom and devilry.

One morning in the early thirties as I stepped off the verandah I nearly placed my foot on a baby ringhals, which could hardly have been more than a few hours old. It was only five inches in length, but that did not prevent it from rearing and spreading a puny hood. When I teased it with my foot, it repeatedly struck loudly against the heavy boot I was wearing.

So small was it, that a young pet monkey which spent every available moment on my shoulder or around my feet evidently did not associate the snakeling with danger. Instead it evinced considerable curiosity, and, in typical monkey fashion, had to peer at it from every angle from a distance of only a couple of feet; and, had nothing occurred, would probably have eventually prodded and pawed it. Dearly, however, did the poor little beggar pay for its curiosity! The effects of the spray of venom which it suddenly received in its eyes were still plainly visible a week later. With its constant whining and whimpering, that little monkey was a pathetic object during those long days of its sufferings.

One sweltering night in 1913, I walked out to the watercart with a jug in one hand, and a candle in the other. Beneath the drip of a leaky tap, I saw a small puffadder. Whether it was after water or prey there was no telling, but as it seemed to be enjoying an occasional drop of water falling on its back, I was curious to see what its reactions would be to drops of another kind. Tilting the candle, I dropped quite a splash of warm wax on its back, with no effect. So bending over, from much nearer, I dripped another lot on its head. Inflating itself, it let out the air in an ominous hiss, and shot forward a foot or two. Here it remained stationary with its head raised slightly off the ground. Another dose of liquid wax on head and eyes set it off with another hiss, and finally a hard stamp from my heavy boot put an end to its career — as I must do to this chapter!

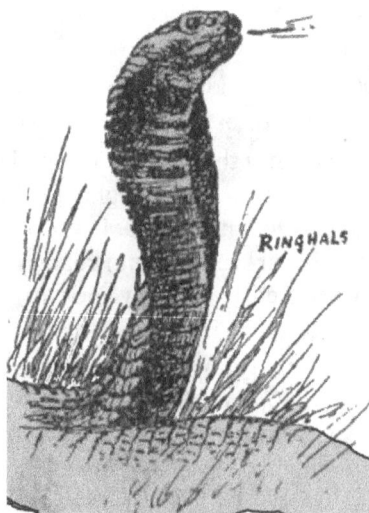

RINGHALS

Chapter 15

ADVENTURES WITH LEOPARDS

WHEN I set out to pen a record of some of my experiences - including encounters with dangerous game — it had been my intention to confine myself solely to such as took place in Ngamiland. It became increasingly apparent, however, that if I included former experiences which occurred in neighbouring territories, the records would be not only more complete, but possibly also of some value to new arrivals in the countries concerned.

This applies particularly with regard to affairs with leopards, because none of my earlier experiences with these great felines were repeated in a similar manner in Ngamiland — where, indeed, I had none worth relating. The following experiences with leopards, therefore, took place mainly in the excessively rocky terrain on, and adjoining, the old home farm in the Tati Territory of North Bechuanaland Protectorate.

In that area leopards were an absolute scourge to both my neighbours and myself. With monotonous regularity they took toll of our livestock and, exhibiting no particular preference, feasted royally upon chickens, turkeys, sheep, goats, calves, and almost fully grown cattle. They raided styes (no fewer than twelve half-grown pigs were carried off from one), runs, and kraals within fifty yards of homesteads. They carried off dogs; and one leopard

even absconded brazenly with a leg of mutton hanging under the front verandah of a neighbour's house. All this was, mind you, despite the fact that natural prey — baboons, dassies, klipspringers, and other buck, as well as guineafowl and francolin — abounded in the area!

If, in the late evening, a cow happened to calve in the midst of the maze of koppies, it was almost certain that the calf would be caught before it could be brought in with its mother; and small stock generally, if left out, were as often as not never recovered.

Dreaded most by the farmers was the leopard's habit of wanton killing: a habit which the brutes indulged in apparently from an innate desire to rend and kill, and possibly also merely for the sport of the thing. One evening before darkness had fully set in twenty six sheep and goats were killed or badly ripped by a pair of leopards: and of those which were not killed outright, only two subsequently recovered. Several of the victims had been sampled by the raiders, but in all no more flesh had been devoured than could have been provided by a single large goat.

In consequence of these depredations, those of us who farmed in that broken but otherwise interesting and picturesque strip of country lying between the Inchwe River on the east and the Tati on the west, waged perpetual warfare on the spotted marauders. But our painstaking efforts were rendered often futile by the rugged nature of the country. Very few leopards were eliminated by ordinary hunting with dogs, of which we had many excellent ones.

Mighty Redwood, Kiaat and other trees somehow found a roothold, skirting and even crowning the koppies. These koppies are composed chiefly of immense granite boulders, piled crazily one upon another: forming innumerable irregular caves, yawning rents and darksome fissures — usually screened by shrubbery. Many are difficult of access, and all form ideal retreats for such creatures as leopards, porcupines, ratels, dassies, pythons, and the deadly black mambas which there occur in greater numbers than in any other part in which I have lived.

Singly or in parties, we assiduously hunted the hills. Glimpses of the quarry were occasionally procured, but no worthwhile results rewarded our efforts. In desperation, and with slightly better results, my neighbours resorted to strychnine poisoning: but the daring raids continued, and, indeed according to my son (who still owns the old home farm) do so to this day.

The employment of poison — even on pests which were causing such heavy losses — never appealed to me, and I concentrated chiefly on trapping. Although, owing to their audacity, leopards are among the easiest of all carnivora to trap, I met with many disappointments due to the difficulty of procuring traps of sufficient weight and strength to hold the brutes. However, my efforts met with a measure of success.

Before relating some of my trapping experiences, however, I shall describe my first encounter with a leopard. Though this was rather a "tame" affair, it is not without interest, since it proved to be an instance where an adult leopardess was held at bay up a tree by two medium-sized dogs of the common lurcher type so favoured by natives, for a period of over one and a half hours! When considering this fact it should be remembered that dogs are largely preyed on by leopards, and my boys lost many.

I must explain that during my farming operations in that area, I always maintained — at a post near the extreme western end of the farm and just short of the Tati River — a mob of mixed dry cattle, including "in calf" heifers and cows. The kraal was distant about four miles from the homestead, and it was situated at the foot of a rugged koppie of considerable height.

The two men in charge of the cattle always kept a few lean, but useful dogs. With the aid of these they kept themselves supplied

with meat in the form of dassies, hares, klipspringers, mongooses, etc, all of which were plentiful in that rough veld.

One morning, one of the boys stationed at the Tati post ran all the way to my house to report that their dogs had treed a large leopard. Excitedly he urged: "The Moreno, must please come and kill the beast!" I commented that the leopard must surely long since have escaped, but the man replied that his dogs would never permit that to happen, and we would certainly find the leopard still treed, so I decided to accompany him back. My rifle being out of order at the time, I had to rely on a double-barrel 12 bore shotgun: so taking that, and a pocketful of cartridges, accompanied of course by my dogs Magnus and Midget (a pair of Great Danes) and a half-breed Irish terrier on whom the children had conferred the strikingly original name of "Little Black Dog" we were soon on our way.

As we trudged along, the man proudly described how his dogs had chivvied and succeeded in baying the leopard, which had taken to a large tree. While they were preparing breakfast they had suddenly heard the agonised, but quickly silenced, bleating of a klipspringer in a small koppie about a quarter of a mile from the kraal. The dogs had instantly rushed off, and were soon heard barking and baiting what they knew could only be a leopard. Snatching up sticks and an assegai, they set off in the same direction and soon came in sight of a large leopardess.

With the dead buck at her side, the leopardess stood on a large slab of granite: snarling and clouting right and left at the wildly excited dogs. The latter most audaciously snapped at her flanks, miraculously avoiding the death-dealing strokes, and so engaged her attention that the men were able to steal up close before she became aware of their presence. Seeing them at last, however, she uttered a vicious snarl and leapt clear of her tormentors: racing along the marshy area beyond until she reached more rocks under a lordly Redwood tree. With the yapping hounds in full pursuit, she tore up the great trunk stopping only when she had reached a heavy branch some thirty feet from the ground. There, with lashing tail and savage continuous snarling, she ferociously eyed the clamouring dogs.

As we arrived on the scene, the leopardess was still upon the branch, growling threateningly, though her attention was now somewhat uneasily transferred to us newcomers. Before I could get within reasonable range, she leapt from the tree and was away in a flash. But the dogs, now joined by my own, pursued close upon her heels and she was forced to seek refuge in another huge tree barely more than a hundred yards ahead.

On receiving a charge of buckshot in her ribs, she half leapt, half fell, from her perch; but desperately clutched a branch some ten feet from the ground and immediately started to claw her way up again. But her progress now was reduced to little more than a crawl, and my second shot brought her heavily to the ground amid the pack of eager dogs. In the resulting brief but fierce flurry, Magnus and "Little Black Dog" each received minor gashes, but between the lot of them they soon finished her off.

This leopardess was fully grown, and in prime condition. In fact her canines revealed the first traces of wear; so, though she was then neither in milk nor yet in whelp, she had doubtless mothered a good many litters. Her skin was perfect, and for many years graced an old armchair!

Early one morning, rather less than a year later, Simon (my head boy at the old Tati post) arrived at the place in which I was then living — some four miles further down the Inchwe River — and reported that a leopard had killed one of the big heifers. According to his story all the cattle had broken kraal during the night and had got away without anybody hearing them (knowing how soundly natives sleep, this is not surprising). As they rounded up the beasts at dawn, they had walked on to the kill, and he had immediately then set off to report to me.

I soon discovered that not only was the heifer the largest, but also the best of several "in calf" two and a half year old heifers in the mob, and the one I had particularly looked forward to seeing in the milking kraal.

As things were bad with me at the time, the loss was a very severe one, and I at once determined to avenge the heifer's death. I was too busy, however, to try to follow up the killer, so I handed to Simon a very heavy trap which I had borrowed from a neighbour, and told him I would follow later by bicycle.

On reaching the carcass, which had not been disturbed, early that afternoon I found that very little had been eaten. Deep claw marks on shoulders and flanks indicated that the leopard had jumped on to the heifer's rear quarter, clinging there while the great canines had sought and found the marrow in a single terrible bite from above.

The poor victim must have dropped and died almost instantly. It was difficult to believe that this was the work of a leopard, and not that of a lion, but all traces of spoor had been obliterated by the cattle which, in curiosity, had later milled around the carcass. Simon, however, assured me that there had been plenty of tracks when they first found the kill, and that the spoor was undoubtedly that of a leopard. Never before had I seen so large an animal killed by a leopard, and I could then see no reason why even cows should not be similarly victimised.

We skinned and quartered the carcass, leaving only the head and offal for bait. This we surrounded by a dense stockade of thorn branches. A narrow gap through which the marauder could enter was left on the side from which it had departed. In this gap I set the trap, to which was fastened — by fencing wire — a stump of wood about three feet in length. The trap and its appurtenances were completely invisible when we had finished, and Simon felt as confident as did I, that, should the leopard return, it would almost certainly be caught.

I was up with the grey dawn next morning and back at the Tati with the rising sun, and I found Simon awaiting my arrival. We hurried to the site of the kill, and, sure enough, the leopard had made off with the trap. Completely open ground lay only twenty yards away, and on reaching this the maddened brute had frenziedly raced around a couple of times, scoring the ground heavily with the violently jerked trap and log, and with its own claw marks as it had desperately fought to free itself. Soon we found the plate of the trap — wrenched off somehow by the violent battering it had received — and a little further ahead we came across the block of wood. Its heavy wire fastening had looped, kinked, and broken: and with the added freedom the captive had obviously raced forward, holding the trap high, and leaving hardly a trace of its passing. The above, alone, will serve to indicate the power and strength of a leopard.

Baboons had accounted for Simon's old dogs, and only a couple of pups remained at the kraal. Old Magnus (the only dog I had at the house and who, at the best of times, could smell little more than his own "scoff" dish) exhibited not the slightest interest in a

spoor many hours old: so all the tracking fell upon Simon and myself. Over the rocky terrain (his was so difficult that only a few hundred yards advance could be attained in two hours. Presently we reached broad outcrops of flat granite, known as "dwaalas" and here we were completely baffled.

Resting in the shade of a tree, I smoked and discussed with Simon our next move, when, suddenly, baboons on a tall, cone-shaped hill some six hundred yards away began to bark very loudly. In a few moments regular pandemonium broke out, and it at once occurred to me that the baboons had probably sighted the struggling leopard. However my companion disagreed with me. He remarked that the baboons made a great deal of noise every morning, and that, as the sun was already high, the leopard would in any case no longer be out in the open.

Just then I happened to glance riverwards, and noticed a native passing through the bush. He was three or four hundred yards away, and on being hailed he stopped, glanced round, but failed to see us in the deep shade, so I told Simon to beckon him. On his arrival, I recognised him as a lad who had, some years previously, been in my employment. With the offer of a reward of a shilling, I hastily scribbled a note and dispatched the boy with it to my neighbours, the Messrs. Wright brothers, who farmed a few miles further up the river.

These gentlemen, whose trap was attached to the paw of the leopard we were after, were rather aged batchelors who, like myself, had incurred grievous losses through the local leopards. In my note I suggested that they should join me, and bring their dog — an old veteran with pretty wide experience of leopards — to assist in tracking the brute. I then settled down comfortably, if somewhat impatiently, for the long wait.

Presently however such a violent renewal of defiant baboon cries: *Baaugh! Baaugh! Waa-hooo! Baaugh!* thundered forth, re-echoing among the rocks, that I leapt to my feet, shouting: "Come!" We ran, threading our way through the more or less open bushveld through which, as abruptly as a giant cairn, the hill rose skywards for some six or seven hundred feet. When we reached its neighbourhood, I told Simon to search carefully round its left side for the spoor, and to shout at once for me if he found it.

I myself took the right hand side, searching as carefully as possible, with the old dog padding along rather listlessly.

The baboons — ever distrustful of humanity — had of course now seen us, and since complete silence now reigned once more, I felt certain that they had already left the hill.

A pair of Jackal Buzzards, repeatedly and noisily swooping towards the steep slope hundreds of feet above, now attracted my attention, as I judged that their bold and magnificent aerial displays — as well as their weird, animal-like calls — were not in this case mere joyous frolic. I felt sure that they were baiting some animal. When buzzards are engaged in that sort of thing they are always worth watching.

Distant shouts, however, indicated beyond doubt that Simon had found the spoor, and I hastened in his direction. He was gazing alternatively at the ground and up the steep slope, and as I joined him, I saw, in the granite sand beside the leopard's pugs, the ploughed scar of the dragging iron. The trap was still holding. Old Magnus, well familiar with the taint of leopards, now evinced more than passing interest in the fresher trail, and preceded us up the jungly ascent at a pace which soon left us behind, though we managed to catch an occasional glimpse of him forging rapidly ahead. Presently he vanished from our view altogether.

After some minutes of such going, we stopped for a rest, and to listen. Not a sound reached us at all, and, as there was always the possibility of blundering on to the leopard in circumstances where, perhaps, a rapid shot might be impossible, we resorted to the age-old procedure of hurling stones at every piece of likely cover ahead.

Advancing in this way, we came in sight of a perpendicular buttress of solid granite, which we knew partly encircled the tapering peak. Here again the old dog came into our view as he was jumping to surmount the obstacle. The take off was too sloping, however, and after a few fruitless attempts he scrambled away round its base and again vanished from view. Avoiding the spot where he had failed as being the probable course which the leopard had taken, we struggled up slantwise to the left, reaching the step some distance further along. Here we examined the ground, and, flinging a few cautionary stones over the top, we helped each other up the seven foot face and rather breathlessly stood eyeing the next rise. Everything was silent, but there was a lot of grass and scrub, and I decided to wait for some further sign from Magnus.

From the summit of Mamabalane — the highest and most precipitous hill east of the Tati — distant nearly half a mile, sounded the barking of the baboons which had cleared from the hill we were now scaling. Whenever there was trouble, they made for that stronghold, which was also the sleeping place of the large troop that daily ranged over the neighbourhood. They had not been long in covering the intervening distance, and Simon said that they were laughing at us. Certainly there was a note of mockery in their distant yells which caused us to smile. The rascals knew us, as we knew them!

Five minutes elapsed, and as there was still no sign from Magnus (who, true to his usual tiresome habit, had probably been led astray by a klipspringer) I decided to push on without him. As a precaution, however, I told Simon to send a few stones into the cover ahead. A series of rasping snarls greeted the first, and my gun jerked to my shoulder in readiness for an immediate charge. However, rather to our relief, the clanking of steel on stone announced that the quarry was again in retreat, and we hastily advanced. As we doubled slantingly down the northern face of the hill, we caught a glimpse of the leopard moving — not very rapidly now — over the flat below.

I was still active in those days — the early twenties — and I kept close to Simon's heels. We had now obtained several glimpses of the leopard, while the clinking of the trap helped us to hold to the course. At the bottom we reached level, but dreadfully rocky ground and, hampered as I was with the heavy boots I was wearing, and the gun in my hand, I was hard put to it to keep up with him. To make matters worse, a false step brought me down heavily among some rocks, when, trying to save the gun, my knuckles were badly torn, also the upper portion of my right hand: while I sustained a deep and painful cut on the right knee. As a result of the delaying influences thus entailed, we presently lost all sight and sound of the leopard; and in that mass of rock trailing was virtually impossible.

Fortunately, however, we managed to keep the right direction. But a few yards further on, and very near on the left front, I suddenly saw the leopard balefully regarding our approach.

Apart from its head, the leopard was completely screened by a large boulder. The flattened ears, wrinkling muzzle, and exposed long white fangs, left no doubt as to its intentions: and as a charge was imminent I fired instantly at the exposed head. Simultaneously with the report, and as the beast fell over backwards, I distinctly saw its left eye splash from the socket, and, thinking that the brute was finished, I foolishly ran up without reloading and put a charge of No. 5 (the only size shot I then had) into the bulging neck. Instead of this finishing it off — as I had anticipated — it had exactly the opposite result. With a volley of savagely harsh grunts the leopard sprang up and immediately came for me, and I bolted — trying to reload as I ran. Unquestionably the providential appearance of Magnus at this critical moment saved me from a bad mauling. From the corner of my eye I glimpsed his rush from the lower side. I glanced round just in time to see him stop a clout behind the right ear which sent him rolling among the rocks — too dazed, temporarily, to resume the fight. His gallant, brief intervention enabled me to insert another cartridge, and, at point-blank range, I knocked the leopard over again — as it irresolutely snarled between its enemies — with another charge of No. 5 behind the shoulder. Between us, we killed it with rocks and stumps of wood.

The leopard was an enormous specimen, and although I am no longer in possession of its measurements, I remember distinctly that it exceeded the record weight according to Rowland Ward (of that time), by eight and a half pounds. Later I shot another of rather greater overall length, but as it lacked the excessive fatness of this one, it weighed a good deal lighter.

We now had the heavy task of carrying the prize to the rendezvous I had arranged with the messenger I had sent to the Wright's farm. Simon, who never stirred from camp without a chopper, soon cut down a light pole, and, after the leopard's feet had been lashed with bands of bark stripped from a handy Mogwana bush, we pushed the pole through and shouldered our heavy, swinging the burden. The final portion of the hunt had brought us back in a semi-circle to the Tati, so that in less than ten minutes we reached the spot where the messenger had left us. In due course my friends arrived and, though delighted to see the dead leopard, they were disappointed that they had missed the hunt. "J. W." (the elder brother) averred that he had never seen such enormous forearms on a leopard before.

The next day, after the leopard had been skinned, I learnt that the No. 5 pellets of my second shot had lodged in the sinews of the neck. Not one had reached the spinal column, but those fired into the ribs had penetrated the heart and other organs. As for valiant old Magnus, his head was so swollen next day that he looked more like a young lion than a dog. Though he had not been badly ripped, his wounds were festering: and it took a week's treatment before he was near normal again. In the following incident I was lucky to escape without paying some penalty for my foolhardiness.

By the almost completely demolished remains of another calf — killed in the same area some months later — I carefully set an old, heavy trap fitted with a longish chain. Resorting to a plan of which I did not wholly approve, I securely fastened the trap to the trunk of a small tree beside which the remnants of skin, bones and flesh had been found.

The following morning I collected a few boys as I passed the cattle post, and proceeded to the trap. We immediately discovered that the leopard had gone off with the trap fastened to one of its feet not long before our arrival, and for quite some distance ahead its spoor through the dew-laden grass could clearly be seen. What remained of the broken chain revealed that it had parted at a much worn swivel — about the only portion of its length I had failed to examine closely for weakness, and this omission led to a considerable amount of needless trouble.

However, there was nothing for it now but the usual tedious tracking, and we took up the spoor with little enthusiasm.

The leopard was heading directly towards the Tati, and where it had crossed a few square yards of open sand near a dwaala the

clear tracks indicated that it was a large male and also that its right hind foot remained still in the grip of the trap.

Nearly four hours later, as we were puzzling out the trail over granite on the final slope to the gorge, a sharp-eyed boy — casting ahead — made out claw-marks on the soft bark of a *Commiphora* tree growing just off the edge of the rock-strewn channel.

While I examined these, I presently saw the trap stuck in a fork some distance up, but there was no sign of the leopard. All the evidence suggested that the latter had clawed its way up the trunk, and while jumping through a fork had jerked itself free of the trap which had somehow become firmly wedged in the opening. In the course of this, the poor beast must have been seriously injured, because, as we were crossing the river a few moments later, blotches of blood bespattered the boulders in its bed, and this made tracking easier, and heartened us all considerably.

At last one of the men touched my shoulder, excitedly pointing to my left. One hundred yards ahead the leopard was visible as it passed from one patch of scrub to another, and I noted that it was only using three legs. Presently it burst from the scrub, moving round a few huge boulders perched on a dwaala, and, seconds later, I saw it disappear, seemingly, into solid granite! As we reached the spot, I looked into a wedge-shaped hole formed obviously by ancient subsidencies and displacement of the subterranean strata.

It was too dark inside to see far, so I lay prone with my face over the hole. After my eyes had focussed to the gloom below I gained the impression of vague outlines of rock and passages fading into impenetrable darkness. On the surface, the rock, though chequered with innumerable fine seams, was still apparently a solid, flattish platform; save for the small wedge which, on the displacement of the supporting rock, earth, etc., had probably slipped downwards — leaving a capital means of admittance to a safe retreat. Our leopard probably knew the spot well.

Taking my rifle and ordering the man to remain at the hole, I walked round looking for exits from what I felt sure was a subterranean cave of some kind, and found that the dwaala ended on the left side in a sheer drop of about fifteen feet. I followed the brink of this cliff, noting that along its foot the granite face was divided into immense cubes by horizontal and vertical fractures. Several of the great blocks were separated from one another by spaces as much as six or seven inches: just the sort of openings which dassies love, but incapable of admitting entrance for creatures much larger in size. After what I had seen from above, I was convinced that these openings connected with a hollow interior, and having checked that no larger exits existed anywhere, I returned to where the boys were waiting.

Most of us had seen the leopard vanish into the rock, and any lingering doubts of its actually having done so were dispelled by the sight of a long smear of blood several feet down the hole. It was generally agreed that the beast must be down below, but how were we to get it out? Since a large leopard had gained entrance by the hole there should be no difficulty for a man to do the same, and for a few moments I toyed with the idea of going in after it. Such a procedure, I felt on reflection, would be very risky.

One of the men suggested smoking the brute out, and with no other solution to the problem I told them to go ahead. With an abundance of dry grass, dry "Resurrection" bushes and brush all handy, quite a blaze was soon set alight down the hole, and for some time the men kept it constantly replenished. However, investigation at the edge of the cliff revealed that no smoke was issuing from the many openings in the rocky face, so I concluded that the faint breeze which stirred the foliage of the few bushes scattered near there was probably driving the smoke straight out of the natural flue in which the fire had been started. I told the men to halt with the dry stuff and to bring in a quantity of the green brush. Frequent additions of this caused quantities of black smoke to belch from the hole, but there was no means of discovering whether any of it was penetrating to the passage below.

It had been terrifically hot among the granite hills, and as we had done many hours of spooring we were all very thirsty. The nearest point to the river was hardly a mile away, and, as I judged that there was sufficient fire to prevent the leopard escaping by the way it had entered, we all made for the water, and were absent for about an hour.

When we returned, I could still see an occasional wisp of smoke curling from the hole, and I now decided to enter the place. The boys were aghast, begging me not to do so, but having made up my mind I walked to the opening with the four boys tailing behind. Each voiced his opinion as to what the leopard would do to me, but, adamant, I bade them be still, and sat down with my feet at the aperture. Rather cautiously I let myself down until I gained a firm foothold, and then asked for the rifle. As I grasped it, I wished it was my trusty old double twelve-bore charged with buckshot.

Sitting down, I held the cocked rifle across my knees, and waited for my eyes to become accustomed to the dimness within. I discovered that I was sitting on a small chunk of granite only about two feet in thickness, and that it may possibly have been the piece that once sealed the entrance above, but I was far too nervy to speculate much on matters of that sort. The fragment was lying on an apparently solid floor of granite - more or less covered with the droppings of small animals.

About six feet ahead was the corner of a great cube, on either side of which were narrow but high openings resembling small galleries, the far ends of each lost in inky blackness. A glance around revealed no stones which I could use for throwing ahead, so I hurled a small length of burnt stick: at the same time raising the rifle in readiness. There was not the slightest response, so I now advanced a step or two to the entrance of the second passage. No light entered here at all, and I felt for my matches. Of course I found the box to be nearly empty, and only now did I realise the extent of my stupidity in entering such a place without dogs, or a good light.

With the flare of a match I raised the rifle and, holding the light above my head, glanced sharply around for the reflection of eyes. Frankly, I was more than relieved to discover that nothing but shadowy rocks were revealed. As I advanced a few steps in the darkness, I struck another match, and yet another, until I was certain that nothing very formidable was in that section. Six matches now remained, and as I glanced back towards the entrance I was shocked to note that not the faintest glimmer of light penetrated to where I now stood. No odour of smoke was discernible, but the place reeked with pungent animal refuse. With the glow of another match I hastened forwards until the passage, narrowing rapidly, halted any further progress.

As the light flickered to its end, I ascertained, by feeling with my feet, that the opening was considerably wider near floor level, so, sitting down, I struck another light, and was able to see into a greatly widened cavern — many yards ahead. Plainly this could be reached by getting down and crawling through, but that (with only a few matches left) would have placed me in a very vulnerable situation. I decided to retreat from this unpleasant place!

I rose to my feet, with the last flicker of the match, and as I did so a faint but quite evident sound set my heart thumping wildly. With the flare of the next match I saw nothing but the faint whirling of freshly disturbed dust in the narrow space. Something had undoubtedly set the fine, powdery stuff in motion. I could smell it, and see it as a faint halo weaving nebulously round the waning light. When nerves are on edge, small occurrences can be jolting, and I ducked sharply as a bat flipped past my ear! With my vision circumscribed, my hearing was functioning at super pitch, and certainly I began to hear things! Fuller proof immediately reached me as the same soft sounds - nearer, more distinct and with a nasty slithering quality now, were approaching rapidly in my direction. A second later, something brushed against my ankle and calf. Lord! How I did jump!

The thing, whatever it might have been, was small — I was certain that it was small — but my scare was colossal, and it took me a minute or two to regain some control over my nerves. It might of course have been a dassie, or some other panicky small creature, but at the time I thought (as I still do) that it was an outsize leguaan or a very large snake, and such haunts of course are beloved of the dreadful Mamba. I had but one match remaining, but with that I lost no time in feeling and clutching my panic-stricken way as speedily as possible to the entrance hole: painfully barking my left shin and almost braining myself against a jutting rock in the process.

The only explanation I can offer regarding the mystery of the leopard is that either it had escaped during our absence at the river, or else that I had seen but a fraction of the extent of the underground cavern.

A somewhat quaint misadventure befell me as I was returning rather late one afternoon from the Tati post, riding on a bicycle.

Pedalling hard and making quick time, I came suddenly in view of an animal sitting with its back towards me and facing down the road. At first I thought it was old Magnus, then a baboon, and when I finally became aware that it was a leopard, I was within less than ten yards of it. There was no time to stop or turn aside; so, doing the only thing possible, I jumped from the machine. Both feet, carried by the treacherous gravel, shot from under me and in a flash I was on the broad of my back, staring between my highly swung legs!

Soundlessly, but with an enormous leap, the leopard was out of the road; and, looping its way through the rank, knee-high grass, it speedily vanished. How so alert an animal had failed to hear my approach which, over gravel, was by no means silent, I cannot comprehend; but the fact remains that it was completely unaware of my presence until I was on my back.

From another kill near the homestead, a leopard one night escaped with a heavy double-springed trap. Three boys and I followed it for some hours before we saw a portion of the trap projecting from behind a boulder in the entrance of a small cave. Cocking the rifle, I told the boys to throw a stone at the trap — which was only six or eight feet from where we stood — and a square hit turning it right over indicated that it was empty. I scrambled on to be huge granite slab which actually roofed the little cave where the trap had been jammed, and sat down in order to enjoy my pipe for a while.

Below us, about two hundred yards away on a flat stretch of ground, a mob of my cattle were grazing, and we could see the old herdboy, virtually surrounded by a pack of dogs, dosing in the shade of a small tree. After a while he arose, and began to round up the cattle. At the same time a slight crash sounded from just below where we were sitting, and one of the boys shouted: "There's the leopard! There the skelm runs!" I was unable to glimpse it until it emerged from the scrub round the foot of the koppie, and then it was running straight towards the cattle, making it impossible for me to shoot.

The herdsman saw its approach and promptly bolted from its line. The leopard raced straight ahead and right through the middle of the herd, with the old man's dogs close on its tail. It

was travelling fast towards another low koppie; and as it passed through some tall, leafless Mopanis about two hundred and fifty yards away, I got a shot, and knocked it rolling, but it was up and away with hardly a break in its speed.

Just after the leopard had reached the cover of the koppie, it was overtaken and bayed: and very soon all the dogs were creating wild music in that direction. As I reached the place, two dogs, badly mauled, emerged limpingly from the fray, and I could hear the rasping snarls of the leopard mingling with the higher-pitched, furious barking of the pack.

The scene that now came into my view was one of wild confusion. The leopard — on its back — was dealing death to every dog which came within range of its paws and jaws, and I had to wait awhile for an opportunity to shoot. As the brute collapsed to my bullet every dog still alive fell upon it; and in a final, furious few seconds its eyes glazed in death.

Two dogs lay dead, and another, whose front paw was dangling by a tendon, had to be destroyed. Not one of the remaining four had escaped injury: and since all that damage had been wrought in a matter of a bare two minutes, it provides an example of the swift, deadly manner in which a leopard fights when lying on its back.

I found that the bullet of my first shot had passed diagonally through the leopard, without damaging either heart or lungs. Where it had finally emerged, however, such a gaping wound had been left that it was indeed a wonder that the beast had been able to continue to run and to eventually end up in such a courageous fight. This leopard was a very large male, and it was the last I shot in that country.

In a broad, open area lying between masses of rocky koppies on three sides — on the edge of which my son Bobby's house now stands — leopards formerly accounted for many calves. This was usually due to irresponsible herd boys permitting their charges to stray into the broken, difficult terrain on either side; and failing to round them up before nightfall. Time and again a calf would vanish and I could but guess as to its fate.

Occasionally the site of a kill was discovered. Stomach contents and other fragments indicated that the killer had feasted to repletion and had then carried off the remainder to some remote spot — perhaps a cave where cubs were awaiting their food.

Once, in the fork of a tree, some distance from the ground, I located remains which had been carried for well over a mile. In that particular instance the leopard must later have found something more tasty; for, months afterwards, the dried out relic was still lodged in the same place! In such larders I have also seen the shrivelling bodies of baboons. As leopards are well aware that jackals and other scavengers are ever on the search for carrion, they rarely leave a kill which they have been unable to finish at a meal. However I can recall several occasions when half-devoured carcasses were needlessly abandoned, and two when the brutes paid dearly for their improvidence.

One morning my boys reported that they had found two partly eaten calves in the open area above referred to; and though the killers — there were two of them — were not in this instance accounted for, the episode was interesting for other reasons.

The victims were lying about six hundred yards apart. Strangely enough, they had fallen to two separate leopards which, I believe, were unaware of each other's presence in the vicinity. The kills occurred during a night following an afternoon of heavy rain, and the spoor was very easy to follow next morning. We tracked both of the leopards. One was a large male: the other an adult leopardess,

or perhaps a younger male; and their tracks never converged. In fact they had made off in exactly opposite directions. I really had bad luck with these marauders. On the following night each returned to its own kill: but, in each case finding a sprung trap at the carcass, both had discreetly retired without attempting to eat!

My disappointment had been great enough when I had found a large rat — almost clipped in two — held in the first trap visited: but it was nothing compared with that experienced when I found the second trap also sprung in advance of the leopard's arrival. In this case a poor old ratel was to blame, and my annoyance rather exceeded my regret! For hours the poor ratel had been trying to free itself from the steel jaws which held its doughty little fore-paw in a vice. Its own jaws were raw and bleeding from its dogged tussle with the merciless steel, and it was in an understandingly wicked frame of mind as it observed our approach. When we were yet forty or more yards away, it voiced several defiant "*gwaas*"; and it so fiercely contested every well-designed effort on our part to liberate it that, in the end, we were unhappily compelled to kill it.

One of the boys had a heavy mogwana stick with a head the size of a cricket ball, and I ordered him to dispatch the ratel with that. Easy said! The heavy blows seemed literally to bounce off that tough little head and neck, and the plucky beast, seemed unaffected by them. I grabbed the stick from the man's hand, and in desperation put all the strength I had into my blows, but the tenacious creature merely kept its snout between its forelegs, apparently immune to this determined onslaught!

The second boy then shouted to me to wait, and took the club from my hand. He walked round to the front of the ratel, and dealt it a shrewd, though not heavy, blow on the partly exposed muzzle; and, mercifully, that did the trick! Stunned, the game little honey eater rolled on to its side, and before it recovered a couple more blows on the same spot finished it off.

"Why did the leopard not kill and eat the ratel?" I asked the men. Laughingly, they replied that leopards knew ratels far too well to attempt such a thing! "All creatures, Morena, are afraid of *Tswane*," one added — and I believe he was right. Truly, no more courageous, harmless, or more justly respected mammal, than the Ratel or "Honeybadger", exists in the African jungle.

This is a long chapter, but I would like to end it on a note of tribute to my faithful old dog and companion — Magnus. The old fellow was already on the down grade at the time when he received such a clout from the leopard — in my defence. Although he took part in future hunts, he died before another leopard fell to my rifle. Always eager for a ramble, the old dog loved his outings with me above all else. I believe that his life's ambition was to overtake and kill his own klipspringer. If his utmost efforts in this direction were unrewarded, he was yet led many a joyous run amid the intricacies of the numerous, inaccessible koppies by the agile little buck. Though quite speedy, his massiveness of frame proved always a handicap in such rough surroundings. Baboons he ignored: and for their part they gave him a wide berth. For a big dog (120 lbs) he had remarkably good feet and staying power, and he could keep going throughout the day in the roughest country. Not of a hunting breed, he yet proved very useful — particularly when I had wounded a buck.

No matter how cold the weather, if I happened to be away for a night he would sleep outside my wife's bedroom door. Though normally extremely good-natured, he would then permit neither our own boys, nor any stranger, to approach. He took kindly to harness; and patiently dragged over long distances a light, double-shafted cart in which the children rode. He adored the children, as much as they loved and teased him! We all hold cherished memories of the old dog!

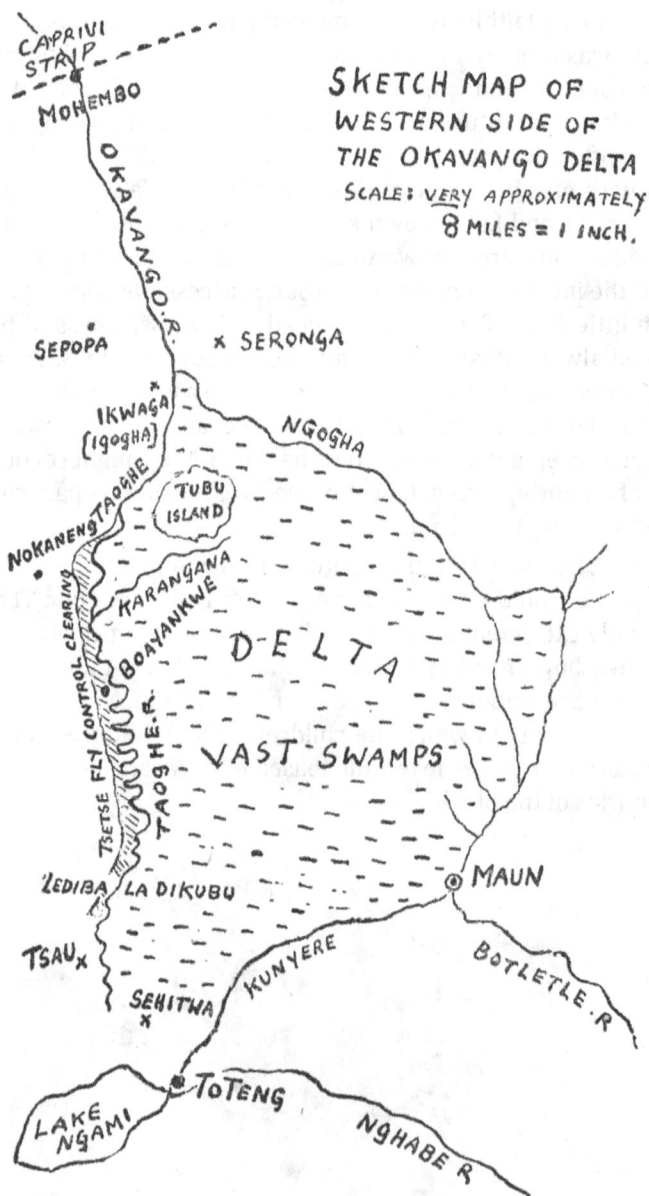

SKETCH MAP OF
WESTERN SIDE OF
THE OKAVANGO DELTA
SCALE: VERY APPROXIMATELY
8 MILES = 1 INCH.

CAPRIVI STRIP
MOHEMBO
OKAVANGO R.
SEPOPA
x SERONGA
IKWAGA (IGOGHA)
NGOGHA
NOKANENG TAOGHE
TUBU ISLAND
KARANGANA
BOAYANKWE
DELTA
VAST SWAMPS
TSETSE FLY CONTROL CLEARING
TAOGHE R.
'LEDIBA LA DIKUBU
MAUN
TSAU x
KUNYERE
BOTLETLE R.
SEHITWA x
LAKE NGAMI
TOTENG
NGHABE R.

Chapter 16

THROUGH THE SWAMP LANDS

The Okavango at Shakowe

I HAD always greatly wished to see something of the interior of the Swamp lands, so when the Assistant District Commissioner, Mr. Gordon Botha, invited me to accompany him on a short trip across the swamps to a place called Seronga, I was delighted. It was while I was enjoying my previously described leave at Mohembo that Mr. Botha arrived at that place and offered me this opportunity, and so I was free to take advantage of it. Seronga is in the well-settled native area on the mainland east of the marshes, and Mr. Botha's work there would occupy several days: permitting me plenty of time to explore the region.

Mr. Botha had given orders for a small fleet of mokoros to await his arrival at Igogha — some sixty miles downriver from Mohembo. We left Mohembo before noon, by truck, en route for Igogha; and on the way we passed within about twenty five miles of the Tsodilo hills, where many splendid examples of Bushman paintings are to be found. These hills, together with those at Kwebe and the Goha Hills near the Chobe, are the only eminences which I recall seeing in Ngamiland. Close to Igogha (where there is a small native village) we were suddenly confronted by a minor waterway some twenty yards across. The old headman, Rakarusha, came running up at this point, and, as a result of his assurances, we rushed the drift safely: finding its floor to be composed of smooth, hard sand. After traversing a second rivulet in the same manner, we soon found ourselves on the Igogha channel — chief and largest of the much divided Okavango.

A number of Rakarusha's men had followed us, and with their assistance a splendid camp, complete with roaring fires, was soon established. While this was being accomplished, Mr. Botha and I examined the *mokoros* moored at the waterside. Three of the seven craft lined up side by side were among the finest examples of native workmanship I had hitherto seen. Having done some boatbuilding myself, I examined them with the greatest interest and approval.

In general form, these craft differed little in design from the usual native dugouts. The characteristic much overhanging stems and sterns were present: but about these canoes there were none of the small natural bulges and hollows of the tree-trunks from which they had been hewn. Manufactured from the boles of huge trees, the lines of the craft indicated the work of highly skilled craftsmen. The sides of the best examples were about one inch thick: the inner curves following — as near as I could judge — the exact sweep of the outer circle, taken in cross section. Only at the bottom, for the purpose of ensuring better balance and greater strength, was there an increase of thickness almost imperceptible to the eye.

The entire length of about twenty feet might have been cut to a gauge line, so little variation in thickness was there; nor was there any undulation in that portion of the hull forming what, in an ordinary boat, would be the gunwale.

With a carpenter's eye I scanned the canoe critically from every angle, and found it to be nearly perfect symmetrically. With ample freeboard and extraordinary buoyancy, to travel in such a craft would have held none of the terrors I had experienced at Mohembo a few days previously. It is all the more remarkable when one considers that the only tools used by the native craftsmen are axes, tiny one-hand adzes, and the very useful *dekoras* for the finishing stages — all self made.

One old man informed me that some of the mokoros took as much as a year to make: yet at one time they could be purchased for five pounds each! I was informed that the best dugouts could still be bought for the absurdly low price of twenty pounds. If I lived permanently in the area, I would certainly never be without a good mokoro!

The favourite trees used for these craft are Mokuchon (*Diospyros mespilliformis*) and Mopororo (*Lonchocarpus capassa*). Worked green, neither of these woods are hard or liable to crack; but the latter, which rarely grows quite straight nor attains great sizes, has a fibrous grain difficult to work.

I have seen mokoros made of other woods as well, notably the Mukwa (*Pterocarpus angolensis*). This beautiful timber, known in the furniture trade as Kiaat, is not, however, really suitable for dugouts as the outer few inches of sapwood are apt to flake away from the harder, golden brown heart. Paddles are also frequently produced from this wood. These are of varying lengths — anything from five to ten feet being normal: the longer ones only being employed when the men stand to their work. When passing over shallows, the paddles are laid aside and long forked poles called *n'kashis* are used for punting. These light poles are never less than ten feet, and not infrequently they measure as much as fourteen feet in length. A punter standing in the stern can propel a craft at a considerable rate on a perfectly straight course.

Whether they are engaged in punting or paddling, much grace is displayed in the movements of experienced river men. Their actions are so free and easy that they are able to maintain them

for many hours without apparent fatigue, and I enjoyed watching the two men: one at either end of the craft in which we travelled.

I soon had a spoon trailing behind, and within less than two hours had boated several nice tiger fish, which the men were delighted to have. About half-way to Seronga we landed on a large island for the purpose of stretching our legs, and there found that stunted *Tsaro* (Phoenix) palms were in profuse bearing. We loaded several bunches of the ripe dates into our respective canoes. The tiny fruits of these palms are of a golden colour, and they taste much like the dates of commerce. I soon finished all mine with great enjoyment, but there is not much flesh on them, and the stones resemble coffee beans.

Presently the leading boats drew into a narrow, almost imperceptible break in the papyrus banks and were immediately lost to sight. Following, we soon found ourselves traversing what, I think, was an unused and much overgrown hippo path. This twisted and turned in an exasperating manner, making it difficult for the men with their n'kashis to force the lengthy craft round the sharp bends. After nearly a mile of this we entered a series of picturesque lagoons, covered in parts with masses of the most magnificent waterlilies I had ever beheld. Another small patch of Komo, on our right, resembled a verdant islet, and then we reached the shore beneath steeply sloping banks: immediately below the highish ground where Seronga is situated. Here all our kit was quickly transferred from the boats to the rest huts, which were to be our home for the next few days.

Here I spent some of the most enjoyable hours in my re-collection. Unfortunately Mr. Botha was too occupied with his official duties to be able to join me, so I was left to my own devices. In quest of tiger fish I made one long, though unfruitful, river trip: but finding the lure of the lily-emblazoned lagoons irresistible, I spent most of my time on those quiet waters. Sometimes I devoted it to searching for types of Lotus hitherto unknown to me; at other times I endeavoured to circumvent the fat, somnolent tilapia so often visible near the edges of reed and papyrus banks, but the fish scorned every type of bait I was able to procure. Then I frequently had shots at the far too numerous crocodiles, but with the usual disappointing results.

Occasionally I had a man paddling, but more often I was alone: forcing the craft through acres and acres of water-lilies which formed an unforgettable impression. Among these was a large species which I had never previously seen. Blooms up to nine inches across were common, and they differed somewhat in form from the funnel-shaped calyces of the more common types. With rounded tips, inclining slightly downwards, the snowy petals, which frame a golden heart, form slightly bowl-shaped blooms of great beauty. Their large, oval, floating leaves with crinkly edges lend additional charm to the stately flowers which rise well above the surface of the water.

Favouring deeper water than other varieties, these lilies are generally encountered in pure, unmixed clumps. My attempts to procure bulbs or roots were unsuccessful, but the many stems which I pulled up were often as much as ten feet in length. It was not uncommon to find minute forms of molluscan life adhering to the maroon-coloured undersurface of the large leaves.

The more common mauve, purple, and pink varieties of lotus bloomed everywhere in considerable quantity, and their sweet perfume suffused the air. In addition I discovered other species which bore exquisite, fragrant sulphur-coloured blooms. Growing plentifully in the shallows, and along winding backwaters, were several varieties of pygmy lilies. Dainty wee things of surpassing loveliness when closely examined: intriguing with their infinite range of floating cells. Magenta-coloured convolvuli occur on the papyrus platforms, twining and binding together the smooth round stems.

Bird life, curiously enough, was on the whole scarce: though such fowl as darters, "fish gluttons", herons, scattered teal and geese, etc., were seen daily, and the squabbling of lily-trotters (African Jacana) was audible almost continuously on the lagoons.

The return journey to Igogha was made by way of the marshes. For a mile or two the route chosen passed over some of the lagoons which I had already explored, and similar ones of considerable size had to be traversed before we reached the grassy marshes ahead. Here the man in the leading craft, having to break a trail through dense growth resembling endless fields of sown crops, had all the heaviest labour: the rest of us following exactly in his track. Here and there traces of old mokoro paths were visible, but this route was obviously seldom used.

Great numbers of tiny islets — actually immense termite hills — each canopied with thickets of stunted wild date palms and an occasional tree or two, were scattered across the watery wastes as far as the eye could reach. Without the aid of the sun or prevailing winds it would be easy to lose one's bearings in such an invariable landscape. When one remembers that over and above the vast areas perennially flooded, the annual inundations create many thousands of additional square miles of swamp lands, some idea of their extent can perhaps more readily be visualised. What we were passing over then was merely a narrow overflow.

Since I have always been interested in fish and aquatic life generally, I have made an invariable practice of trying to investigate such life in all waters traversed. On our numerous halts, therefore, I took the opportunity to open the grass with both hands in order to peer into the clear, shaded water. I never failed to observe fry: sometimes in parties of perhaps a dozen, at others in small shoals; and the young of tilapia species invariably predominated, though other types were present. These small fish evidently sought such sheltered surroundings both for the purpose of feeding on organisms on the vegetation and also as protection from the marauding adult fish and other enemies which perpetually prey on them. These hordes of young fish largely account, of course, for the huge concentrations of water fowl which occur when the inundations have subsided. Even the birds cannot cope with all the food: much remains for mammalian and insect life to prey on.

Fish are commonly supposed to travel upstream only. This certainly does not apply in Ngamiland, for with the arrival of the first waters, periodic rivers which have been completely dry for months are immediately stocked with fish in variety. Of these, myriads perish later when, after the flow has ceased, the water remaining in pools is rapidly absorbed by the thirsty Kalahari sands!

I measured the water depth at frequent intervals with a stick carried for this purpose, and I found that, excluding the frequently quite deep channels, the average depth was about two and a half feet. The bottom was invariably of firm silt.

A problem which has always puzzled me is how the termites so effactually seal off their abodes against the ingress of water. The heart of these nests, where the queen is located and nurtured, is about six feet below ground level. Where only the upper portion of the mounds are above water, it seems inconceivable that mere earth and the saliva of the creatures can exclude moisture, or at least extreme humidity. Tens of thousands of the huge mounds are scattered over the marshlands where they are subject to conditions as described. How is it done? My own guess is that there are many chambers within the nests which are so constructed that compressed air prevents water from rising above the balance of pressure exerted by the respective elements.

This, however, in no way explains a further mystery which intrigued me. I was peering for fry, when I saw a small party of rather large black ants running in and out of a broken-off reed which projected several inches above the water, but nowhere near the peak level of the floods. Where, and how, had these ants existed when the water was at its highest level?

Abundant evidence that the water level was dropping was apparent in the numerous small channels carrying rapid streams in various directions. One we had left recently was flowing towards Seronga. Another we met shortly after was moving in exactly the opposite direction, and others were crossed at right angles. Faint variation in the plain levels were of course responsible for this phenomenon, and, it may be added, the same applies to some of the larger streams which at times definitely flow in the wrong direction!

The mighty Okavango was falling, and the waters it had poured across the low-lying tracts were being rapidly drawn to its bosom once more. In but a couple of months the huge, grassy marshlands would revert to the alluvial flats, beloved of lechwe, reedbuck, etc.

While we were crossing the marshes, numerous nests were observed of, presumably, one of the numerous species of warbler. These warblers, being solitary fellows, do not build in communities as do so many of the weavers: but their nests, though smaller, greatly resemble those of the latter. The nests seen, which were invariably attached between two reeds or sedges, were abandoned, and I was unable to catch a glimpse of the original owners. I managed to secure a fine specimen which finally reached the Albany Museum undamaged.

We passed several thinly wooded islands of fair size, and in due course reached a narrow, deep channel along which the water was fairly racing. After a while this became closed in by banks of papyrus, and in one place (quite near the main stream) we saw wet and broken vegetation where a party of hippo had emerged from the water only a few minutes before. The stream was so narrow at this point, that the canoe-men could easily reach either margin with their nkashis; and I could imagine nothing but dire results, if, on rounding one of the numerous sharp bends, we had suddenly encountered the huge beasts blocking our way! The possibility of such meetings are among the greater of the risks, thrills and fascination inseparable from travel by native craft anywhere within the swamps area.

A few moments later we sped suddenly, at right angles, into the broad Igogha stream: feeling not a little relieved to be out of that rather unpleasant channel, with its constricting papyrus and rushing water.

* * *

The complicated river system of Ngamiland has always fascinated me. Few of the available maps provide a true picture of the intricate network of channels, spillways, and backwaters which alternately convey the great floodwaters annually borne inland by the mighty Okavango. Without complete aerial surveys, a lifetime might be spent in mapping and exploring; and even then, owing to year to year variation in the local directions of the water flow, some confusion would still exist.

Both Andrew Wright and Hardy Pretorius provided a lot of information on the subject, while Martinus Drotsky also had considerable knowledge of the swamp lands. More information was gained by assiduous questioning of the river folk, the Mokuba, but all this suggested that, though the general flow of the yearly inundations was towards the south east, many waterways might weave a serpentine course in an opposite direction. A frequent cause for this is that floating islands, great man-made rafts and other flotsam create bottlenecks which force the water to bank up and escape at the next lowest point: thus forming new, unrecognised and unnamed lagoons and streams which sorely perplex guides confident in their knowledge of the mysterious region! As these spillways flood the marshes, they form a perfect maze:

becoming most confusing, particularly on cloudy days when the sun's guidance is not available. When following such a stream in search of a suitable crossing place, I have, in half an hour and in the course of a single mile, literally walked the compass round — ultimately finding myself back near my starting point!

Such waterways finally sort themselves out: and at intervals they unite with other channels; but this may be over one hundred miles or more. United, they become the well-defined streams marked on the maps; but they come into spate only after the upper "feeders" have completed the flooding of the greater marshes. Then, in their lower reaches, they resolve into the principal channels which drain away that vast accumulation of water.

Of these rivers, the Boro (which in its upper reaches is known as the Chwaralangwana) is the largest, or at least bears the heaviest volume of water.

The Khawapa, Santantadibe, and Gomoti — to mention only the more important — are all large periodic rivers: though the last-named is much choked up in parts by a species of water-loving Fig, from which the stream derives its name. With the exception of the Khawapa and a few of its minor overflows, these rivers all converge on the Thamalukane.

The Thamalukane, which passes by Maun, forks about fourteen miles beyond that place. The eastern branch, carrying the greater volume, becomes the Botletle. The remainder, flowing in a single channel, is generally known as the Nghabe - though its name is in fact changed locally every ten or twelve miles! It finally pursues its course south westerly towards Lake Ngami, though for a considerable number of years no water by that stream has ever reached that depression. As I write this, however, in this year of 1954, there has been a return to earlier conditions. A large volume of water is entering the lake, via the Nghabe channel which has risen to a higher level than it has done in living memory! A century ago, Livingstone, Baldwin and other travellers enthused over the Nghabe as a very considerable river.

Other overflows from the swamp lands occasionally reach the lake by way of the Xnaragha, Matshe and Xnudum rivulets; but the thirsty lake floor, and evaporation, absorbs them in a very short time.

It is often asked whence all this water comes, and where it goes? In the Angola highlands there is a rainfall averaging about one hundred inches per year. Much of this is carried westwards to the Atlantic Ocean by the Cunene River; but the Okavango River, draining the S. E. Watershed, brings inland an enormous volume, much of which is dissipated in the swamps at its delta: while the Kalahari sands also absorb a considerable amount. Periodically, too, the Botletle River receives its quota. This latter is sufficient occasionally to fill, at its eastern extremity, an immense reed-choked marsh known as Lake Kamadu, whence rare overflows reach the great Makarikari Salt pan.

At the peak of these off-season inundations, the regular channels which score the level, sandy country, are in places quite incapable of coping with the formidable onrush which - surging over low banks — spreads over huge areas. This occurred on a major scale in my own area shortly after my return from Seronga.

I was able to observe the progress of the water from its first appearance, and soon came to regard it as an unmitigated nuisance! When the road to headquarters was cut off, another route, half as long again and containing much sand, had to be used. Next, several sections of the fly rounds, where local tribesmen informed me no running water had been seen in the memory of the oldest inhabitants, became inundated. This necessitated annoying and in some cases undesirable deviations in the surveyed lines. In addition to the above, our regular track to Goboxlo, at that time frequently used by the natives cutting thatch grass, was also cut off. So, with waxing floods, we found ourselves on each succeeding journey being forced further and further outwards. This continued for over a month; by which time the original track was in some parts as much as a mile away, and months elapsed before it could be re-utilised.

As elsewhere, the new water, on reaching dried up channels, advanced at a crawling pace. But a tiny trickle, snaking its way along at a speed of only a few hundred yards in twenty four hours, will, in a few days, assume the magnitude of a sizeable river with a strong current. The formidable wastage, through absorption by the deep sands, will however be readily imagined. It was a revelation to me!

I was walking along part of a sandbelt threatened by advancing water one day, and noting some tracks at the entrance of an ant-bear hole, I peered down to examine them.

To my amazement I found that the hole was partly filled with water, which had evidently attracted a thirsty jackal. Had the creature advanced but another hundred yards it could have slaked its thirst from surface water which was slowly, but surely, encroaching in the direction of the burrow. Within a few days the whole of the immediate vicinity had been transformed into a shallow, grassy lake.

A long while after this, after a journey of several hundreds of miles across the marshes, particularly that portion called "the Flats" which lies to the east of Taokwe, it occurred to me that a single canal of about thirty three miles, between the Taokwe and the junctions of the Chwaralangwana and Khwapa Rivers, on a straight bearing from the Tsodilo Hills, might well drain away all surplus water from the vast region south of the line. In a few years this should make available to cultivation, and irrigation, hundreds of thousands of acres of alluvium — right at the head of an unfailing water supply!

The meandering nature of the deltaic streams, reducing enormously the velocity of the annual onrush of water, is mainly responsible for the ever-recurring blockages and wastage. But if the waters were confined to a single, straight channel the above might be prevented: and if such a channel was gradually bulldozed from the junction end, an effective canal could be completed at comparatively low cost. Such a scheme would in no wise interfere with, but rather enhance, the supply of water necessary to the streams further to the east and south east.

Wherever one travels along the larger and more permanent rivers, a great variety of aquatic vegetation, other than the usual papyrus, reeds, and sedges, will be noticed. Unfortunately I am unable to name the species of these interesting growths: many of which are moss-like in appearance while others have thick, fluted stems, armed at their edges with fat, soft spines. Others again resemble ferns, and nearly all rise just to the surface of the water, where they form a sort of film.

Where this vegetation abounds, it forms the favourite haunt of the richly coloured greater African Jacanas. These graceful birds, their long legs provided with incredibly long, narrow toes especially adapted to the purpose, run lightly over the surface in search of various forms of insect and molluscan life and the young of various fishes. In the shallower reaches, the vegetable growths grow so densely that it is difficult to wade through them. Waterlilies force their way through the tangled mass: their great round leaves and fragrant blooms beautifying the surface of such otherwise repellent backwaters.

The hosts of waterfowl are a perpetual delight. The jacanas predominate: and sooner or later you will observe one chasing from its own special haunt a smaller cousin: the Lesser Jacana, more sober-hued than its larger relative, and whose periodic intrusions on the latter's domain are always speedily noticed and resented!

Coots and gallinules, waterhens and rails abound; and the little Black Crake, with scarlet legs and yellow-green bill, is heard uttering his chattering and strangely animal-like growling calls from reed brakes and rushes more frequently than he is seen.

There are numerous other birds. Terns range tirelessly and silently, hawking their dinner over the water — rarely settling down. In the lower branches of the trees, hump-backed rail and night-herons will be noticed in company with bitterns, darters, and cormorants — the latter often drying their plumage with outstretched wings.

Kingfishers in great variety, from that living gem the little crested Malachite to the great speckle-backed and rufous-chested Giant Kingfisher which attains a length of about eighteen inches, are always in evidence as they dive fearlessly into the swarming hordes of young fish. Their pleasant chattering cries resound everywhere.

One can follow no channel for any distance without glimpsing the grand, regal African White-headed Fish Eagle. He will probably be perched on the upper branches of a great riverside tree, but his haunting, attractive call of "WHEE-WHEE-WHEEOH" is constantly audible: and indeed no sound is more typical of the rivers, lakes, and swamps, of Africa.

Crocodiles often remain in the lagoons until the latter become quite shallow. Perhaps they instinctively realise that opportunities for grasping warm-blooded prey increase as the waterholes become lower and fewer; or perhaps they remain to finish off the quantities of barbel and other fish which yearly allow themselves to be trapped by remaining in favoured pools until the last means of egress have vanished. One year very many barbel, up to twenty pounds in weight, were speared by our fencing boys using wire-pointed lances. What was formerly an extensive lagoon had dwindled to a pool about fifty yards across, and nowhere more than five feet deep.

This pool was not far from a camp then occupied by Odendaal, who was engaged in the construction of a new fence. I frequently bathed in the pool, and had felt the big catfish thumping against my legs.

One evening a solitary boy, intent on a fish supper, entered the water and was badly mauled about the legs by a seven foot crocodile. He was a long while in hospital, but he would never even have reached there had he been attacked by a fullgrown croc! Despite the fact that a number of men had bathed there each evening after work, it transpired that two young crocodiles had remained in the pool. One was accounted for — I saw its skin — but the other managed to escape.

The natives living near the swamps, outside the fly area, are accustomed to plough right to the water's edge, as the inundations recede. This is sometimes continued right across the shallower waterways, and in this humus soil quite heavy crops are raised. One year, while I was in Ngamiland, it happened that the following season's flood waters arrived earlier than usual, and large areas of ripening corn were caught by the new water. In many cases reaping was carried out from mokoros, and in the shallower parts by women and children wading. During that season there were three reported cases of reapers being mauled in their lands, and possibly others occurred as well: crocodiles can be very daring!

Some years earlier, while in Rhodesia, I had a very unpleasant experience with a crocodile. I was spending a vacation with my brother and sister-in-law, and during my stay they arranged a long trip to an old favourite spot on the Hunyani River, near Kutama Mission, for a few days fishing. Unfortunately for us, the river was in partial flood, and our sport was largely confined to such fish as barbel and eels. Tiring of this one afternoon, I took up rny rod, and with a few spoons in my pocket, made my way a mile or two up-river: spinning for tiger wherever the vegetation would permit me to do so. Along the area which I covered, the river is divided into eight or nine narrow channels. Seeking for suitable casting places, I crossed a number of these where they raced between rocks, and in some cases by the aid of trees. The water was too turbid for tiger fish, however, and my total bag consisted of two small ones.

On my return journey, I recrossed, as I thought, all the channels I had passed on the forward journey, but when I finally arrived opposite the camp I found that I was cut off from it by one more stream. It was then dusk, and I felt disinclined to scramble back along the broken river bed between the channels, so I closely examined the one in front of me. It was deep, and running like a millrace, but scarcely more than seven feet across. I was confident that I could jump it without any special effort, so, throwing the rod across, I made the attempt. The sodden bank gave as I took off, and I landed in the water on the far side. Instantly clutching a bunch of reeds, and with the strength of a badly scared man, I dragged myself to the edge, where, with handholds on roots and branches, I pulled myself up the steep incline from the water. I was only just in time, for, as I achieved the first few feet, a snap like a pistol-shot with a tremendous commotion in the water intimated that a croc had only just failed to grab me by the foot.

225

I was still trembling when I reached the camp!

No account of the swamp regions of Ngamiland would be complete without some details about the Papyrus which covers scores of miles of the marshlands, the more sluggish streams, and the margins of the larger, permanent rivers. The plant is a giant sedge. Its stems, which are up to three inches thick at the base, are smooth and round and taper gently to the top, where they terminate in a feathery-looking globular seed head from ten to sixteen inches in diameter. The average height of the growth is seven or eight feet, but in favourable places it may attain a height of as much as fourteen feet.

This is the same papyrus whose substance formed the material on which the ancient Egyptian writings were made, and which played such an important part in the ancient culture of that land. Apart from the Nile, however, many more southern African rivers possess their own beds of this peculiar plant, not least of these being the Okavango — particularly in the delta area. Papyrus is indeed a strange type of vegetation: equally at home floating on tropical waters or taking root wherever deposited by receding floods.

The plant is amazingly buoyant: being composed of myriads of tiny air cells which permanently exclude water. Hundreds of square miles of it exist, packed on the surface of the great river and its widely spreading channels, lagoons, and marshes. In parts its complicated, floating root system is so densely packed and interlocked that natives can cross deep, permanent streams with animal-drawn sledges! Game use it in the same way, and I have seen lechwe frollicking noisily on platforms a long distance from terra firma. Hippo, crocodiles, otters, pythons, and waterfowl in variety, find, amid the vast floating masses, conditions ideally suited to their modes of life.

Migrating river folk make gigantic rafts of the stems. These are formed merely by piling the stems crosswise to a thickness of several feet, to a size depending on the requirements of the builders. Some of these are so large that huts are built on them which, with mud-covered fire places, provide all the requirements of family parties — including space for fowls and a goat or two! Naturally such rafts can be manoeuvered down current only; and when their purpose has been served they are abandoned, and have thus been known to cause serious blockages in narrow but vital channels.

Great chunks sometimes break away from the floating packs. In area these may be equal to that of a small room or they may be as large as a big house, and they float slowly away.

I have seen several of such large "floating islands" — even as far down as the Botletle River: where, indeed, I encountered the first two I had ever beheld. On that occasion, being absorbed in fishing, I was suddenly not a little astonished to notice that an island which had been exactly opposite to where I was sitting had, in the space of an hour, moved some fifty yards downstream! There was no current, but a stiffish breeze was driving the floating mass slowly along.

Before closing this chapter, I feel it is relevant to mention briefly an extraordinary species of grass which is known to the natives by the name of Letetumetsu. I first saw this extraordinary growth at a pan not far from the Karanamoxgee lagoon.

Growing in the water, this Letetumetsu plant, which has buoyant, cellular trailing stems, spreads over considerable areas. The old growth, which continues to live, is continually being superimposed by new sproutings, so that platforms many feet in thickness and hundreds of square feet in area are frequently seen in various parts of the swamp lands. The platform on this particular pan had an area of about one hundred and twenty square yards, and was of unknown thickness. I walked on to it, and for about an hour fished from the top of it in water about five or six feet in depth. I discovered, though, that I had to shift my position slightly every few minutes or the great pile of matted vegetation would very slowly submerge and water would begin to gather round my feet. The late Hardy Pretorius told me that he had seen a horseman venture on to an enormous and very ancient platform. From my own experience I do not question the accuracy of this statement.

At the top end of the Karanamoxgee lagoon there is a smallish platform on which I one day surprised an enormous crocodile. It is a curious sensation to walk over letetumetsu beds because, apart from the noticeable underfoot buoyancy, displaced water causes strange, sinuous undulations to recede in all directions, and these can be seen a long way ahead — something like the lazy, dying swells that continue over the surface so long after the dropping of a strong wind over open water.

Chapter 17

BY OX-WAGON TO THE MAKARIKARI

MY imagination has always been enthralled by the Makarikari: that vast, mysterious depression on the edge of the Kalahari Desert which thirstily absorbs the waters of the Nata and many other rivers. The constant urge to visit and explore its shores and islands was realised recently when I was able to undertake a journey of several hundred miles by ox-wagon.

We arrived one evening at Tsimoane, just off the edge of the Makarikari. Previous visits to this place had been made during the dry season, and what a transformation the recent copious rains had now wrought! Trees, stark and naked a few months before, were now clothed in soft, verdant foliage; and the extensive open veld covered with luxuriant grass, all smiling with flowers, formed a cool and refreshing prospect. A wonderful change, indeed, from the bare, sunbaked flats which had so recently stung the eyes with the fiercely reflected rays of the sun!

Many small pans of water lent additional charm to the peaceful scene. The air positively throbbed with life as insect hosts in wide variety revelled in the moist atmosphere. The incessant shrill notes of cicadas, crickets, and grasshoppers merged in a glad-some, melodious harmony; while, from the pans, resounded the vigorous concert of the frogs. From the deep, organ-like bass of the great bullfrogs, to the shrill, piping "Piet! Piet!" of their little tree and rush-climbing cousins, all blended harmoniously with the myriad other sounds. Nightjars were skimming, ghost-like, over the grass and round the edges of pools, hawking for their supper (or should it, in their case, be breakfast?). Later they were joined by the bats with their erratic, tireless flight.

At Tsimoane, the water from the little Mogobale River is absorbed in the extensive turf flats. As the rainy season advances, these flats become very marshy, and my wagon was stuck in one of them the following morning. These marshy places were breathlessly lovely just then. Growing, massed in the luxuriant grass, were acres and acres of fragrant Belladonna lilies, while between the trees the numerous pans gleamed like jewels. Here industrious waterfowl were paddling and feasting: spreading panic among the frogs and aquatic insects.

After we had travelled northwards for about an hour, the great Makarikari loomed suddenly in view, and I stood spellbound: gazing, into the infinitely remote horizon where sky and pan merged into one quivering, hazy blue line. In the middle distance floated quaking mirages, with clear sky (or was it water?) underlying. Away to the left, receding for miles and miles until lost in the hazy distance, was a great lake. In the foreground lay the cream-coloured pan. As I advanced, the lake diminished in size while the pale-hued flatness increased: leaving at length only the vast, silent pan reaching away to its thousands of square miles.

Mysterious, treacherous and grim, the huge, empty depression inspired a feeling of awe.

Men and animals have been suddenly engulfed in its quicksands; and it is rumoured that a Scotch cart and oxen, passing across a portion of it, were caught — sinking out of sight in a few minutes! Quicksands must be rare though; sticky, yellow clay generally occurring just below the salty crust.

A high watershed overlooks the southern margin of the Makari-kari, from which a wonderful view can be obtained. From here, too, the mirages are indescribably weird and beautiful. Along the foot of the watershed, at intervals, occur splendid springs of fresh water. There is one such spring at a place called Musu, and it is-sues from a small cliff, its face embowered with maidenhair ferns. This spring was much favoured by lions, and the great pugmarks in the mud betrayed where a huge fellow had slaked his thirst.

But a few miles from Musu is Noka-a-Mokolane (River of Palms) so named from the number of these stately trees growing near. The spring, which is the beginning of a small water course which runs into the pan, is the strongest I saw during my wanderings; but the place was rather spoilt by the number of cattle drinking there, Noka-a-Mokolane is a noted haunt of lions. The numerous dense clumps of dwarf palms afford them excellent cover, while the game which flocks nightly to the perennial spring provides an abundant and varied food supply.

A strange feature about the Makarikari is the peculiar, magnify-ing quality of the light. One is frequently deceived by tiny, distant objects appearing many times their natural size. On one occasion I mistook a small, black dog, trotting over a portion of the pan half a mile away, for a wildebeest! This sort of thing continually hap-pens, especially to persons whose eyes have not become accus-tomed to the peculiarities of light. Distances are extraordinarily deceptive. Those who have not experienced it would have difficul-ty in appreciating how marked this phenomenon is.

The last outspan for the night was made in a clump of splendid palms right at the edge of the Mahata pan. Sleep came swiftly, and the dim light of dawn revealed that we had trekked right into a belt of palms. For miles around their huge, fan-like fronds, rattling and rustling with each breath of wind, towered above the scanty bush.

After a few hours of necessary work, we trekked on afresh. Within a couple of hours we had passed out of the palm belt. From hence the journey, mostly through Mopani scrub and sandy woodland, was less interesting: especially since the foliage of the trees had recently been stripped bare by caterpillars. Nambo pan was reached that night. Duties occupied the morning following, but we got away in the afternoon and reached the Nata River at 9. p.m. on Christmas Eve. Christmas Day dawned, not with the customary bright sunshine, but with black, threatening clouds. An early bathe and some fish for breakfast seemed desirable, and both were procured in a short time. I had intended to spend the day fishing, but the threatening weather forced us to proceed at once, as it was essential to cross the river. Eight miles up I found a suitable ford, and got across without much difficulty. That was at Tsaxla, and on several occasions have I camped there. It is a beautiful spot, especially after the rains. The great trees are wonderful, and there are many sedge-lined pans in the open, park-like country bordering the river which are always worth a visit.

Last year I waded into a beautiful pan called Mathlaputhla, near the Tsebanana, to examine and photograph the Lotus blooms, of which there were several species. One flower measured exactly nine inches in diameter! In this pan, growing side by side with the lilies, was a kind of water convolvulus with vines similar to the ordinary, cultivated "Morning Glory".

These were flowering profusely, so that their lovely magenta tints mingled with the blue, mauve and gold of the Lotus lilies.

Presently I came upon a large flock of Marabou storks. There is something absurdly Hebraic about these quaint fellows! The humped backs, bald pates, and ponderous bills recall Biblical pictures of the Children of Abraham! White storks, and the ubiquitous "Rain hawks" were present, literally in thousands. No doubt they were attracted by the abundance of the Mopani caterpillars.

Lethlo Pan is one of the best known on the Tsebanana, and it normally contains water throughout the dry season. Recently,

however, it was the scene of a pitiful tragedy, for it was here that many beautiful wild creatures suffered the torments of death from thirst. Well known to them as a watering place, the buck, predatory animals, and elephants visited it in thousands when other waters gave out. Man, too, in his usual selfish way, brought his herds and flocks along. Alas! The supply was unequal to the demand. The pan emptied, and the thirsty creatures sucked up the ooze until that, too, was exhausted; and only sticky, black mud remained. Maddened with thirst, the poor beasts continued to flock to the well-remembered place: to find, not relief, but foul mud: the stench from the rotting carcasses of earlier arrivals; and death in its ugliest form. The gaunt, emaciated creatures — their impelling need rendering them fearless of man or beasts — plunged heedlessly into the clinging mud.

The weaker individuals were immediately trapped, and trampled down to rise no more; while the stronger ones floundered desperately round and round, butting one another in their agonies. And, so, for weeks, the heaving thirst-stricken mass could be found at the pan. Dozens perished daily, but still more and more came till the much delayed rains brought relief to the unfortunate survivors, and the residue struggled away. Hundreds remained: mute, bleaching, yet eloquent witnesses of the pitiless drought.

For a period, the fair, lilied pan had become a spectacle of horror, but at the time of my visit it again contained a little water. Viewed from a distance, it once again was alluring: but the air around was tainted, and in its vicinity lay thickly strewn the remains of wildebeest, roan and sable antelope, and reedbuck.

In the hardened mud numerous great basin-like tracks told of the evening visits of a large herd of elephants, as did the broken and uprooted trees. The great beasts had helped to finish the precious water, nightly revelling in mudbaths as is their wont: thereby spoiling more than they consumed. Then, sagacious creatures as they are, they made tracks for pastures new.

Where mammalian life had suffered such tragic hardship, bird life had enjoyed a period of great plenty. Swarm after swarm of locusts brought to the birds joy and endless feasting. The advent of the massed invasion of caterpillars brought a further great influx of bird life — illustrating once again the all-wise, wondrous balancing scheme of Nature. Stately flamingoes: rose and white with grotesque, awkward looking beaks; could be seen standing knee deep in some of the quiet pools. Blue-grey herons flapped and croaked along the waterways. The shy little Night heron: gaudy kingfishers, ibises, darters, pied "clinking" Blacksmith plovers, snipe, collared sandpipers, snowy egrets, and lively avocets with strange, flexible upturned bills, were all to be met within an afternoon's ramble: while duck, teal, and divers shovelled in the mud of the still pools and pans they loved. The cheery, ringing scream of the White-headed fish eagle resounded along the glades.

My duties led me southwards from Lethlo Pan, and I did a long evening's trek along the old Pandamatenka road — once the main artery of traffic to the Zambezi. This road was often travelled by the old hunters and pioneers. It was formerly the highway to Kasingula, but is now fallen into disuse and disrepair. Yet, there is glamour in its very name: the glamour which forever invests all ancient highways, and places of historic interest. The mind is at once recalled to the names of the men who blazed and trod them into being: who opened the way for those who followed; tamed the land and founded a dominion.

Like so many of the Protectorate rivers, the Nata overflows its banks in parts, and the water spreads over the level country in the most unexpected directions. Indeed, I was informed that, during really heavy rains, the actual river is lost to sight and the country is flooded for miles around. At one point I was encamped on the precipitous banks thirty or forty feet above the river bed, yet high in the trees on the banks were bunches of reeds and driftwood.

This huge volume of water drains slowly away to the great Makarikari Salt Pan, but there is very little current, as witness the splendid trees growing in the very bed of the river. The greatest charm of the Nata, perhaps, lies in its grand, long reaches of water. People who live in parts where there are constantly flowing rivers may not be able to appreciate the effect of these large, open waters upon those of us who are accustomed to the sandy rivers where one often has to scrape a hole in order to obtain a drink.

A curious feature about the Nata is that on rare occasions the water flows along its bed in the wrong direction — that is, towards its source. This phenomenon occurs when the Makarikari fills from other sources, and the Nata is not flowing. In these circumstances, there is an overflow from the Pan up the river course for a few miles. To this overflow is ascribed the fact that in the lower reaches of the river the water is decidedly salty. Perhaps such is the case, but there is a big natural deposit of salt in a loop near the river's mouth, and this appears to be the more likely cause.

POSTSCRIPT BY EDITOR

DURING the period in which I have been organising Mr. E. Cronje Wilmot's manuscripts, I have received many interesting letters from him. The following extracts from these letters, concerning additional matter on diseases of game, present status of game in Northern Bechuanaland Protectorate, and some further notes on snakes in Ngamiland, seem to me to be worthy of inclusion to complete the book: coming, as they do, from a well-qualified observer of many years' experience.

(1) PRESENT STATUS OF GAME IN NORTHERN PROTECTORATE:

"You will be pleased to hear that elephants, which have recently approached within eighty yards of our camp on the Nata are greatly on the increase in the Northern Protectorate. In fact they are ranging over thousands of square miles of the country, and their total strength must include many thousands. Giraffe, Eland and Gemsbuck are also still quite plentiful; while Wildebeest occur in incredible numbers. As carriers of disease, and polluters of pan waters, the latter are something of a menace.

"A lot die seasonally from mange (i.e. wildebeest), and though the Bushmen kill large numbers there is rather an increase than a reduction in the astonishing hordes which converge on the more permanent waters towards the end of the dry season. They appear to breed during most months of the year. At any rate, one sees a percentage of young calves during all seasons. But gemsbuck, springbuck, and steenbuck are dropping their calves at the present time (October)."

(2) DISEASES OF GAME:

"With reference to game dying from mange: wildebeest are the only large mammals I have known to succumb to the disease, and large numbers die annually from it. Only a few weeks ago we found one lying dead on the edge of the Madala pool (half a mile from here). It had little hair left, and the hide was hard, dry and rough.

"Duiker and steenbuck are not infrequently infested with large maggots — some almost as large as one's little finger — under the skin. The victims are usually very emaciated and are quite unfit for food.

"Otherwise, apart from Rabies (endemic in parts of Ngamiland) I know of no diseases affecting the local fauna.

"Have you ever heard of a kudu cow with horns? In the Grahamstown Museum there is a pair measuring between two and two and a half feet, which I sent to Dr. Hewitt from the swamps area of Ngamiland. He already had a small pair on exhibition, but knew of only one other."

(3) ADDITIONAL NOTES ON SNAKES AND SQUIRRELS:

"This morning I went by dugout to Tsoda Pan. I saw nothing beyond some waterfowl, including three very confiding Open-bill storks, and a young python. The latter was very tightly coiled round a dead branch, its head tucked beneath the coils. The morning had been chilly, and obviously the snake was trying to warm itself. It very suddenly came to life when I carelessly thumped the stem with the side of the craft, plunging headfirst into the shallow, sedgy water in the twinkling of an eye!

"Since my arrival, three mambas have been killed. Two of these were revealed to me by the frantic chirping of a Grey-footed squirrel, and about this I will say a few words later. One of the three snakes measured nine feet two inches, the others a few inches less. Not one of these mambas was in any way aggressive.

"I have also come across a number of other snakes, including two huge puffadders, and bird snakes. In fact, all the snakes put together encountered during my former long sojourn in Ngamiland have not equalled in number those seen over the past few months, and I am beginning to think that I shall have to revise my former ideas about this being an almost snake-free country! No doubt the excessive extention of the swamps latterly has forced them into drier parts.

"Now about the squirrels. I am sure that you must have come across instances of these little creatures baiting snakes. I have done so frequently, and on the last occasion was attracted to the large 9 ft. 2 ins. mamba by the persistent whinnying chirpings of a squirrel. The snake was fully stretched out on a thinnish branch about thirty five feet above the ground. Within eight feet of the reptile, and probably relying upon its own lightning-like rapidity of movement, perched the excited squirrel: defiantly flicking its tail and chattering in a manner no doubt most provoking to its sinister enemy.

"Possibly the squirrel realised that the snake — rigidly stretched out — would be unable to strike forward, though to me it seemed in deadly peril. Nonetheless, I should have liked to watch the outcome, but a friend shot from behind me: smashing the brute's head, when of course the squirrel instantly vanished.

"I have examined the stomach contents of numerous snakes but have yet to find a squirrel included in such, yet I feel sure that many of the latter meet their ends that way.

"One of the native hunters in this camp brings in a lot of carnivora, including the various cats. Recently, unhappily, he killed the finest specimen of a civet I have ever seen. I have purchased the skin for the Albany Museum."

I asked Mr. Cronje Wilmot for his personal views on the Destruction of Game Policy in Tsetse Fly Control. He replied as follows:

"You ask whether I consider that game destruction is helpful in the eradication of Tsetse flies. Whilst I am wholly against that measure, and always opposed it (as I shall do again when I rejoin the Tsetse Control Department next year) I must answer "yes" and "no"! But a good deal depends on local conditions.

"During my previous years in the Department I found very strong proofs of the difficulty of controlling "fly" when game was very plentiful. I have already related, in my book, the case of the Xnaraga Valley, shortly after the rinderpest. A second instance is as follows: at one period the Administrator issued free permits for shooting in a certain badly "fly" infested area which was heavily stocked with game.

"An enormous amount of shooting took place: so much so, in fact, that a displacement of game resulted which caused areas more or less fly-free to become re-infected! After my departure from Ngamiland, and owing to some extent to correspondence between the Resident Commissioner and myself (in one of his letters he stated: "you will be pleased to hear that I have issued instructions that shooting should be curtailed") the hunters were reduced, and game fences allowed to get into disrepair. Today the position is worse than it has been for many years. In fact there has been a very serious encroachment of fly into areas in which I have never previously heard of them.

"Nevertheless, I am still convinced that Game destruction is entirely wrong in principal, and think that the sooner it is scrapped the better. But the campaign commencing next year will still consist of that: and discriminative Bush clearing. The latter, even if very costly, may well prove to be the best answer to the problem."

To all of us who deplore the widescale destruction of our finest types of African fauna in the campaign against the Tsetse fly, the above views will be of interest.

C. T. A. M.

ADDITIONAL MATERIAL

The following two chapters were for reasons unknown to the family not included in the original book.

Both have been have been added into this modern edition of the book because of their intresting content.

However, because they were not included, they do not have the benefit of C.T. Astley Maberly's excellent illustrations and it has been endeavoured to illustrate the text with suitable photographs, although the quality of these was not always of the best.

The first chapter deals with the tour of the Okavango in 1947 by His Excellency, Sir Evelyn Baring, the British High Commisioner for Southern Africa, and his wife, Lady Mary Baring.

Sir Evelyn had previously been Governor of Southern Rhodesia, and went on to become Governor of Kenya, where his governorship was marked by the Mau Mau rebellion.

The Chapter is written in the form of a diary of the expedition, which explains its almost staccato format.

Unfortunately the extremely blurred picture at right is the only one of Sir Evelyn and Lady Mary to have survived from the expedition.

The second chapter is actually an excellent article written by E Cronje Wilmot on the Bushmen (San) of Western Bechuanaland, more particularly the hybrid Bushman/ Tswana people referred to as the "Masarwa".

F. N.

Chapter 18

ACROSS THE SWAMPS OF THE OKAVANGO

THE TOUR OF HIS EXCELLENCY
SIR EVELYN BARING THE HIGH
COMMISSIONER OF SOUTHERN AFRICA

A DIARY

June 21st 1947

Detailed to accompany His Excellency, the High Commissioner and Lady Mary Baring on their recent expedition trough the swamps of the Okavango Delta, two members of the Bechuanaland Protectorate Government Service and Mr. S. Davies of the Witwatersrand Native Labour Association left Maun on the above date for Shakawe, near the South West African border, there to await the arrival of His Excellency.

En route, at Nokaneng, they met Mr. Sillery, the Resident Commissioner, Mr. Germond, District Commissioner, and Mrs. Germond, also bound on the same mission.

June 22nd 1947

The usual hearty welcome was received from the good residents of Nokaneng, and after a welcome and abundant breakfast, the purchase of a few odds and ends unobtainable in Maun, the party again proceeded and travelled through without incident, reaching Shakawe (250 miles from Maun) at 7 p.m. Here again a hearty welcome was accorded them. Mr. Matthias, the Witwatersrand Native Labour Association Representative there, quickly arranged for their every comfort.

June 23rd 1947

The gathering together and sorting of scattered belongings conveyed by the various trucks of the large convoy with which the party travelled, the receiving and sending off of radio messages and the laying in of more supplies, occupied the greater portion of the morning, but time was found to inspect and admire the beautiful grounds of the Wenela camp ad the majestic Okavango flowing swiftly and silently beneath its high westerly banks, clad with lordly trees and palms. To the east, beyond the 200 yards wide channel of swirling water, stretched miles of papyrus swamp and reeds and no visible banks save a faint outline of the trees on the horizon.

Here is the birth of the great, mysterious swampland and the threshold of a delta in which a mighty river finds its dissolution. Those with the time on their hands stared with curiosity and pleasurable anticipation of the adventurous journey to be undertaken and the knowledge that the trip would be achieved by the largest and most spectacular expedition ever to attempt the crossing, as well as the only one boasting the company of ladies in the party, added much to the satisfaction and pleasure of being numbered in the privileged company.

Wireless messages kept all informed as to His Excellency's progress by air, and at last came the news that his plane had left Maun on the last lap of its long trip, its arrival timed for 4 p.m. The whole party betook themselves to the landing ground, arriving just in time to see the great machine touching quietly down.

Waiting cars and trucks soon conveyed the whole assembly to a previously prepared camp one and a half miles up river from Wenela. Here, on the very brink of the high perpendicular banks of the lordly stream, a wide space had been cleared beneath magnificent Mokuchum and other trees. Tents scattered over the broad area were soon occupied by those to whom they were assigned and all were engaged in stowing their belongings.

By the time every ting had been made snug and comfortable for this, the first night of camping on the Okavango Swamps trip, a radiant, crimson glow from the rippling water betokened the setting of the sun and not long thereafter the full party gathered round a grand roaring fire.

His Excellency and Lady Mary Baring quickly made all feel that there was to be a minimum of formality and almost unconsciously one and all found themselves taking part in animated conversation, the chief topic, of course, being the forthcoming trip and speculations on the probable results of tomorrow's fishing. Lady Mary has come splendidly equipped with superb fishing tackle and all the keenness of an ardent angler, and notwithstanding the sharpness of the frosty air, prophesies as to the probabilities of sport were not lacking.

A paludrine tablet each, handed round by the Doctor, was washed down by a comforting drink and when the dinner hour arrived some time later, all moved to the common table, where to the accompaniment of happy, interesting talk, sharpened appetites soon did full justice to the good fare provided, but with the nip of winter tingling at the finger tips, the fireside was not long neglected.

As there had been a considerable fall in the water level, a discussion followed on the wisdom of attempting the crossing of the swamps at this time of the year. An experienced, senior official, who was not participating in the excursion, and, who fearing for His Excellency's and Lady Mary's safety and comfort, was very decidedly opposed to the venture, pointing out the possibility of long delays caused by the probable blockage of the known channels, through growths of papyrus etc. and the lowness of the water rendering the passage of the heavy barges a doubtful proceeding. A time limit to the duration of the trip caused further complications and more ground for anxiety. The element of risk was fully realised and the issue hung in the balance.

Weeks of exhaustive enquiries and careful planning, however, backed the District Commissioner's quiet assurance that all would be well and Lady Mary's emphatic: "We are going", decided the point, much to the relief of the majority. The decision was celebrated by a few delightful fireside songs. Comforting warmth after an excellent meal soon induced the desire for sleep and the party dispersed in twos and threes.

June 24th 1947

Nature was kind and a brilliant morning heralded the bright, sunny day which followed. His Excellency was up with the rest and a pleasant ramble through the beautiful, unfamiliar woods carried us on to breakfast time, after which Sir Evelyn and the Resident Commissioner motored to Mohembo, some nine miles up river, whilst the remainder of the party found various occupations, the anglers in particular being very much occupied. By lunch time Lady Mary had landed two tiger fish, one a beauty of over seven pounds weight. More fishing in the afternoon resulted in a couple of fine "tigers" being brought to the bag, by the Resident Commissioner.

As is usual with this type of fishing, several got away with terrific strikes and spoons were lost.

As the shadows lengthened another interesting walk was taken with the High Commissioner, whose obvious pleasure and interest in these little excursions added a hundred fold to the charms of an enchanting evening.

Friends from Wenela called and joined in "spots" and another most pleasant evening passed to the hour of bed time.

June 25th 1947

The camp was early astir and bustle, and innumerable cases were being filled with foodstuffs and equipment of all sorts. A staff of excellent servants, each absorbed in his own particular duties, moved here and there, whilst floating from the "kitchen", the appetising smell of frying bacon and eggs betokened no reduction in activity there.

His Excellency and one of the party had already returned from an early walk and all were in preparation for a start as soon as breakfast was over. A prime beast had been slaughtered and the staff waited eagerly for their portions whilst choice cuts were being removed for the European mess.

Table chickens, unwilling to lose their new found liberty, squawked and fluttered frantically to avoid recapture and a return to the coop destined to be their last earthly home.

Trucks and Caboose drivers were warming up their engines, for a thirty-two mile journey had to be made by road to Sepopa, where the fleet of mokoros and barges awaited our arrival. The hum and stir of the breaking up of a large camp was everywhere in evidence, but with the help of many willing hands, everything was soon stowed in the commodious vehicles and at a reasonably early hour the convoy was in motion. A delay of twenty minutes occurred whilst the party watched a not very spectacular Mambukushu dance, although the mode of hairdressing of the women and their long, oily tresses hanging almost to the waist caused considerable interest and photographs were taken.

At Wenela, some further delay took place, while extra "smokes", blades etc. were being purchased and further wireless messages dispatched. Then, with the good wishes of friends there, the party was once more on the way, arriving at Sepopa in under two hours.

A nice site had been chosen for the camp here and everything was soon shipshape, with ample time for botanising and inspecting the fleet.

The largest barge, with a short flag staff and a Union Jack fluttering merrily in the breeze, was nicely fitted with matting awnings etc. for the comfort of His Excellency and Lady Mary.

The craft were moored in a channel greatly narrowed by encroaching papyrus and nothing could be seen of the main river which, however, we knew wound tortuously through the rank growth some distance further in.

No trace of opposite banks or lines of trees could be made out. The great swamps had spread to either side of the river, sucking greedily at its clear, living water. Hippopotami, whose tracks were in evidence, could be heard gurgling shortly after our arrival. The great beasts have here, as elsewhere in the swamps, a sanctuary that will for all time guard against their extinction.

In the environs of the camp are some beautiful and colossal sausage trees whose abundant fruits hang like great polonies on their slender stems and there is no lack of other interesting vegetation.

245

Each evening for an hour or so before and after sunset, mosquitoes had been very much in evidence, a nuisance which was certainly never missed when for some mysterious reason they always ceased operations at much the same time and not noticed gain until early morning.

The usual cheerful party gathered round a crackling fire and doctored with paludrine and something a good deal tastier, chatted merrily until dinner was announced, followed later by fireside singing, talk and laughter.

June 26th 1947

Dawn was announced by the clear melodious, bubbling notes of a coucal, a sound which will, to some of us, always be associated with these great swamp lands.

The whole camp as soon once gain a hive of activity. Paddlers whose homes were in the vicinity arrived in twos and threes. Those with leaky mokoros set about their baling by the simple expedient of standing at the end and with one foot shooting the water out on to the bank. Others cut thick stems of papyrus on which to stack their loads against possible damage by water.

Members of the party who were travelling by native craft spent some time in selecting the largest and driest and getting their effects so packed as to leave sufficient sitting room.

Much care and ingenuity had to be exercised to stow all the large quantity of baggage into the waiting dugouts and barges and there was something of an overflow into the passenger craft but this had been anticipated and previous arrangements made for more dugouts or mokoros to await our arrival at Seronga on the next day but one. The apparently impossible was accomplished after a little delay and the whole party, with servants, found comfortable enough seats.

Photographs were taken of the "Flag Ship" and long line of frail looking craft, each with a paddler standing fore and after and farewells waved to the men in charge of the homely cabooses and trucks. The convoy was afloat!

Soon it strung out in a long line down the narrow papyrus fringed water way which lead not much further along into the main Okavango stream, already very noticeably narrower than at Shakawe.

The deepest interest and certainly no misgiving filled the breasts of this party on this opening day of an adventurous trip through the watery wastes of the great Ngami swamp lands. Thrilling thoughts and happy anticipation predominated and "tiger" spoons were soon being trolled behind the skimming craft. Lithe Mukuba river men paddled gracefully and unhurriedly, some of their narrow craft with a bare inch of free board, hugged the edge of the immensely dense papyrus growth, for a strong upcurrent wind was raising something of a swell, but the cutting of corners on frequent sharp beds was risked and rapid progress achieved. The heavy baggage barge, (something of a tub) with five paddlers, was quickly distanced but is tardy progress caused no undue alarm as its very bulkiness was sufficient insurance against possible mishap.

Papyrus persisted - wall-like, floating and immovable in its packed formation, this strange type of vegetation covers endless miles of deep water and supports other growths, including ferns, a lovely magenta coloured convolvulus and others, as well as affording resting and hiding places for innumerable crocodiles, otters and various water fowl.

So dense is the growth at times that the river folk are able to cross deep channels with animal-drawn sledges, and still fresh in the writer's memory is a terrifying experience of slipping up the armpits through an unnoticed hole when negotiating one such deep channel.

The tops of island trees occasionally peeped above the feathery heads and once or twice the vague outline of giant trees on some sandy mainland ridge away to the South West. Ever and anon, a mokoro would draw into the living wall, when a paddler with vigorous strokes would detach stem after stem at a certain stage of ripeness and ,stripping the outside skin, chew contentedly at the sweetish pulp within. Their white passengers, imitating them, also munched, not without enjoyment, but with some soreness of unpractised tongues.

Other uses are also found for papyrus. The cellular nature of the stems prevent their ever becoming waterlogged and thus they form the best possible material for rafts, which the river men frequently make use of.

These are formed by merely piling the long stems crisscross to the thickness of several feet and to a size governed by the requirements of the builders, some so large that huts are raised on them and, with mud-covered fire places, provide all the needs of migrating family parties, with space to spare for all their possessions. Of course the rafts can only be manoeuvred downstream and when they have served their purpose are abandoned and not infrequently cause serious blockages in vital narrow channels.

The possibility of the manufacture of paper from papyrus, on more modern lines than the originators of the commodity ever could have dreamed of, has been considered, and, if the scheme is ever tried out, there certainly will never be a lack of raw material. Papyrus sometimes reaches a height of 14 feet with stems three inches in diameters at the thick end, but such sizes are unusual.

Kingfishers, occasional ibises and may lovely bee eaters were seen and the distant haunting notes of the magnificent white headed fish eagles, came floating through the clear atmosphere. A couple of shots echoing from the direction of the leading boats told surely of crocodiles, of which several were seen from time to time, and were not being too kindly dealt with.

The flag ship was well in the run and on the tail coming up about midday, all the leading craft were found drawn up on the grassy edge of a fascinating islet, where His Excellency had come across a couple of riverine trees, unknown to us, of which many more were seen during the course of the day.

Lady Mary had grassed another good tiger fish and the Resident Commissioner had sent to the bottom a sadder but no doubt much wiser crocodile. Only a few more miles had to be travelled so a little while was spent in partaking of welcome cups of tea and waiting for the slow-moving baggage barge. When it eventually hove into sight we were once more on the move. The camp for the day was even nearer than expected and we reached Igogha, a place fairly well known to several of the party, at an hour which permitted of a long and most enjoyable ramble on the edges of the drowned land and amidst charming vegetation.

His Excellency gloried in the exercise and the examination of numerous game tracks, many unfamiliar to him. Here among others were numbers of lechwe, situtunga and reedbuck tracks, and the footprints of both the clawed and clawless otter, which he was quickly able to distinguish one from another.

Some time was spent in watching the evolutions of fighting snipe and listening to their shrill drumming. Various trees and shrubs had their intriguing influence and it was only the dwindling light which forced a tardy return to camp. It has been a great and wonderful day. The faces of the whole party reflected contentment and satisfaction – an omen, we felt sure, of many more even greater ones to come.

Three of us unattached members of the party, having planned to sleep close together, gave instructions for our cots and nets to be fixed up in a cosy corner behind sheltering bushes or palms ,an arrangement which was to be followed throughout the trip. Each with his own personal servant, we had nothing to do but enjoy ourselves. A little chat and "nightcap" was the general order before creeping beneath the nets and sound, dreamless sleep should have followed.

But alas! Such was seldom the case – at least for two of us who had to be content listening to the sound if unmelodious slumbers of the third. Snoring as had surely never before been equalled, or so the unhappy listeners thought, rolled in great tremulous waves from beneath that net, until it seemed the whole camp must be awakened, but we were widely separated and the rest were blissfully unaware of their fellow-traveller's torment. Snoring in every possible key. The thick, choky sort often breaking into easy trombone-like notes testified to our companion's unadulterated and apparently sweet repose. We listened first in amusement, then in amazement and later still in wakeful desperation, for there seemed nothing much we could do about it. The shielding mosquito net prevented the flinging of shoes, and shouting gave but temporary relief.

At breakfast one morning, the Doctor, somewhat bleary-eyed gave a discourse of the causes of snoring and hinted at possible remedies. All very technical and impressive but further night's suffering proved them to be of little value, and in desperation the advice of one of the servants was sought.

He, a comical scamp, whose carrying voice could be heard at most hours, gravely averred that a little cold water poured into the uppermost ear usually proved instantly effective. Though quite prepared to believe this, the presence of a very handy scatter gun forbade the experiment. No other remedy seemed available, other than bowing to our hard lot. The accusation of moaning and groaning, roaring and even bellowing produced no more than an amiable grin from our well-rested comrade and we could but hope that like the great General in history, who snatched a few minutes sleep amidst the roaring of cannon, we would in time become accustomed to his nightly boomings.

One of the occupants of a distant tent had mentioned having heard lions, a long way off, the previous night, and though not disbelieving, our snoring friend, whose ample form fitted rather more then snugly into a camp chair, reclined luxuriously backwards, The ground was soft and yielding and the back feet of the chair suddenly sinking upset the centre of gravity.

A hearty laugh greeted the sight of a pair of top boots directed to the heavens, but a secret feeling of elation at our portly friend's discomfiture was dispelled some hours later, when on approaching the distant mosquito nets, ghost-like in the moon light, whither our friend had preceded us, we were greeted, whilst still some distance off, by that sonorous booming we had come to know so well and dread. It seemed like unconscious revenge. Resignedly we crawled beneath our nets, trying to feel it was good to know that at least one of the trio was enjoying sound, undisturbed repose.

June 27th 1947

Many hands led to a good early start and speeding craft soon passed the lake river branch of the Okavango, the Teoge of the early explorers and sometimes the Taokhe of modern cartographers. (either rendering really only meaning a large flowing river).

The entrance is narrow and further along the channel is utterly blocked by papyrus and other aquatic growths, hence the drying up of Lake Ngami, now a wooded pastoral area, though occasionally, as in '44, holding up to thirty miles of shallow, quickly receding water, a travesty of Oswell's, Livingstone's and other early explorers "Great Lake". The 1944 water reached the lake via other roundabout channels, but in 1853, the traveller C. J. Andersson wrote:

> "The lake is fed by the Teoge at its N.W. extremity. The river never, perhaps, much exceeds forty yards, but it is deep, and, when at its greatest height, contains a large volume of water. Its annual overflow takes place in June, July and August and sometimes even later. The source of the Teoge is unknown but it's supposed to be very distant. It may, probably have its rise in the height table land as the Quanza and other steams of importance. "The main course of the Teoge is N. West , but is so serpentine that in the thirteen days I ascended it, travelling on the average five hours a day and reckoning two and a half miles to the hour, I only made on degree of latitude due north of Lake Ngami. As far as I proceeded, however, it was navigable with smaller craft, for only in three places that I can remember, did I find less than five feet of water, and generally speaking, the depth was considerable".

The possibility of conserving and utilising the immense volume of water uselessly spilled over the vast swamps area, forming no inconsiderable part of the broad scheme originally outlined by the late professor E.H.L. Schwarz, frequently provided a subject for debate which lead to much interesting discussion and consulting of maps and more recent reports. Suggested approaches to a very real problem, from different angles, were delved into but it was generally felt that until such time as the whole area was accurately mapped and more done in the way of taking levels, little could be done.

Numerous other channels from north east, really only loops, were passed, as well as several exquisite tree and palm covered islands, where, on a former trip, great bunches of tiny but delicious dates had been gathered, but now, in the off season, alas! they yielded nothing more than their beauty.

The Red Boat, as the baggage barge had come to be called, made rather worse progress than usual, but detracted nothing from another most interesting day, during which, among other interests, a large crocodile was killed outright and two splendid "tiger" brought to bag.

A couple of miles from the destination for the day, the river was left behind and a passage forced through thinning papyrus and along twisting dugout paths which after a while opened out into charming lotus-clad lagoons, over the final stage to Seronga. A previously prepared camp awaited the arrival of the flotilla and in a very short while tents were up and the kitchen fire blazing.

Several hours of daylight remained, giving ample time for various arrangements, including the hire of more mokoros, the owners of which, by the District Commissioner's forethought were awaiting our convoy, the purchase and slaughter of a couple of bullocks as a food supply for the now greatly increased strength of paddlers and a good long tramp with Sir Evelyn into the sand belt, where several old vegetal friends were encountered for the first time on this trip.

Seronga boasts a store and is on high ground commanding a splendid view of the swampland and vistas of a grand, deep and long lagoon, where Lady Mary and the Doctor went fishing and though returning empty handed, felt well satisfied with the fierce tiger strikes they had had.

On this lagoon, though not as numerous as in summer time, are many beautiful water lilies in variety, among others a magnificent sulphur-coloured species. Attempts to collect bulbs failed owing to the depth of the water which is seldom less than and generally much over ten feet. Crocodiles abound and take a heavy toll of native stock.

June 28th 1947

Our fleet now strengthened, consisted of three barges and twenty four mokoros, all properly manned. A total of 72 Africans made up the staff.

Transferring of baggage caused some delay but by 10 a.m. everything being ready, the Flag Ship pushed off, followed by the long escort of mokoros. The same winding track had to be followed to the river where the paddlers laid aside their *nkashis* or punting poles and settled down to paddling, the brisk current reducing the labour to a minimum.

This being the last day on which trolling could be carried on, spoons were soon flicking and flashing through the translucent element but tiger fish were singularly uninterested.

Two hours fast travel brought the boats to a narrow channel which had to be followed. Branching away first to the west and then in a general southerly direction, this very deep, lateral stream, hedged by immensely tall papyrus, wound and twisted to such a degree that seldom were more than a couple of craft in sight of each other, but the strong current swept us along at a fine rate.

In great fear of encountering hippopotami, the paddlers kept a sharp lookout, as more frequently than not, these giant amphibians fiercely resent any intrusion of their secluded haunts, causing many serious mishaps and engendering a wholesome dread in the river folk, who have periodically to use the narrow waterways.

This particular channel was called the Seyamakgeto, the name meaning the place where the taxes were eaten. In earlier times the river men had to pay tribute in corn and on one occasion when negotiating the waterway, a dugout bearing such grain was overturned by hippo and everything lost, the incident at once providing a name and bestowing an evil reputation on the stream, which its somewhat gloomy shut in appearance seemed to fully merit. It is one of a perfect network of similar mysterious channels.

Nothing untoward, however, happened during our passage, but it was not without a feeling of relief, when, some two hours later, the leading mokoro suddenly turned into an almost invisible gap in smallish papyrus and swept into alternating patches of rushes and small lily-covered lagoons, to presently emerge into the seemingly interminable grassy swamps of the Delta, usually spoke of as "flats".

Some days would be occupied in traversing them, a prospect imbuing one and all with pleasurable anticipation. Gliding through the grass and sedges of these immense inundated area affords great interest and excitement, notably more so after the hours in the papyrus-walled water lanes with little visibility and the ever-present sense of lurking known and unknown dangers invoked by the dark, sinister, waters.

One of the first sounds to reach our ears on coming into the open was the familiar *kraak-kraak* of the purple-fronted heron, but, this apart, we were struck right away by the almost uncanny silence of the mysterious, fascinating immensity which had so suddenly encompassed us. Bird calls are rare and except on the wooded islands, there was not much to produce sounds, though what was lacking to the sense of hearing was amply compensated for by the beauty reaching out and out, for the vision to absorb. A quiet, peaceful, and, one felt, enduring loveliness, stretching away on either hand for literally thousands of square miles.

Myriads of tiny, palm-bedecked islets – mostly gigantic ant heaps - flecked the vast expanse, creating here and there charming vistas narrowing and melting to invisibility in the quivering light of the westering sun. All sense of monotony was denied by the seductive splashes of varying colour shades provided by the many-hued grasses, reeds and sedges and long wedges of shade in the lee of the little islets.

Eastwards, in the full glaze of the afternoon light, the reverse of the picture stood out in minute detail. The eyes, reaching out to the infinite distance, would linger and register and wander on and around the great circle of the flat horizon and nothing to displease would be found.

In the distance ahead, great foliaged, water-loving trees marked the position of the ever-recurring larger islands - our course took us by the very edge of some, where, peering into the dark crannies beneath partly submerged branches, we expected to see we knew not what. Sometimes, landing, a way was forced through thick brakes of palms and scrub and always in the open spaces would be found the tracks of the little sanctuary's shy inhabitants, not infrequently the sharp, wide-splayed V's of the rare water-loving situtunga, which the uninitiated would never dream were left by a buck. At other times, those of more antelope – bushbucks, reedbuck, lechwe. Then again the rounded, cow-like spoor of buffalo or the great pugmarks of hippo and, perhaps also, the grubbed up working of warthog. Owls and eagles love these islands and other birds, though not plentiful, will be met with by any intrepid traveller.

The variety of trees is not great, but their large, dark forms rise high above the drooping fronds of the phoenix palms. Lavishly en-

dowed by nature, these lonely, remote spots possess an indescribable charm of their own even as they lend of their beauty to the general surroundings. The desire to explore them one and all will come to those who have the time and the wish to Look and See.

For days to come islands had to provide our camping places and as sometimes they were far apart, it would not always be easy to decide whether to stop rather early or to risk reaching another before it was dark.

Since entering the "flats" the men have stood to their work, using their long *nkashis* or forked punting poles. Mostly expert river men, their slow swinging motion is full of grace and ease. Gliding smoothly through the grass which masks the craft and lower limbs, an impression was easily gained of so many men performing on skates, the punting poles alone dispelling the idea.

The long procession of barges and dugouts one behind the other in the narrow mokoro paths, made quite an imposing spectacle. Occasionally an open channel or a lagoon was crossed or followed for some distance, when the course would be marked for stragglers by breaking or doubling tufts of grass or sedges or leaving fragments of papyrus floating.

Loitering and other delays sometimes caused the string of craft to be stretched out for several miles and the Red Boat, now more unmanageable then ever, often reached the camp several hours after the rest.

The day passed all too quickly and camp was pitched on an island called Mohanen (the place of the baobabs). On it were many magnificent trees typical of the riverine forests of Ngamiland, as well as several immense Mohanas or baobabs. At the foot of one, springing from the colossal roots was a curious cone-like, warty

255

growth upwards of twelve feet in height and about half as thick at the base. Utterly without shoots or "eyes", it's cairn-like appearance created some speculation and curiosity. The High Commissioner and Lady Mary both managed to scramble to its top, on the rounded end of which was discovered the initials D.O.S. and the date 1929. These conveyed nothing to any of the party, but no doubt in years to come, they would periodically arouse the same feeling of curiosity as they did in us.

The usual cheery talk around the glowing logs was somewhat shortened by the urge of sleep after a long day in the fresh, bracing air.

June 29th 1947

Leisurely but good progress was made through much the same type of swamp land and though travel was extended to a much later hour than usual owing to no suitable island for camping being reached earlier, the enchanting loveliness of these isle-dotted broads held the unwavering attention of the party and sped the passage of time in an almost alarming manner.

Eventually an unlikely looking islet was reached and as nothing better had come into sight, it perforce had to be used. What a surprise here awaited the party for on thrusting through the rank marginal growth a circular clear space covered by couch grass was come upon and a more perfect camping spot could not have been chosen. The circular area, about half an acre in extent, was bordered by colossal trees and phoenix and hyphaene palms, with a tall young baobab of some six feet diameter, guarding the entrance end. A perfectly sheltered, lovely spot and with a sufficiency of dry wood at hand, several fires were soon blazing, with a contented, happy party, lounging glass in hand, around ours.

June 30th 1947

In honour of the High Commissioner's visit and to commemorate the night spent there, it was decided to name this delectable spot Baring Island, so, whilst breakfast was in the course of preparation the words were deeply carved on the baobab and photographs taken.

Breakfast disposed of and everything packed and stowed in the waiting craft ,a farewell was made to an enchanting little isle and at least some hoped that the opportunity for another visit might some day be possible.

His Excellency's enthusiasm for the several daily rambles insured that little was ever missed at the various stopping places and seldom a moment was lost. Where the islands were small, two or more rounds were made, and, if an evening ramble, the waning light alone induced a return to camp.

Never once a blank – something worthwhile, whether tracks or trees or shrubs or birds, always presented itself and afforded material for discussion or the swelling of marginal notes in text books and they were always enjoyable.

Rapid progress was possible for several miles along a good deep channel flowing in the right direction, but speed was soon again retarded by heavy aquatic growths - lilies, sedges, reeds and occasional patches of papyrus.

Some delay, excitement and a good deal of shouting by the paddlers occurred when a buffalo, feeding belly-deep on the coarse swamp grass, was spotted and the dugouts whose passengers had rifles shot forward, The District Commissioner with a good start, came first within easy range and a well-placed shot caused the great beast to plunge madly forward amid terrific splashing and then it suddenly collapsed. In no time all the craft were around and the huge carcass was dragged to a handy antheap, where snaps were taken of the throng of elated boat men, hacking this mountain of delicious meat, hide and all, into chunks sufficiently small to be accommodated in the already heavily-laden mokoros.

In an incredibly short while not even the "innards" remained and the convoy was once more on the move, only to be again halted by further shouting when a limping buffalo was sighted splashing in the direction of the long line of boats.

The beast stopped, scanning the unusual scene and then in a manner of an animal in no mood for being trifled with, continued its advance. After approaching quite near, however, its courage seemed to fail and it turned, making off in the direction whence it had come. Several dugouts gave immediate chase, their excited occupants getting out their long heavy stabbing spears, the idea being to edge the animal into deep water, where it might have been stabbed to death, but none being available, the chase was abandoned after one of the craft had approached within fifteen yards – a risky proceeding.

There was now some change in the surroundings, with different types of vegetation being encountered, and frequent torturous hippo paths had to be followed through rank growths of rushes and reeds which were often almost tunnel like in nature. A couple of Mukuba villages were passed but the people had nothing of interest for sale and appeared utterly disinterested in our passage, thought they could scarcely have ever before seen anything quite to impressive as the long line of craft passing their island home.

We stopped for the night on an island reached not long after and here the tents were pitched beneath really magnificent garcinia trees. A Bushman village was passed not long before landing and a local headman in our company arranged for these people to visit us before our departure in the morning.

Two immense herds of buffalo were seen during the day and a good variety of other game was also sighted but left undisturbed. Phoenix palms were now being replaced by the pale-coloured hyphoene palms, of which several groves were passed and it was likely that no more of the former would be seen as for some unaccountable reason they do not extend much east of our position at that time.

A party from the Bushman village, mostly woman, visited our encampment as we were preparing to leave. They were Maxanaxwes, with interesting facial tattooing and the usual bushman skin robes.

His Excellency delighted their hearts with a generous ration of strong tobacco and a handful of salt each, whilst one young girl went into ecstatics over a trinket presented her by Lady Mary. This little community consisted almost entirely of women, their menfolk having died out one way and another with but a couple of exceptions and a few very young lads. One of the men had very recently been killed by a buffalo.

Several of the young maidens were decidedly comely and all were a cheerful, well-nourished lot.

The first few hours of the day's travel was through exceedingly dense grass and rushes and the hippo path followed was so tortuous that the paddlers had an arduous time negotiating the sharp bends with the barges and long mokoros and it was with much pleasure that open water was later reached, the channel followed being that of the deep, fast flowing Xiri River which passes between Boxwi and Bob Islands, and eventually joins the Boro.

Another buffalo was accounted for by the District Commissioner and other members of the party bagged three tsessebe between them.

Large herds of buffalo were again sighted, as well as numbers of lechwe, tsessebe and wildebeest, the noisy splashing of the former being frequently heard, the animals themselves entirely hidden in the tall water grass. On landing for the day a fascinating walk was taken and several varieties of game examined at close range by His Excellency and Lady Mary.

The camp was as usual pitched beneath magnificent trees and the hiking party, returning lat,e were welcomed back by the fragrance of roaring fires and the sight of sundry bottles of "good cheer". Festoons of stripped flesh strung from tree to tree gladdened the hearts of the African retinue, the contented murmur of their subdued voices and occasional burst of laughter reaching our campfire from time to time.

This camp was on Boxwi island – overrun with game as the trampled soil and shortness of the grazing testified. The large number seen were so astonishingly tame that it was quite evident that little if any shooting ever took place here.

After a tramp commencing at dawn in which Lady Mary joined and during which much game was again seen, camp was struck and the journey continued along the fairly well-defined channel of the Xiri which, however, spread into occasional broad and long reaches of marsh land. In these places the noisy splashing of lechwe, reedbuck and buffalo was not infrequently heard and occasional glimpses of the animals themselves obtained.

A long afternoon's walk during which game tracks, including the huge pug marks of a couple of lion were followed, but apart from impala, no game was seen.

The evening was much too fine to return to camp early and the not very distant moaning of a lion across the waterway, led us further and further downstream, where perching on the side of an antheap at the water's edge, we listened to the occasional night sounds, but "Leo" spoke no more and positive darkness forced a reluctant and rather difficult return to camp, through blackening woods.

It was a joyous ramble.

Lions, whose tracks had been observed the previous evening, roared grandly during the night, their booming, deep voices splendidly in keeping with the wild surroundings. During the morning ramble two immense buffalo bulls were come upon by Sir Evelyn and Lady Mary, but the cover being thick, they were soon lost to sight, not, however, without thoroughly startling one of the party, who having lingered behind happened to be in the beasts' line of retreat and only saving himself by frantic yells from being run over.

A large herd of tsessebe, frequently obscured by their own terrific splashing, was observed crossing a wide shallow swamp. They were followed shortly after by two roan antelope galloping in the same direction and a little later a solitary buffalo was sighted, feeding as is so often the case, in water up to its sides. It was not interfered with and continued its grazing quite unconcernedly. The usual lechwe and a pair of reedbuck were also sighted.

Camp was made a couple of miles from the junction of the Xiri and Boro Rivers and His Excellency made his usual ramble through the woodlands.

In contrast with the cheerful chattering of the paddlers, happy at the thought of the approaching end of the long trip, an atmosphere of sadness could be sensed around our fire.

The knowledge that this was our last camp and nearly the end of a gloriously interesting journey, rather weighed on all. Numerous common interests and a splendid comradeship throughout had created material for unforgettable memories and, when in the future, members of the party met, bright recollections of the High Commissioner's Swamps Tour would come vividly to mind.

The Expedition, lead throughout by the District Commissioner on whom fell all the organising and manifold routine duties, progressed in the smoothest manner imaginable and the whole party expressed its indebtedness for the carefree comfort brought about by his thoughtfulness.

July 4th 1947

After another short morning ramble the expedition was once again on the move, on the last stage of the journey this time. The Tsetse Control fence was reached in the early afternoon and not long afterwards the confluence of the Xiri and the Boro was passed, the winding of the latter necessitating the fence (previously cut) having to be crossed three times.

A couple more hours brought the convoy to the Thamalakane (the home river). Later the causeway carrying the main river road over the river was reached and the flag staff and awnings had to be removed from the High Commissioner's boat to get it through the culvert. Photographs were taken of the mokoros shooting the rapids under the bridge, which caused mild excitement and the shipping of a little water by the smaller craft.

The big barge, reassembled again, took the lead down the last six miles to Maun. Excited boatmen drew on their best endeavours and fast time was made in the brilliant sunshine of a perfect afternoon, the convoy being met by local officials at the High Commissioner's beautiful camp.

Thus ended a tour, the memory of which would remain green for all time, and, in the minds of those who were privileged to take part in it, cherished recollections of His Excellency's and Lady Mary's interest in its every phase and their unchanging kindness to all throughout

Chapter 19

THE BUSHMEN OF YESTERDAY AND TODAY

HAVING during some twelve months work on the edge of the Markarikari Salt Pan came into daily contact with Bushmen it has occurred to me that an account of these very interesting and primitive people might be of general interest and I propose in this chapter to give a brief sketch of their past with some observations of their present customs and the conditions under which they are living.

The Bushmen can justly lay claim to being the descendants of the original inhabitants of the country - the people who in the remote and misty past fashioned the crude stone weapons and hunted the gemsbuck, the eland, the giraffe and indeed all the large fauna occurring in the country. The people whose culture slowly advanced as century followed century, reaching its zenith perhaps a thousand years ago when it arrived at the stage where bows and poisoned arrows and wonderfully wrought stone implements replaced the former crude attempts which represent the very dawn of their occupancy.

They had advanced to the stage where we of the present enlightened era must fain marvel at the wonderful skill they had developed in lithic art and admire their beautiful work in such refractory materials as quartz and chalcenony.

The country abounds with endless traces of their activities in this direction and many perfect examples showing the various stages of their art can be found today, the durable nature of the medium in which they worked showing little trace of the passage of endless years.

Excavations in the debris of cave floors have revealed not only animal remains but scientists have been enabled to follow the steady advance in the culture; the lower levels producing the more crudely-worked tools and subsequent layers showing the development of the artists' ability and technique. Nearer the surface are found the wonderfully worked pygmy implements or microliths of what is known as the Wilton culture, as well as ostrich egg shell beads, bone tools and lumps of decomposed haematite which, with the oxides of iron and limonite are said to be the pigments used in the execution of the remarkable mural paintings found in rock shelters from the Zambezi to the coast.

These paintings have also thrown much light on the past of the Bushmen. The gradual improvement in their art can be followed here, as with their tool making. Superimposed painting have provided the clue as to the earliest ones and experts have been able to prove that the order of superimpositions, colour and style has remained constant throughout the country.

In some of the earlier light red paintings can often be seen the *steatopygous* (large buttocked) figures of women and *steatopyga* is still a physical characteristic of the Bushmen race.

The art of rock painting has developed to the stage of the exquisite polychrome paintings found in parts of Rhodesia, which display the really high degree of skill achieved by these people. Then there is evidence of a period of decadence and the subsequent total ending of the culture. The significance or purpose of these painting is wrapped in mystery. They may only be the outcome of the artistic spirit of the people a striving towards the beautiful, and a desire to decorate their dwellings. However, the more of the paintings we examine and the more we study them, the less inclined are we to accept this view. The recurrence of many strange figures other than human or animal gives one to ponder and speculate and adds greatly to their charm and the mystery surrounding them.

In tracing the descent of the Bushmen it is not my purpose to comment more than briefly on this most puzzling feature of their past; and all I desire to show is that the Bushmen had inhabited the country for ages prior to the coming of that other mystery race, the earliest gold-seekers. They must have watched the advent of those folk and their activities; the raising of their temples of hewn rock, their mining operations and establishment of lines of forts, built after the manner of their temples, to the east coast. They must have learnt something of their religious rites and sacrifices and witnessed after the passing of some hundreds of years, their ultimate exit or annihilation. Yet there is not a trace of evidence that they acquired a scrap of the culture of those invaders, neither have they any tradition about them.

Later they witnessed the arrival of those Bantu people whom destiny had decreed would become their conquerors and their lords.

It is inconceivable that the Bushmen, a people who had undoubtedly always lived by the chase, would not have acquired some knowledge of the art of warfare. Apart from other weapons, their terrible bows and the poisoned arrows with which they laid low the largest and fiercest beasts, must have given them a tremendous advantage over the barbarous people entering the country, particularly as the influx of strangers must at first have been slow. We know that the Bushmen were a big nation and that they occupied the greater portion of the country from the Zambezi southwards.

How then were they overcome and brought nearly to extinction and later to slavery? Were they a people divided against itself, living in small communities with bitter intertribal hatreds and quarrels, rendering it impossible for the nation as a whole to present a united front to the invasions from the north? Or, could there have come with the invaders some ravaging diseases which all but wiped out the old inhabitants and saved the newcomers the danger and trouble of lifelong warfare?

Just how they were overcome and subdued or driven forth into the barren wastes is a question which must forever remain unanswered. Certain it is that the present day "domesticated" Bushmen (or *Masarwa*) are of a very different type of those fore-bears of their who were essentially cave-dwellers and roamed and hunted the vast stretches of country without let or hindrance. Generations of serfdom and exile have so broken into the fabric of their old customs and culture that nothing remains of them but their bows and their arrows; not even traditions. This fact seems to hold a good deal of significance and a strong suggestion that the bushmen did not become desert dwellers from choice but rather that they were forced into the uncongenial surroundings and conditions which probably but few survived. Conditions which made their old mode of living impossible and became the instrument whereby the present type was evolved.

Man is prone to speculate and theorise and to delve after the truth in matters of this kind but here he is up against a blank wall – a sealed chapter in the history of the Bushmen. That there was an infusion of new blood within comparatively recent times there can be no doubt and the fact must be obvious to anyone who has come into daily contact with Bushmen.

The old pot-bellied, spindle-shanked, almost apelike type of inferior height and intellect and their treacherous, undependable natures are rare today, except perhaps in the heart of the Kalahari and the remoter parts of South West Africa. They have been replaced by a hybrid race physically not inferior to the Bechuana and many fine specimens of six feet in height and over are to be met with. Their mental outlook is naturally on a different plane to that of the people whose slaves they became but they have many good qualities and the day will dawn in the not very distant future when they must be given the right to assume the status of a nation with tribal laws and privileges of their own.

They are generally regarded as being the slaves of the Bamangwato and in so far that many of them receive neither food nor wages this is correct, but they are well treated on the whole and have never been reduced to the insufferable condition of being more chattels of commerce, so their thralldom sits lightly on their shoulders and they are a happy and carefree if rather an irresponsible race.

The matter of procuring a sufficiency of food is their greatest problem, but they stoically face the periods of plenty and famine as they come, waxing fat and sleek during the rainy season when there is an abundance of milk and falling back on the coarse diet of such roots and berries as they are able to find in the off season, varied occasionally by the flesh of tortoises, iguanas, small cats and even snakes, caterpillars and frogs but at that time of the year they generally lose flesh and sometimes become dreadfully emaciated. That they are able to keep body and soul together on such meagre and indigestible fare illustrates their hardihood and vitality and I have found it impossible to walk even the worst conditioned ones off their feet.

The men are for the most part employed at cattle herds by the Bamangwato and are given all the milk they need. During the summer months this constitutes practically their sole article of food and is mostly consumed fresh from the cows, the surplus being made into "madiela" which is a simple form of cheese prepared by pouring the milk into skin bags which are hung in the sunshine until the milk has thickened into stiff curd. The whey is drawn off through a small opening in a bottom corner of the bag.

Many Europeans are fond of madiela and it is doubtless a good and sustaining article of food, but the milk is handled in such a messy manner that I have never been able to bring myself to trying it. The fruit of the cream of tarter trees is sometimes used for coagulating the milk artificially in much the same way as rennet and pepsin are employed by Europeans.

Little can be said for the abodes of the Bushmen. Their huts are usually the most crazy affairs and can offer but slight protection against the heavy tropical showers which sometimes fall. Indeed they do not appear to be troubled by a thorough wetting and I have frequently seen them sleeping soundly in the heaviest downpours with no more covering then a small goatskin.

Their dress consists of skins tanned on the under side and with the hair left on. The men seldom wear more than a loin cloth except in cold weather when a coat of calfskin is thrown over the shoulders. The women wear a sort of two-piece skirt, also of skin, one half in front and the other behind with a wide overlap at the sides. Quite pleasing patterns are seen and are obtained by scraping the hair off in zigzag lines and diamond panel effects. As with the men goat skins are worn over the shoulders in cold weather only or when a mother is carrying an infant. The young maidens are often comely and have good figures but incline to steatapyga early in life.

In colour the Bushmen vary from light yellow to a deep African brown. I do not recall having ever seen any daubing themselves with pigments of any kind.

The woman usually have their heads shaved bare, but the young bucks take a good deal of pride in their hair as their fancies run riot. The results are usually quire pleasing though and the patterns followed kept remarkably even and symmetrical. I was amused at one young fellow's effort. He had the whole of the top of this head shaved bare in imitation of natural baldness and it was so well done that I did at first believe him to be naturally bald. Evidently he imagined that this style gave him an air of age and dignity.

The language of the Bushmen bears not the slightest similarity to any other and abounds in strange, and to a European, impossible clicks. Their vocabulary is said to be limited but there is surely no language in which intonation and voice inflection plays a greater part or which is more musical.

E.C.W - 1958

The Wilmot Album

Author E. Cronje Wilmot (right) with his son Bobby in the early 1960's on a small farm near Francistown,

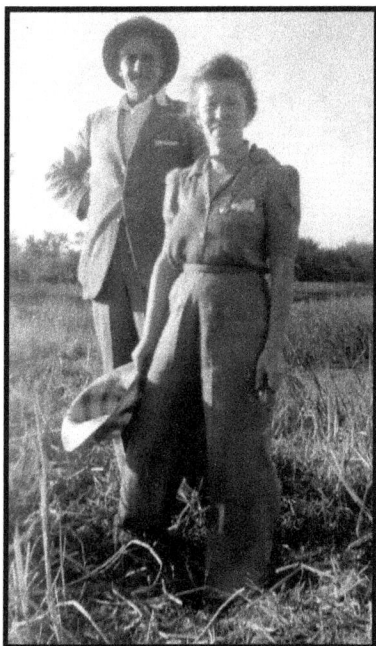

Top left: E Cronje Wilmot with Matron Murch of the Maun Hospital shortly after recovering from Bubonic Plague (Chap 8, P99)

Top right: Bobby Wilmot

Bottom: Possibly the last picture of the author, taken just before his death in 1967

Bobby Wilmot training oxen at the Makarikari Salt Pans

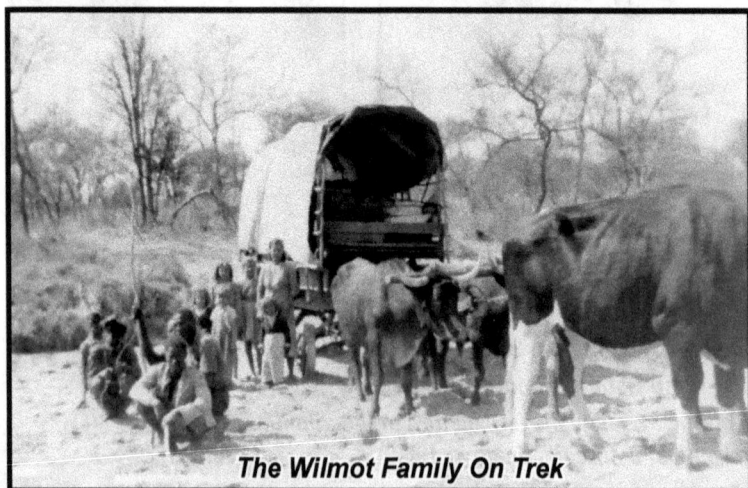
The Wilmot Family On Trek

A Wilmot Family Gathering

The author's shack at Chuchubegho during fly
control operations - luxury indeed! (Chap 9, P103)

The author's
daughter Stella
and son Eric

One of the pictures
taken immediately after
the author's mauling
by a lion shows the friend who
was with him that day.
(Chap 11, P140)

E. Cronje Wilmot's pet
sitatunga doe at Maun
(Chap 9, P101)

www.ingramcontent.com/pod-product-compliance
Lightning Source LLC
Chambersburg PA
CBHW052122270326
41930CB00012B/2727